The Campus History Series

WESTERN STATE COLLEGE

MOUNTAIN MECCA

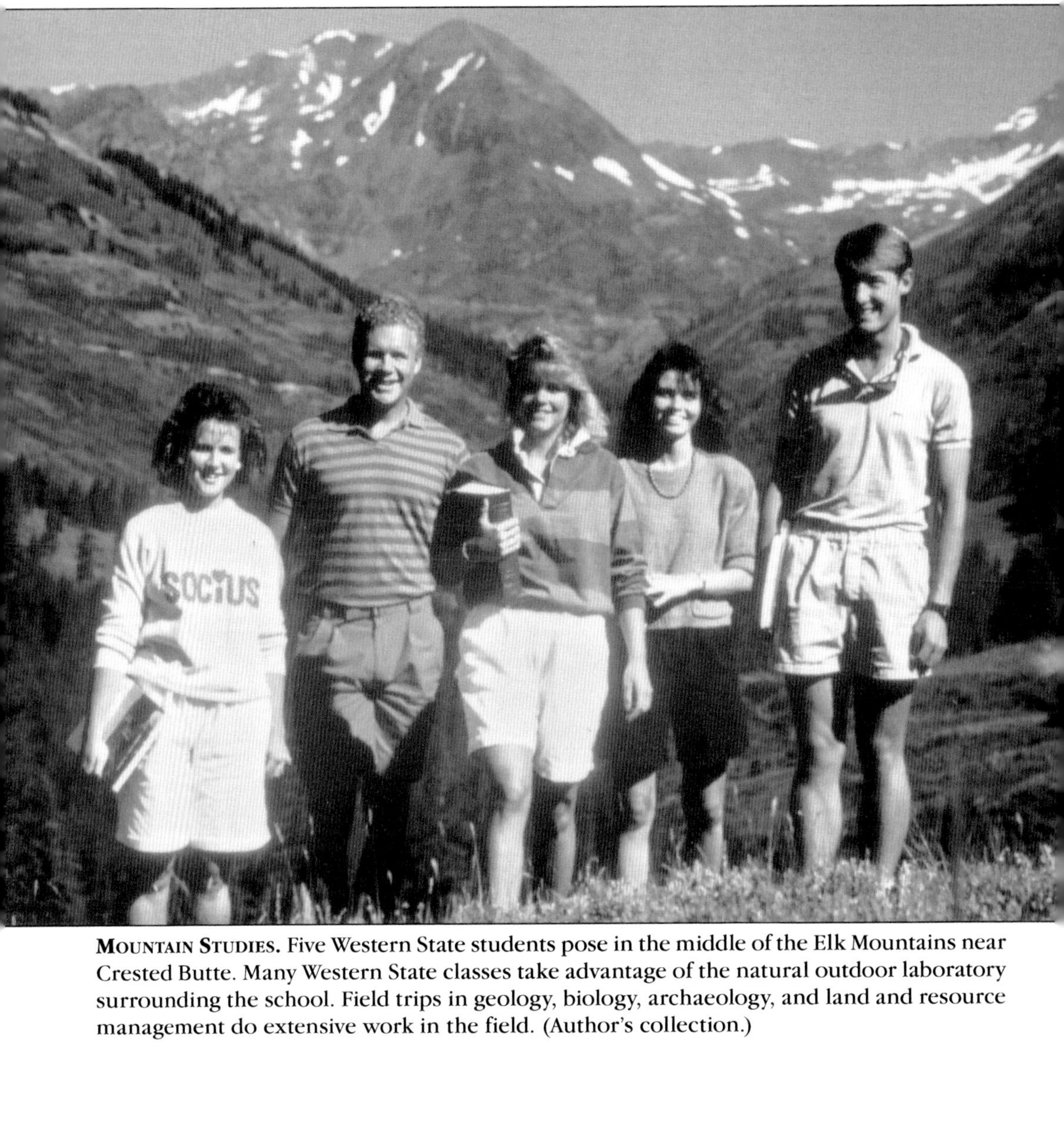

Mountain Studies. Five Western State students pose in the middle of the Elk Mountains near Crested Butte. Many Western State classes take advantage of the natural outdoor laboratory surrounding the school. Field trips in geology, biology, archaeology, and land and resource management do extensive work in the field. (Author's collection.)

On the Cover: A Western State skier sails off the Rozman Hill jump during an intercollegiate meet in 1953. Crested Butte Mountain, a few miles north and over 12,000 feet high, is in the background. (Author's collection.)

The Campus History Series

WESTERN STATE COLLEGE
MOUNTAIN MECCA

DUANE VANDENBUSCHE

ARCADIA
PUBLISHING

ISBN 978-1-4671-3095-0

Published by Arcadia Publishing
Charleston, South Carolina

Printed in the United States of America

Library of Congress Catalog Card Number: 2013954935

For all general information, please contact Arcadia Publishing:
Telephone 843-853-2070
Fax 843-853-0044
E-mail sales@arcadiapublishing.com
For customer service and orders:
Toll-Free 1-888-313-2665

Visit us on the Internet at www.arcadiapublishing.com

*This book is dedicated to Sven Wiik
and all the Mountaineers of Western State College
who have made it a great institution of learning.*

CONTENTS

ACKNOWLEDGMENTS

Many individuals, libraries, and museums are to be thanked for the use of their photographs in this book. In particular, I would like to give special thanks to Nancy Gauss and the Western State Colorado University Library for allowing me to use pictures in the university collection.

During my 51 years as a professor and coach at Western State, my interviews with Ed Ali, Bob Arnold, Carol Baird Izett, Marvin Bohman, D.H. Cummins, Molly Gratton Fisher, Thor Groswold, Chris Johnson, Walter Jackson, Dolph Kuss, Rial Lake, John Mellon, Bruce Palmer, Crosby Perry-Smith, Sven Wiik, and Mickey Zahradka have greatly added to the information in this book.

Unless otherwise noted, the images in this book are from the author's collection. Additional images appear courtesy of the Western State Colorado University Library (WSCU), Francesca Pavillard-Cain (FPC), Dan Cress (DC), Crested Butte Mountain Heritage Museum (CBMHM), Gunnison Pioneer Museum (GPM), and G.J. Santelli (GS).

I am very grateful for the support, guidance, and wisdom of my editor, Stacia Bannerman, and Arcadia Publishing. I am also greatly indebted to Pam Williams of the historical Island Acres Resort in Gunnison, who scanned all the photographs in the book. Lastly, a salute to Sven Wiik, who had a great influence on me as a person, professor, and coach.

Introduction

Western State College (WSC), which became Western State Colorado University in 2012, was the first college on Colorado's Western Slope. The college was established in 1911 as a teacher training institution, Colorado State Normal. Located at 7,703 feet, deep in the Colorado Rocky Mountains, the college is surrounded by four mountain ranges: the San Juan, Sangre de Cristo, Sawatch, and Elk Mountains. The four ranges include 40 mountains over 14,000 feet with incredible hunting, fishing, skiing, and climbing. In the midst of this stunning landscape, Western State College became an outdoor mountain mecca, which has greatly influenced its history.

Within 50 miles of the college are two major ski areas (Crested Butte and Monarch), one of the great mountain biking regions in the world, great coal mines near Crested Butte, and the town of Marble, where the Tomb of the Unknown Soldier and Lincoln Memorial were quarried. Nine miles west of Gunnison is the Blue Mesa Reservoir, the largest body of water in Colorado and the state's second largest tourist attraction. The famed Black Canyon begins west of Gunnison and is unique and rich in railroad, water, and climbing history. Located in a high alpine valley in the middle of the Gunnison Country, Western State has often been described as not so much an institution of learning but rather a state of mind.

Throughout its 100-year history, the college has grown from primarily a teacher training school into a four-year liberal arts institution with several master's degree programs. Western is nationally known for its emphasis on outdoor education. In 1928, former Western State biology professor Dr. John C. Johnson started the Rocky Mountain Biological Laboratory in the old silver-mining camp of Gothic, 36 miles north of the college. The lab is nationally known and conducts scientific studies on such important matters as climate change and the effects of high altitude and has over 100 projects on stream ecology. Western today has national-caliber programs in land and resource management, exercise and sports science, environmental studies, archaeology, and geology; it also has the only nationally certified search and rescue team.

As the years have come and gone, Western has been privileged to have had a nationally known faculty. Clarence Hurst started the Southwestern Archaeology Society, which had membership in 32 states. Paul Wright became the father of intercollegiate skiing when he got that sport adopted by the NCAA in 1950. George Damson started the famed WSC Music Camp in 1934, which attracted famous conductors from around the world. Western's graduates have also distinguished themselves with the likes of oil men Paul Rady and Peter Dea; three track and field Olympians, Michael Aish, Elva Dryer, and Bobby Gaseitsiwe; legendary mountain biker David Wiens; and two-time Olympic ski coach Sven Wiik. Western has also turned out many Olympic skiers.

Western State reminds one of the *Little Engine That Could.* Isolated in the Rocky Mountains with only narrow-gauge railroad transportation in the early days and with little financial support from the state of Colorado, Western has grown into a top liberal arts school. Gunnison County was named one of the most affluent counties in the nation, and Western gets nearly 30 percent of its students from states other than Colorado.

Today, Western is in the midst of a great building program with a privately funded Borick Business Building, a University Center, and a field house just having been completed. The school is still unique; it is the highest-elevation four-year university in the nation and is a great laboratory for outdoor education. During the summer months, students and scholars converge on the Gunnison Country to study what they can only learn out of a book where they live. Western State looks with confidence to the future; its beautiful campus, great mountain location, expanding building program, outstanding faculty, and the opportunity for students to study in a great outdoor laboratory makes Western unique.

Western State College, now a university, is a school that has been shaped by elevation, the great outdoors, recreation, and perhaps destiny. Western looks with optimism at the next 100 years.

One

1911–1929

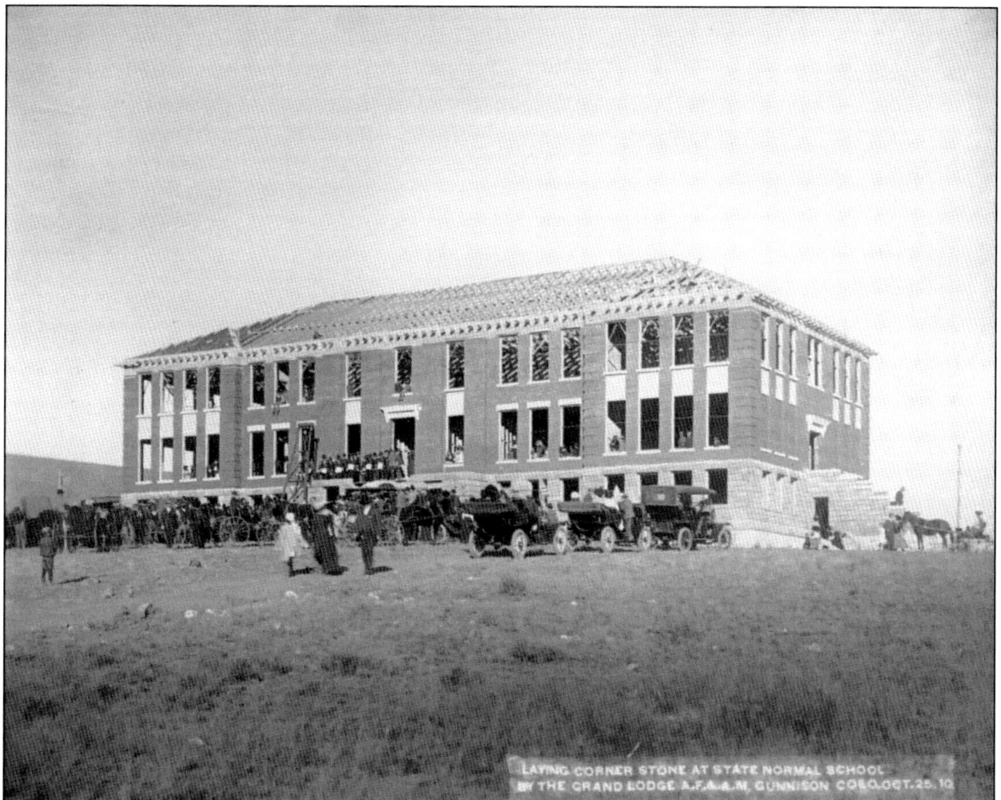

CORNERSTONE LAID. The cornerstone of North Hall (later part of Taylor Hall) was laid on October 25, 1910, amidst great fanfare. Within the cornerstone, which was opened 100 years later, were, among other things, two local newspapers, coins, Mason membership rosters, and photographs of Gunnison and the Gunnison Country.

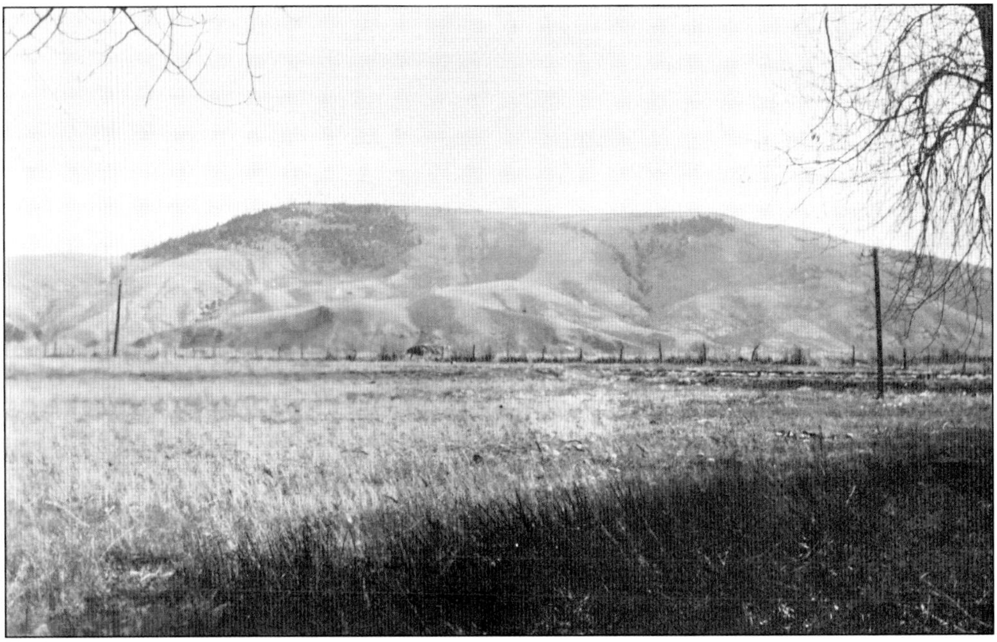

Tenderfoot Mountain. Just south of Gunnison and Western State College, Tenderfoot Mountain, at 8,671 feet, towered almost 1,000 feet higher than Colorado Normal School. The "W" was built on the mountain in 1923, three years after this photograph. The normal school purchased the mountain from the federal government shortly after the school opened. (WSCU.)

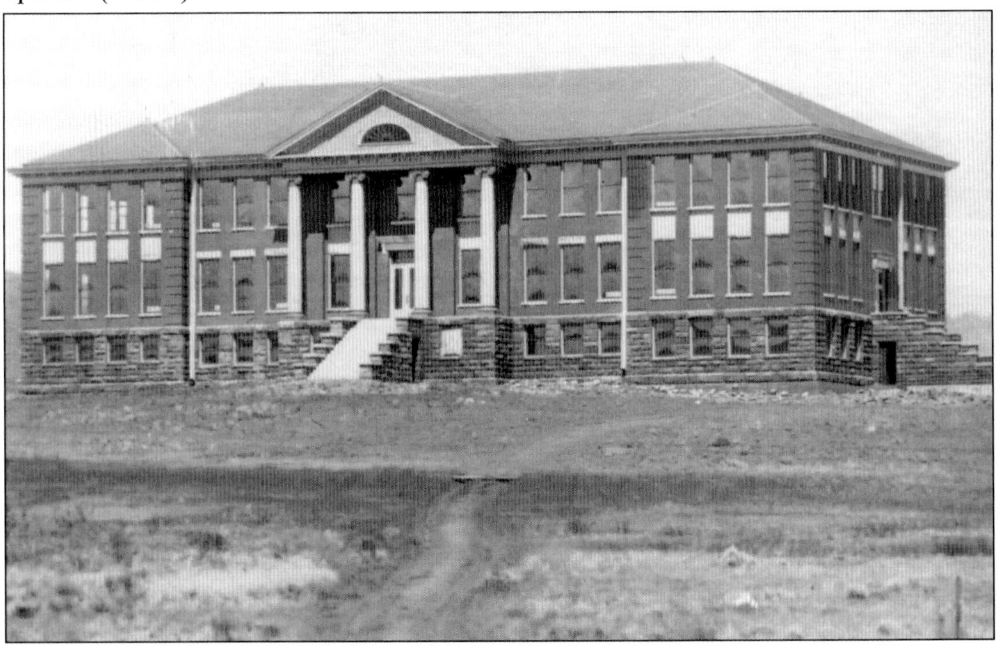

Taylor Hall, 1915. North Hall was the first section of what later became known as Taylor Hall. Built in 1910 and 1911, it was the first building on the Colorado State Normal School campus. Later, in 1920, South Hall was built, and in 1929, Central was finished, completing the three stages of Taylor Hall. (WSCU.)

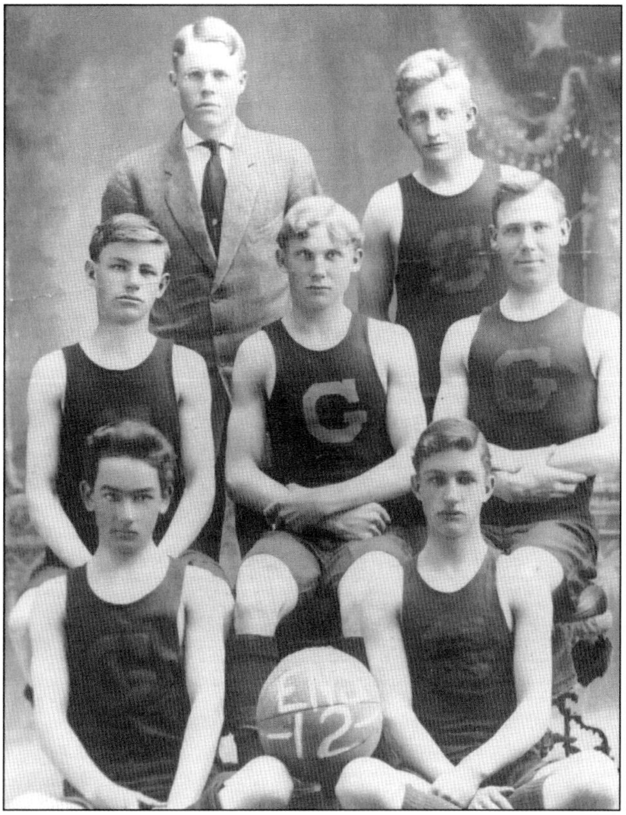

FIRST BASKETBALL TEAM. Head coach Dr. John C. Johnson and the first Colorado State Normal team are pictured here in 1912. The "ENS" on the basketball stands for "Elementary Normal School." All of the players were Gunnison High School students enrolled in the normal elementary program at the college. (WSCU.)

WOMEN'S BASKETBALL, 1912. Women's basketball, a fledgling sport nationally, got underway at Colorado State Normal in 1912. The sport then had three offensive and three defensive players who had to stay on their own side of the court. Scores rarely reached the 20s in those days. (WSCU.)

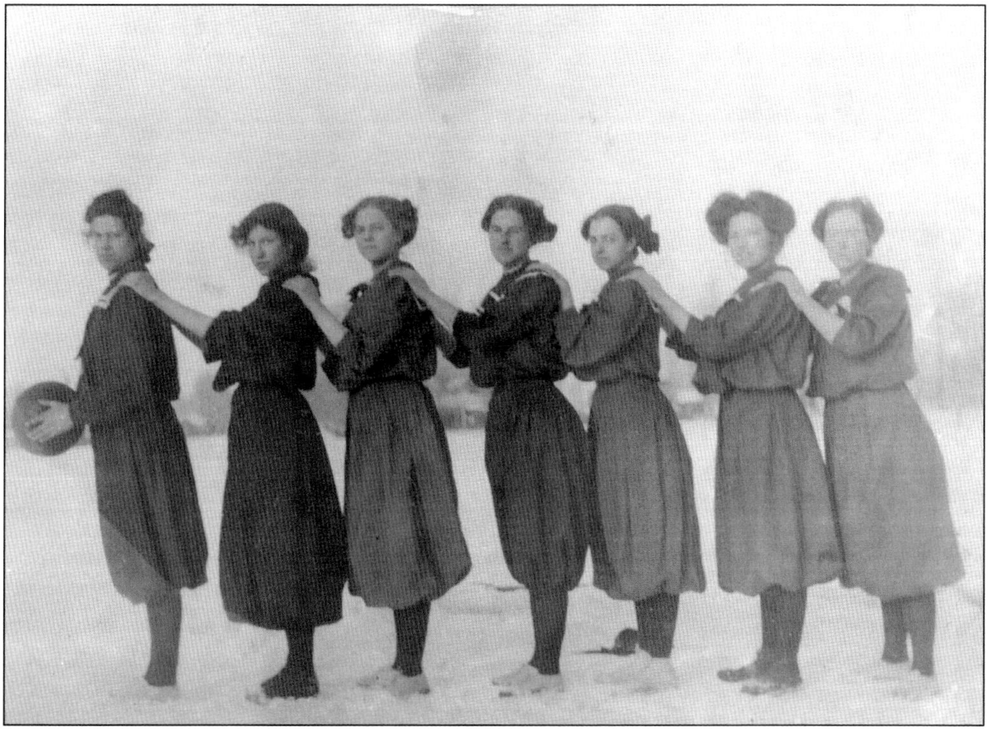

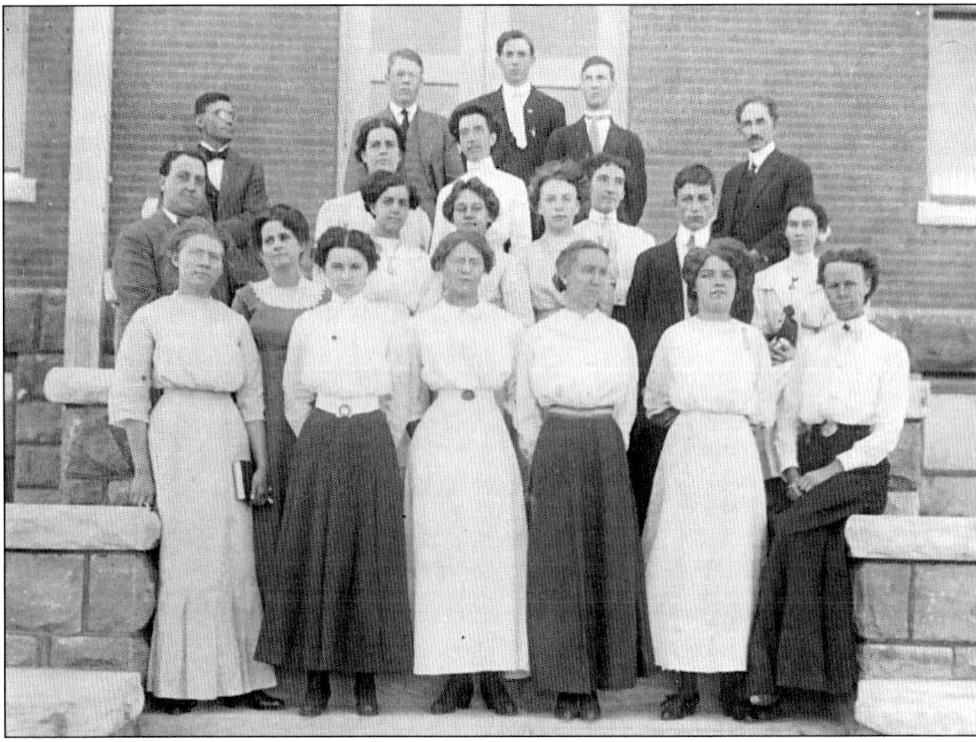

First Faculty and Student Body. In September 1911, the first faculty and student body pose for a photograph on campus. From left to right are (first row) Katie Walker, Kate Redden, Clara Morris, Josie Hendricks, Vera Adams, and Winifred Wonders; (second row) Wilbert Franks, Eva Carpenter, Vergie Miller, Helen Webster, Mildred Burch, Ray Hollingshead, and Alice Courtney; (third row) Heinrich Richter, Lucy Spicer, Wilma Hehnes, Ollie Veo, and Principal Charles Hollinsghead; (fourth row) John C. Johnson, Merton Bedford, and Charles McKee. There were 13 students and 8 faculty members. (WSCU.)

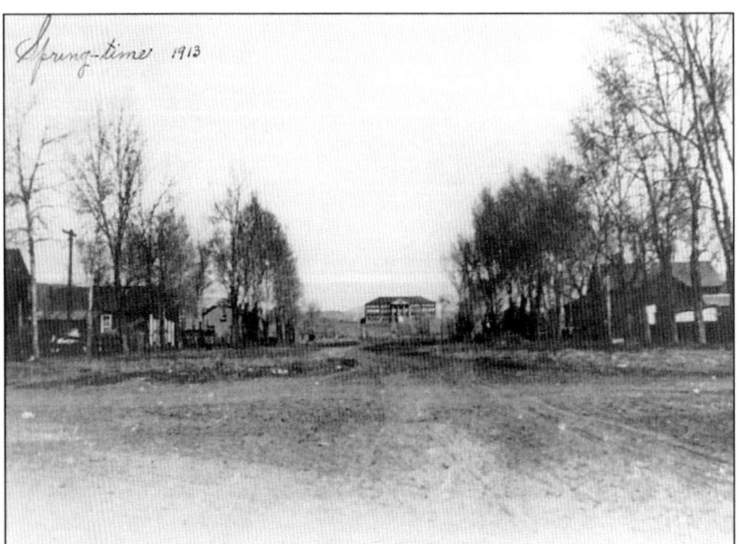

North Hall, 1913. North Hall was the first building of Colorado State Normal School and was built in 1910 and 1911. The hall gave off a lonely appearance with only a few scattered Gunnison buildings nearby.

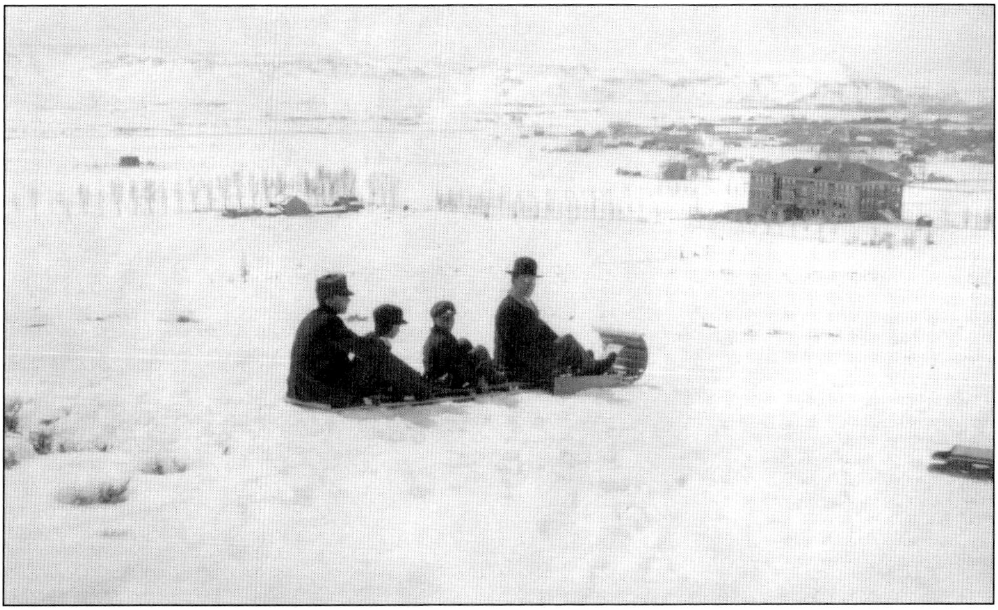

Smelter Hill Tobogganing. One of the highest points on the Western campus was Smelter Hill, the site of the Moffet Smelter in the 1880s. This picture was taken during a steep toboggan run, which ran for nearly a half mile. North Hall is seen in the background. The run was not for the faint of heart. (WSCU.)

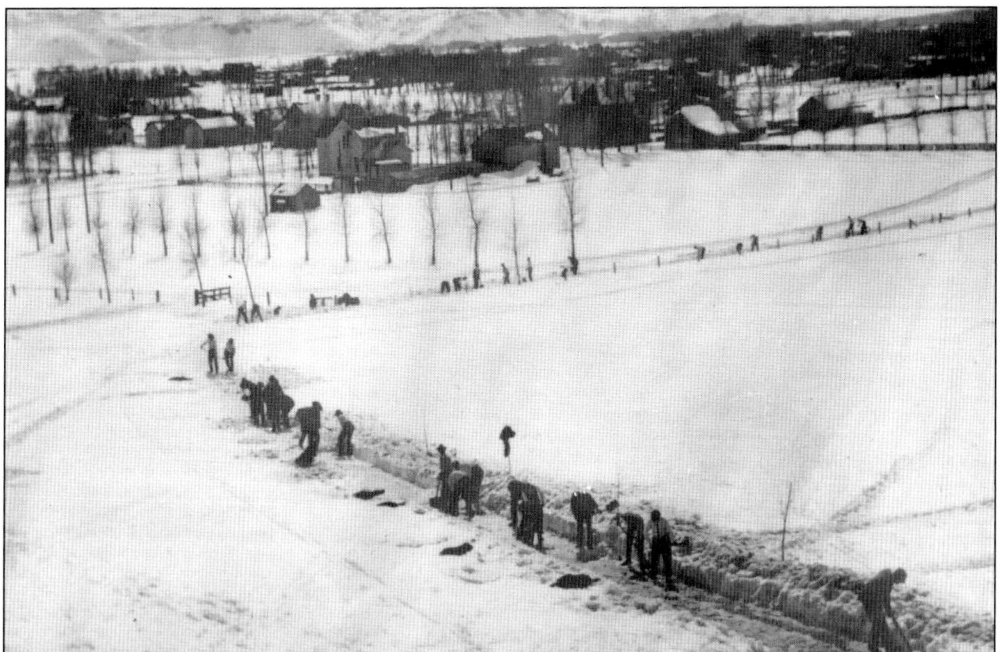

Western State "Maintenance Department." A heavy snowfall has hit Gunnison during the winter of 1924. In the absence of a college maintenance crew, Western State students pitched in to clear a path to Taylor Hall.

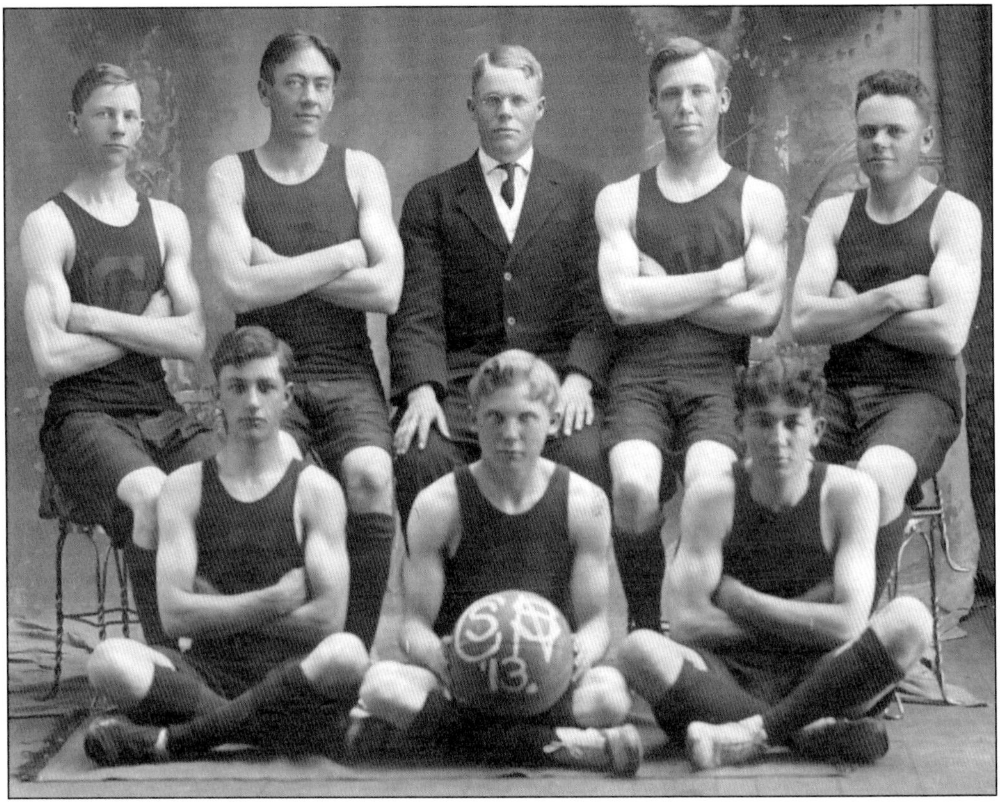

The Second Team. The second Colorado State Normal basketball team played its first games in the winter of 1912–1913. Coach John C. Johnson recalled, "We practiced in North Hall . . . the showers only delivered cold water but what of that. Young men were built only of hardy pioneer stuff and could take it." Pictured from left to right are (first row) Ray Hollingshead, Verne Mauer, and Chester Pittser; (second row) Richie Walker, Fritz Zugelder, coach John C. Johnson, Arthur Chinery, and Ralph Stone. (WSCU.)

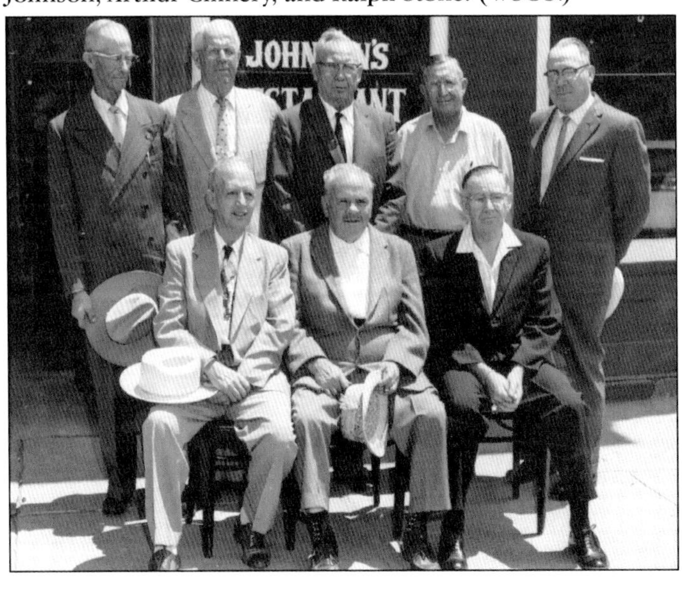

Basketball Team Reunion. On July 20, 1961, the first basketball team in the history of Colorado Normal School had a 50-year reunion in Gunnison. From left to right are (first row) Ray Hollingshead, Ralph Stone, and Arthur Kroll; (second row) Richie Walker, coach John C. Johnson, Verne Mauer, Homer Gray, and Arthur Chinery. The men pose in front of historic Johnson's restaurant. (WSCU.)

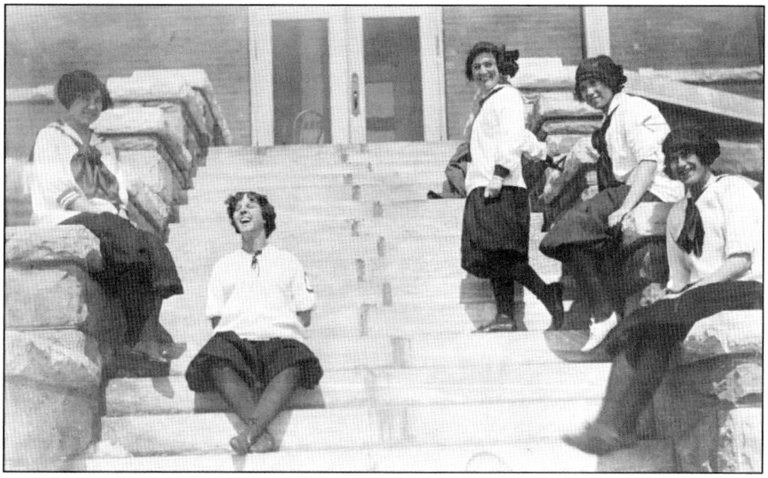

Colorado Normal Coeds. There was a dress code for men and women on special days at the normal school. The code was always in effect on picture days, such as evidenced in this publicity shot on the steps of Taylor Hall. (WSCU.)

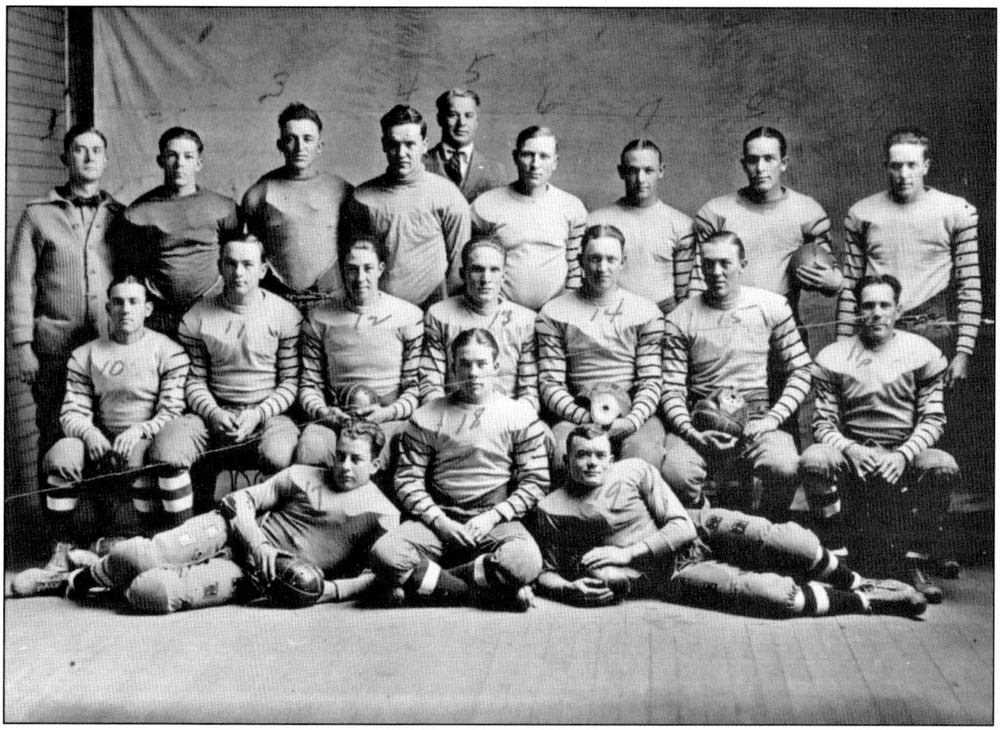

Western State Football Team, 1922. The football team of 1922 featured three players who became very well known. Buell Crawford, third from the right in the back row, broke his leg the following year and died on his 22nd birthday of blood poisoning. Chuck Wright, holding the football, became a legendary high school coach in Ohio, and his brother, Paul, far right in the back row, became a famed coach and athletic director at WSC. The Mountaineers were coached by A.C. Krause. (WSCU.)

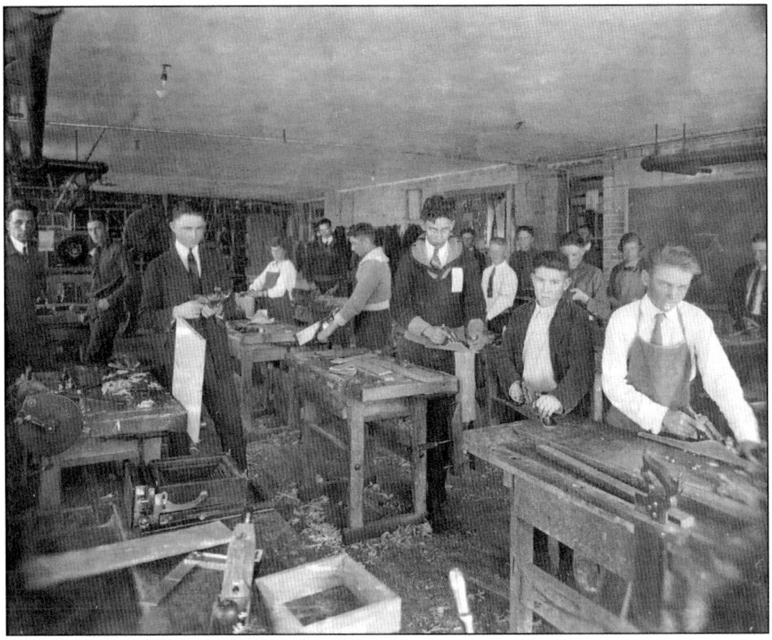

MANUAL TRAINING. One of the most important academic areas at Colorado Normal was manual training, also known as "shop." Here, students prepared for acceptations such as welding and carpentry, both in great demand in 1919. (WSCU.)

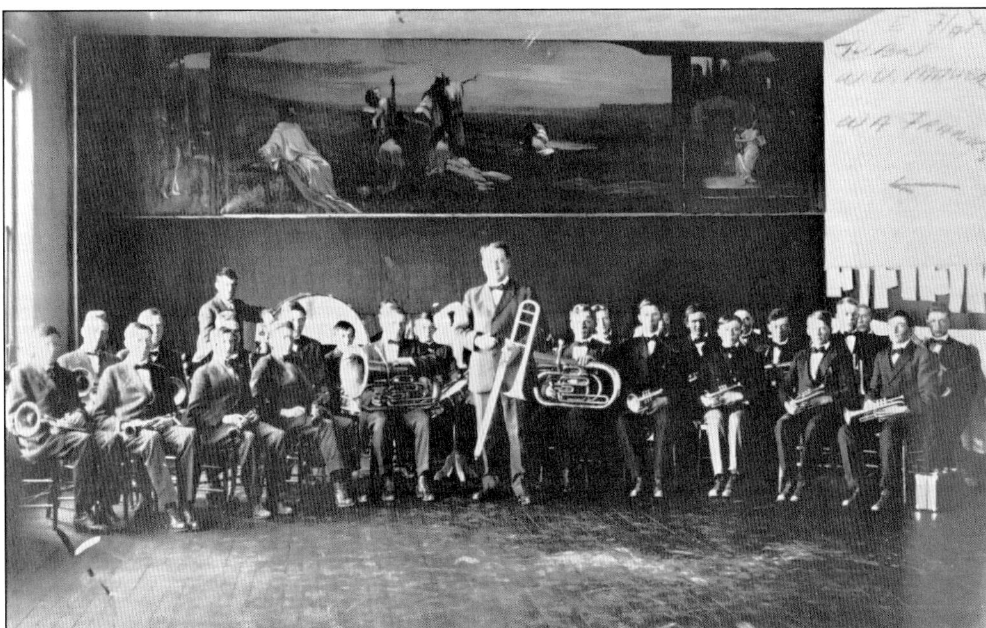

EARLY BAND. With a Heinrich Richter (Colorado Normal School art teacher) mural in the background, the normal school band is ready to play in 1920. Their music performance took place in North Hall, then the only college building on campus. (WSCU.)

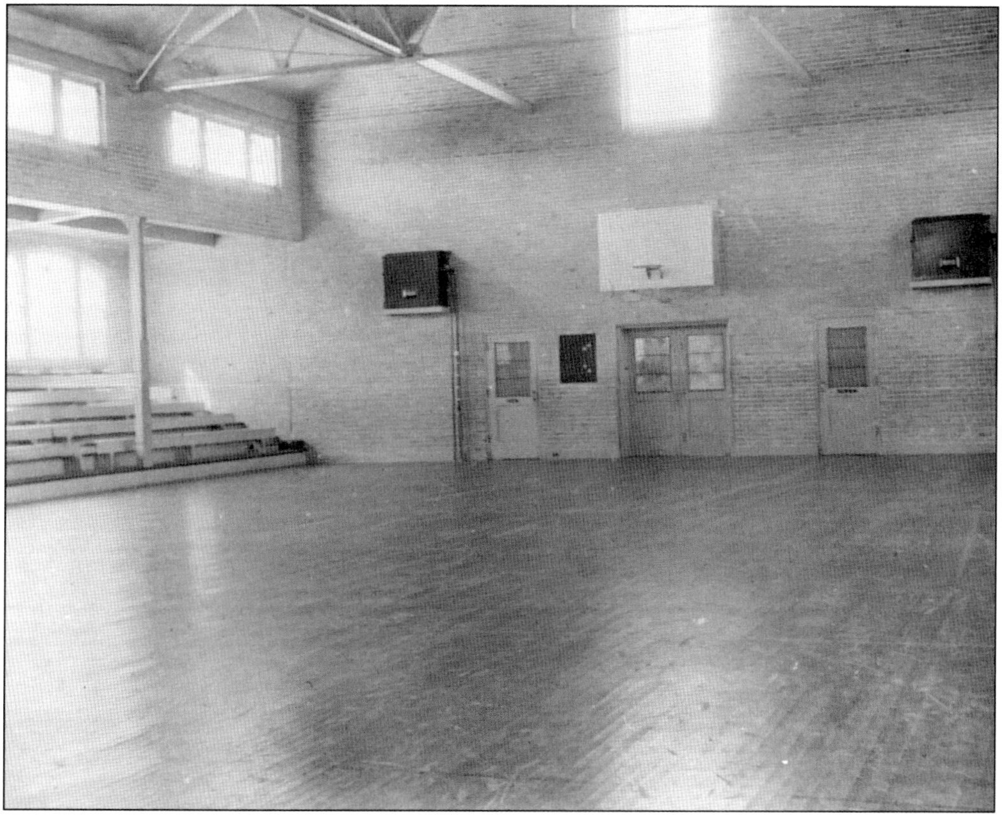

Crawford Gymnasium. The Crawford Gymnasium was built in 1924 at a cost of $40,000. The gym, the first on campus, was named for Buell Crawford, a football and basketball player who died the previous year. This was one of the few cases of a college building being named for a student.

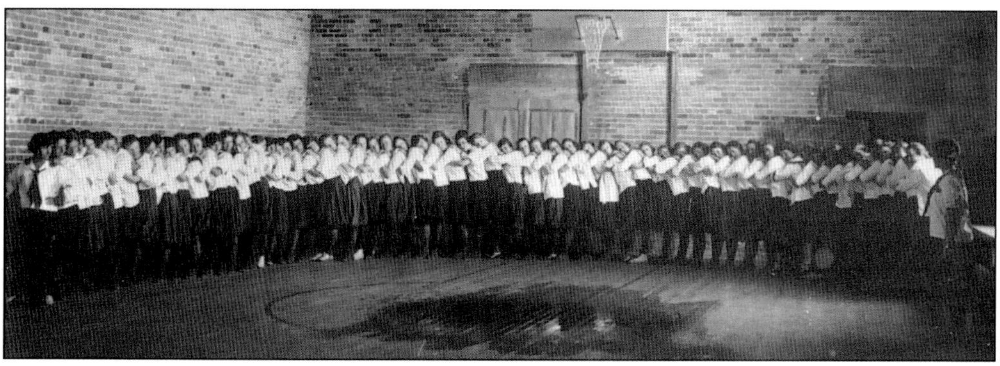

Colorado State Normal Women. The entire women student body lines up in Crawford Gym in 1922. Physical education classes were mandatory then and included basketball, archery, and gymnastics. The following year, the normal school became Western State College, a four-year institution. (WSCU.)

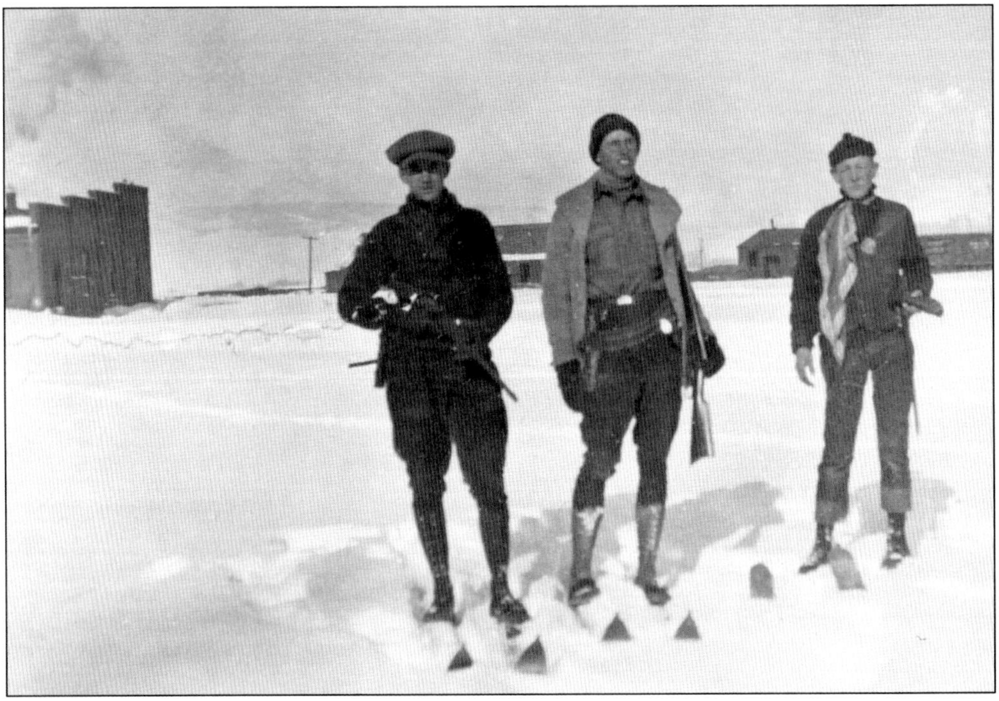

Shooting Rabbits. Bill Calkins (center) is with two friends next to the Denver & Rio Grande (D&RG) Railroad yard in Gunnison in 1924. The men have their rifles loaded and are hoping for a successful rabbit hunt.

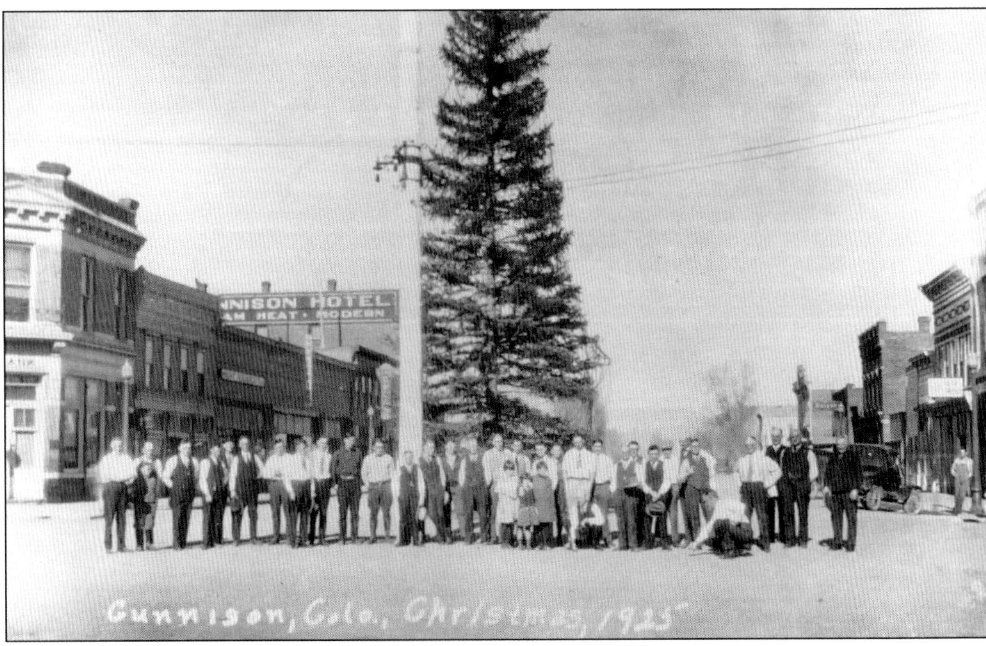

Christmas in Gunnison. Gunnison has an overrated reputation as one of the coldest towns in the nation. In reality, the perpetual sunshine, lack of wind, and low humidity give the town an ideal climate. On Christmas Day, 1925, there was no snow in Gunnison, and the temperature was 54 degrees—short-sleeve weather.

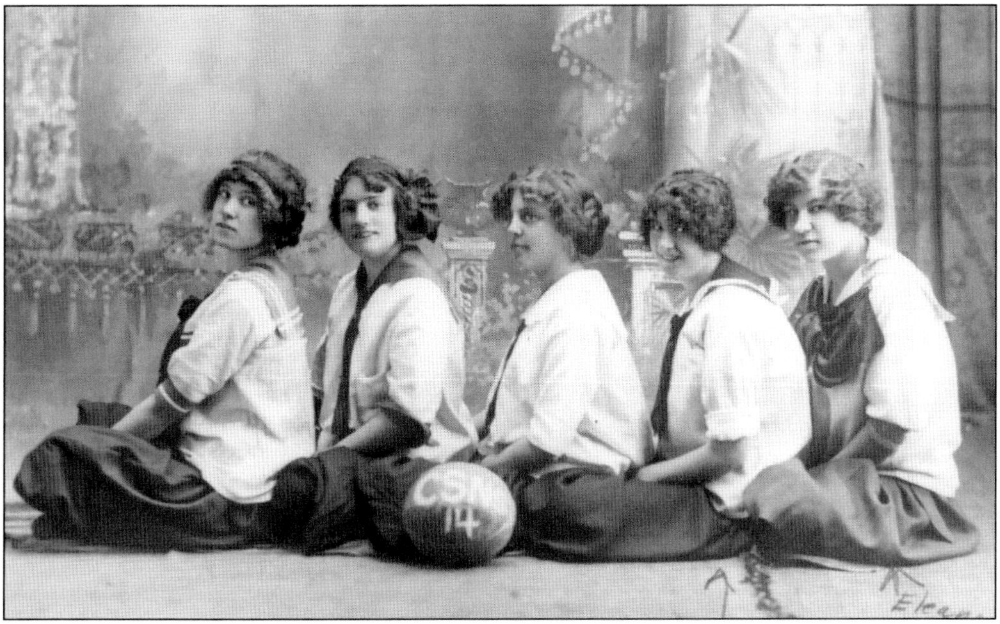

1914 TEAM. Colorado State Normal was in its fourth year, but the women's basketball team still continued playing its games against high school teams. The 1914 team included, from left to right, Eleanora Bray, Julia Hogan, unidentified, Fritz Castle, and Lucy Mauer. (WSCU.)

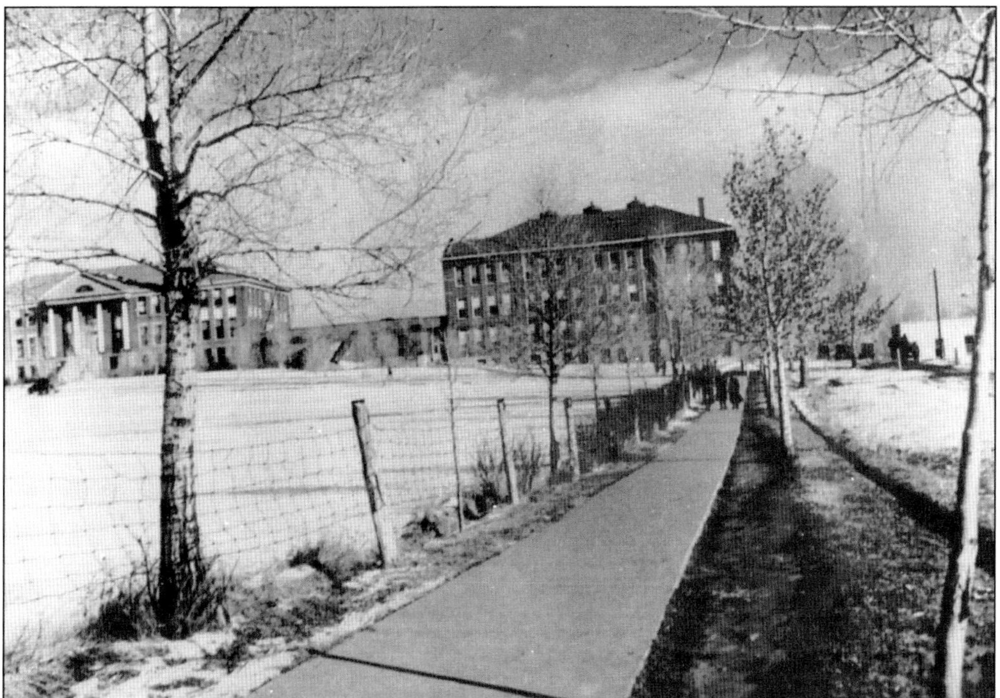

NORTH AND SOUTH HALL, 1928. North Hall (left) was the first building for Colorado State Normal, and South Hall was Gunnison High School in 1920. In between, construction on Central Hall began in the early 1920s, but because of a lack of funding, it was not completed until 1930. The three sections completed what became known as Taylor Hall. (WSCU.)

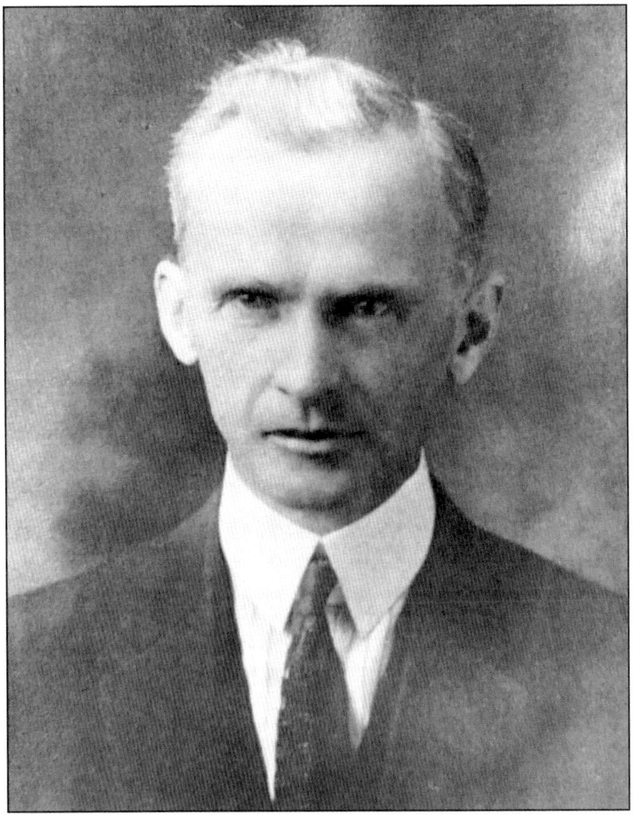

Sam Quigley. Born in Minnesota in 1873, Sam Quigley was educated at Iowa State, Iowa University, Harvard, and the University of Chicago before joining the staff at Colorado Normal in 1914. After serving in World War I, he returned home to serve as president of Colorado Normal. He was instrumental in Colorado Normal becoming Western State College in 1923. He left the presidency in 1927 and continued in higher education until his death in 1946. (WSCU.)

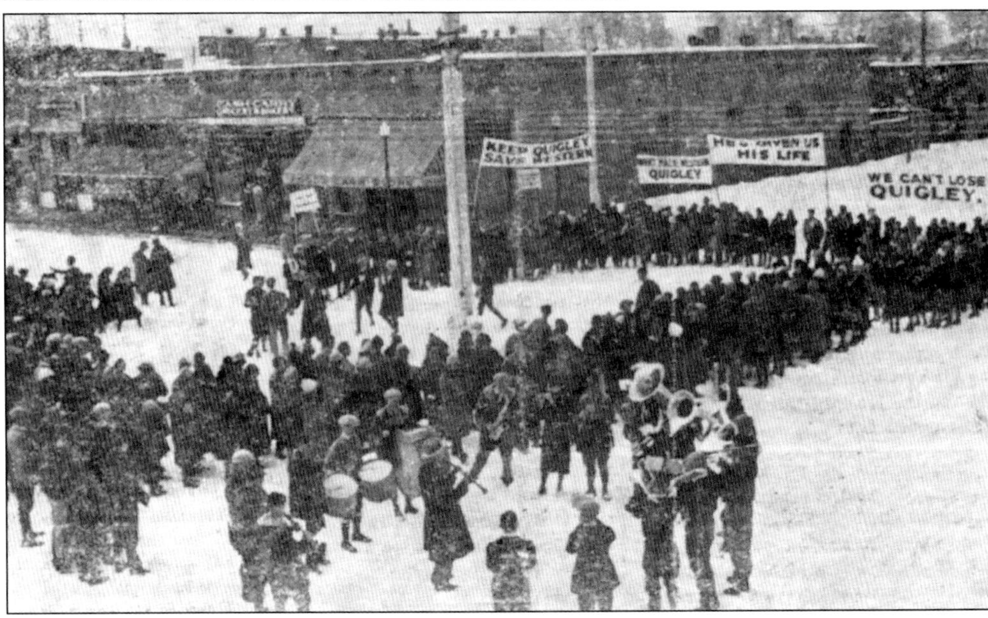

Quigley Controversy. Sam Quigley was the much-loved president of Colorado State Normal School from 1919 to 1923 and then head of Western State College from 1923 to 1927. More than anyone, he was responsible for the success of the fledging school. In 1927, Quigley was forced out as president by members of the Ku Klux Klan in the Colorado Legislature. (WSCU.)

Two

THE DEPRESSION YEARS

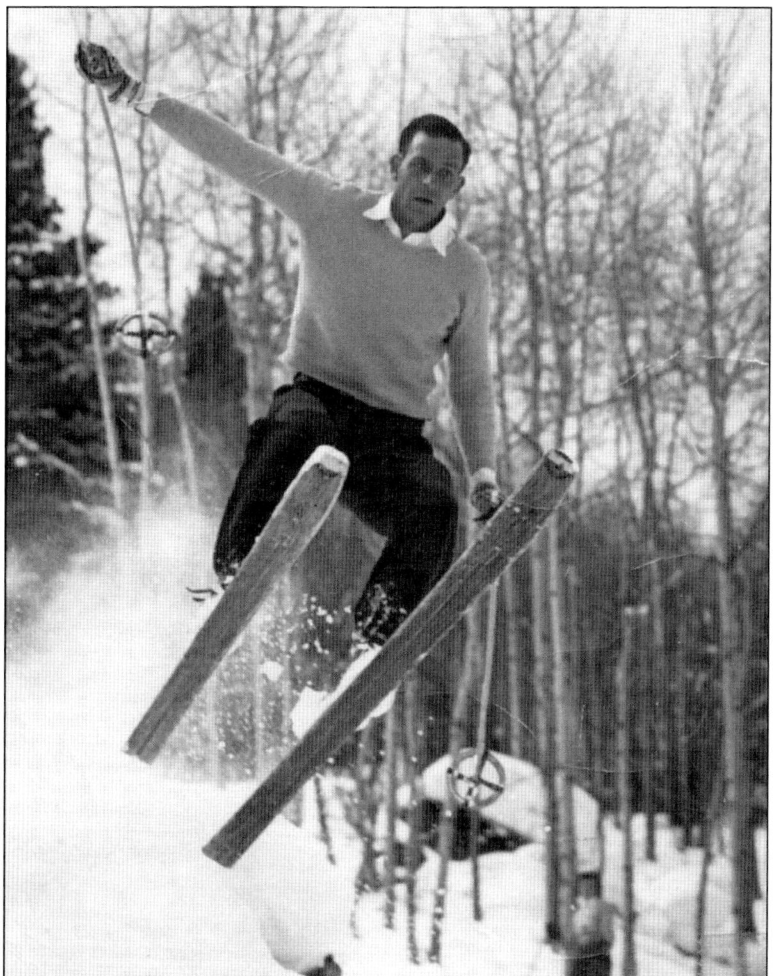

BRUCE PALMER. The earliest great skier in the history of Western State College was Bruce Palmer. A student at Western in the early 1930s, Palmer competed in Rocky Mountain races during that decade. After graduation, he became one of finest skiers in the Rockies.

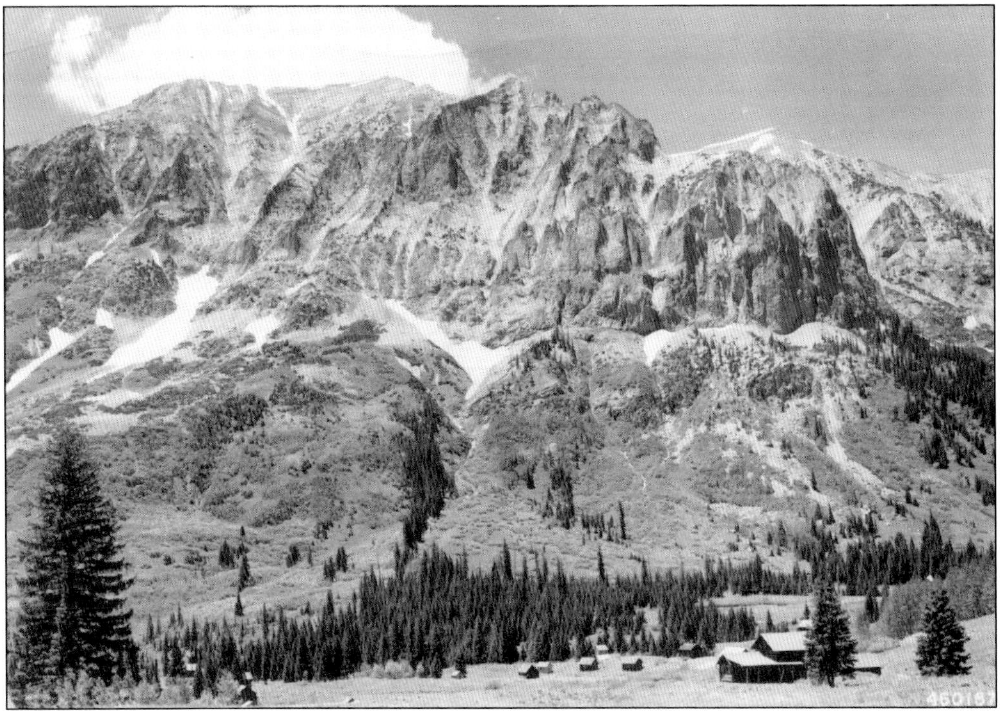

City of Silver Wires. Located in the rugged and high Elk Mountains, the old silver camp of Gothic transformed itself in 1928 when John C. Johnson of Western State started the Rocky Mountain Biological Laboratory. Since that time, the laboratory has become world famous for its studies. Majestic Gothic Mountain, at 12,500 feet, towers over the camp.

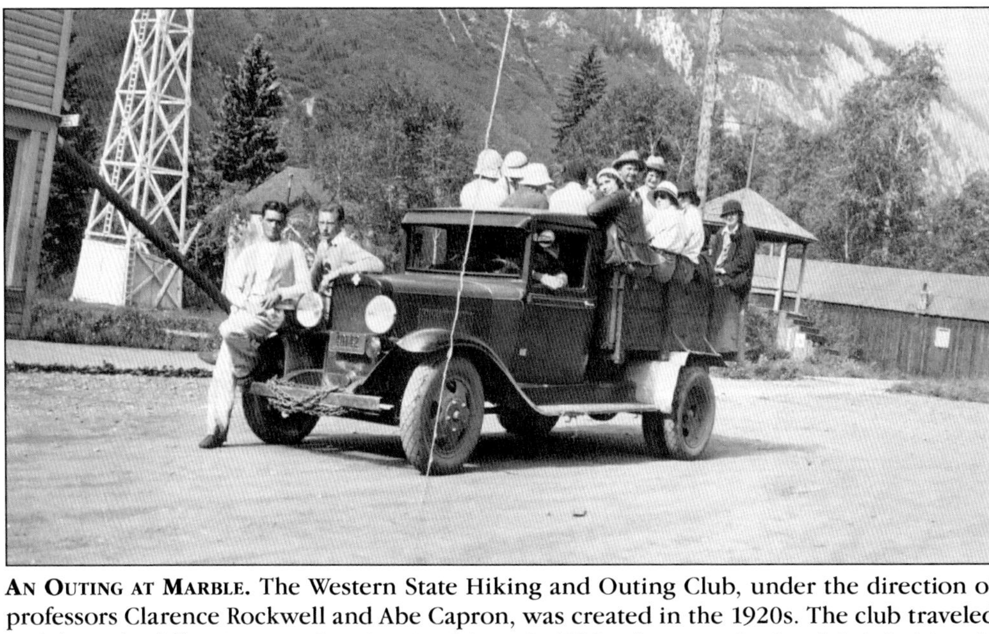

An Outing at Marble. The Western State Hiking and Outing Club, under the direction of professors Clarence Rockwell and Abe Capron, was created in the 1920s. The club traveled widely in the fall, winter, and spring. In this early-1930s photograph, the club is in historic Marble, from where the marble for the Tomb of the Unknown Soldier came. (WSCU.)

Taylor Park. Thirty miles long and eight miles wide, magnificent Taylor Park was the scene of great silver and gold mining from the 1860s to the 1880s. The Taylor River headed off 11,800-foot-high Taylor Pass not far from Aspen and joined the East River at Almont, 45 miles away.

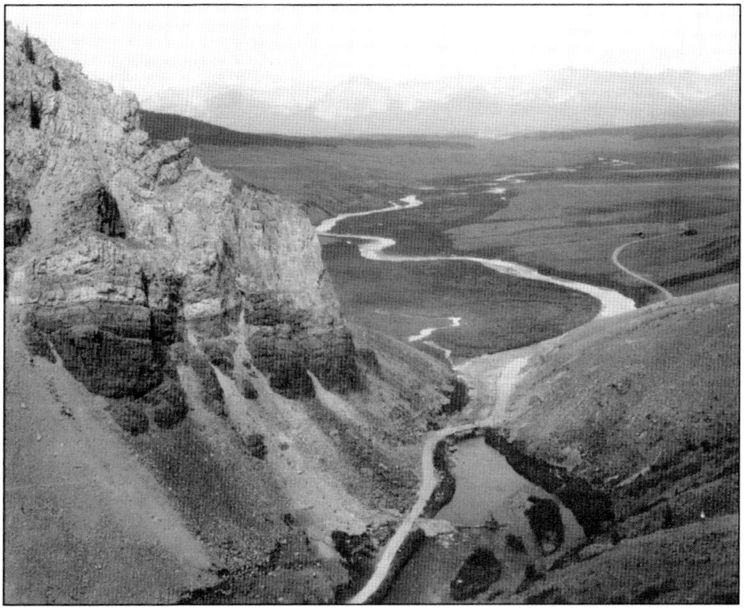

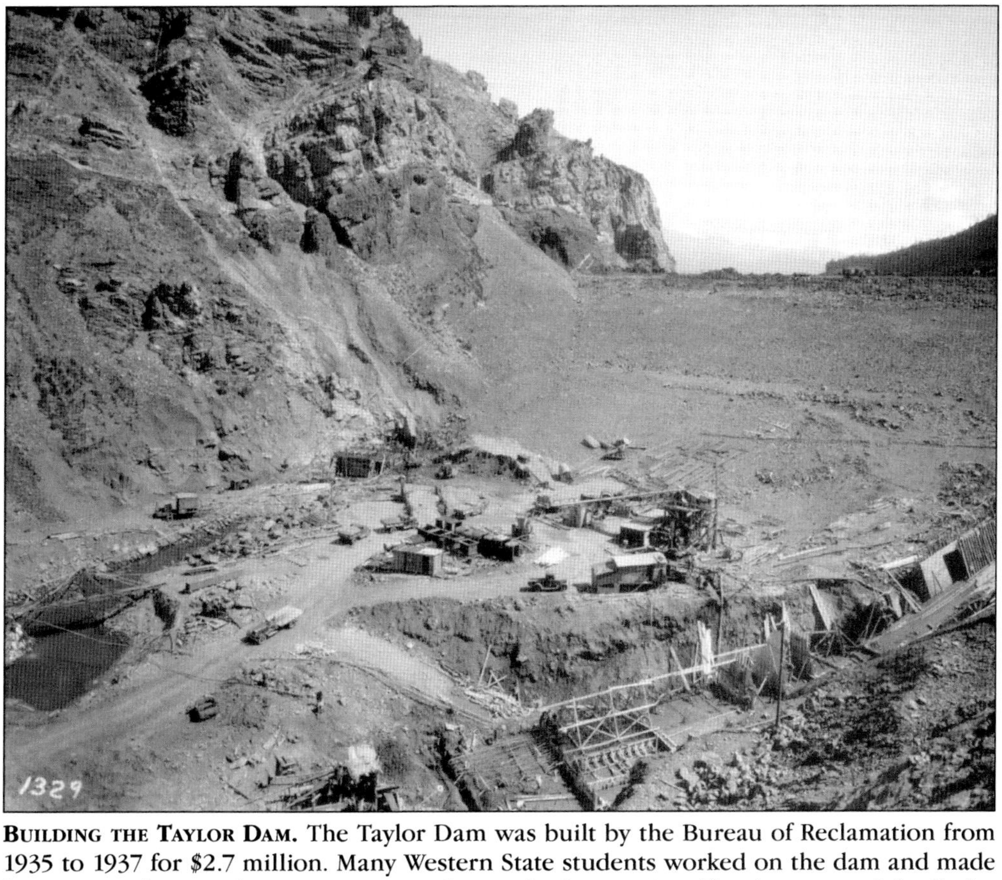

Building the Taylor Dam. The Taylor Dam was built by the Bureau of Reclamation from 1935 to 1937 for $2.7 million. Many Western State students worked on the dam and made from 50¢ to $1.10 an hour, great wages during the Depression. The dam created the Taylor Reservoir, which holds 106,200 acre-feet of water.

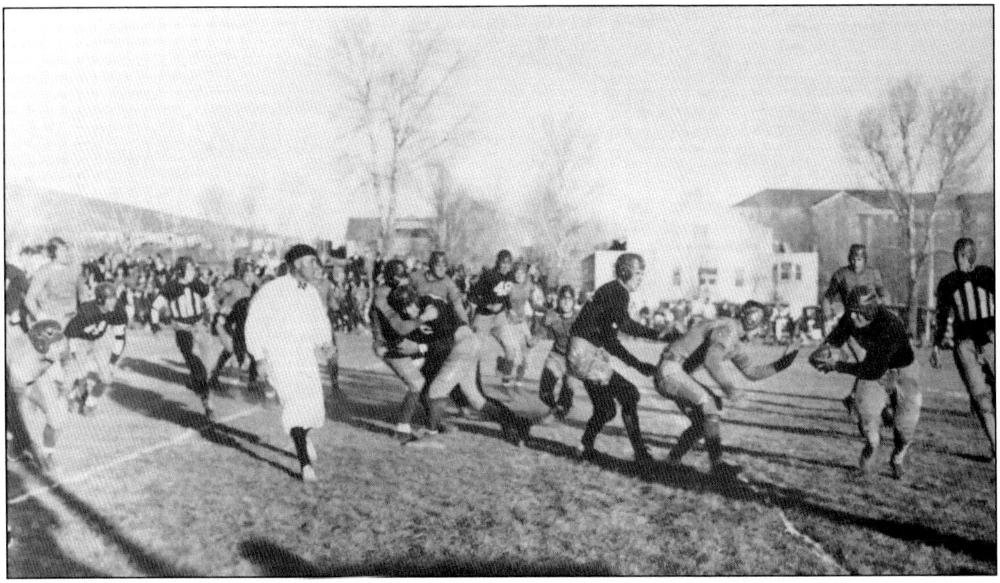

1930s Football. A Western State halfback runs a sweep around left end in a 1933 game on the WSC campus. Crawford Hall and Taylor Hall can be seen in the background. Mountaineer football players played on both offense and defense in those days.

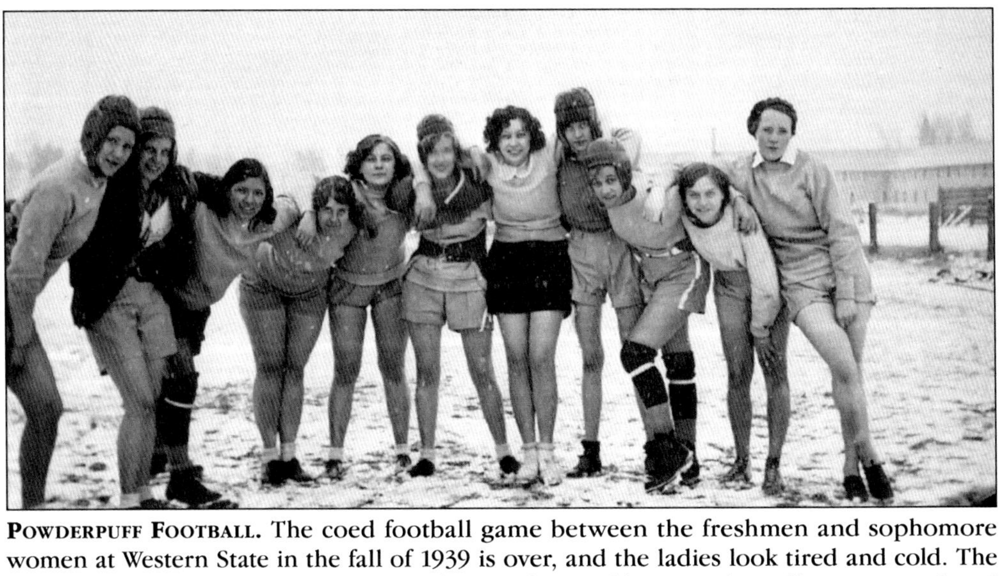

Powderpuff Football. The coed football game between the freshmen and sophomore women at Western State in the fall of 1939 is over, and the ladies look tired and cold. The sophomores defeated the freshmen 13-6 in the first and last powderpuff game ever played at WSC. (WSCU.)

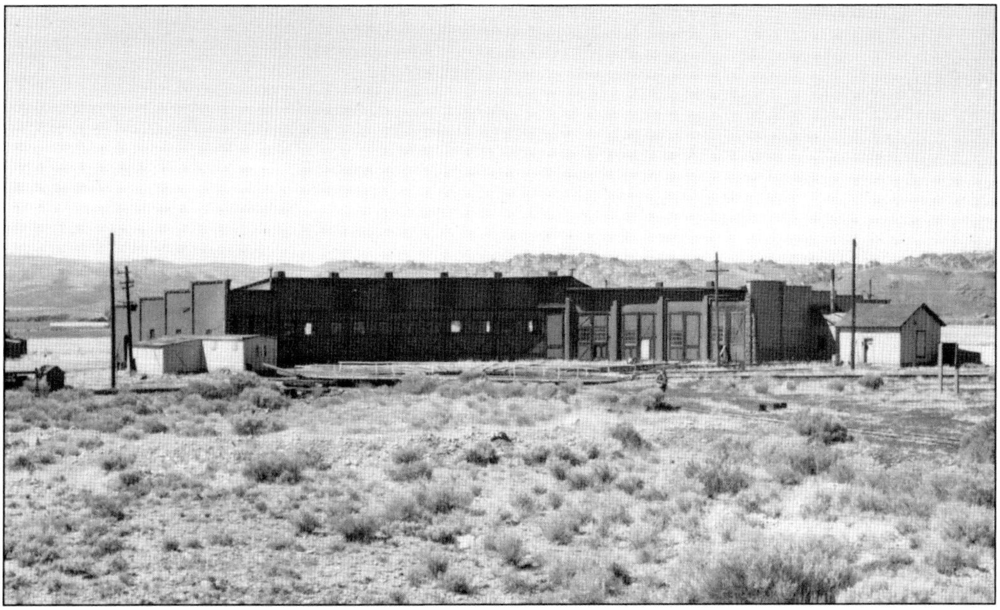

Gunnison Roundhouse. The Gunnison Roundhouse had seen better days when this photograph was taken in the 1930s. The Denver & Rio Grande and other railroads were being replaced by trucks, planes, and autos. For a long time, however, the Rio Grande was the only way in and out of Gunnison for Western State students.

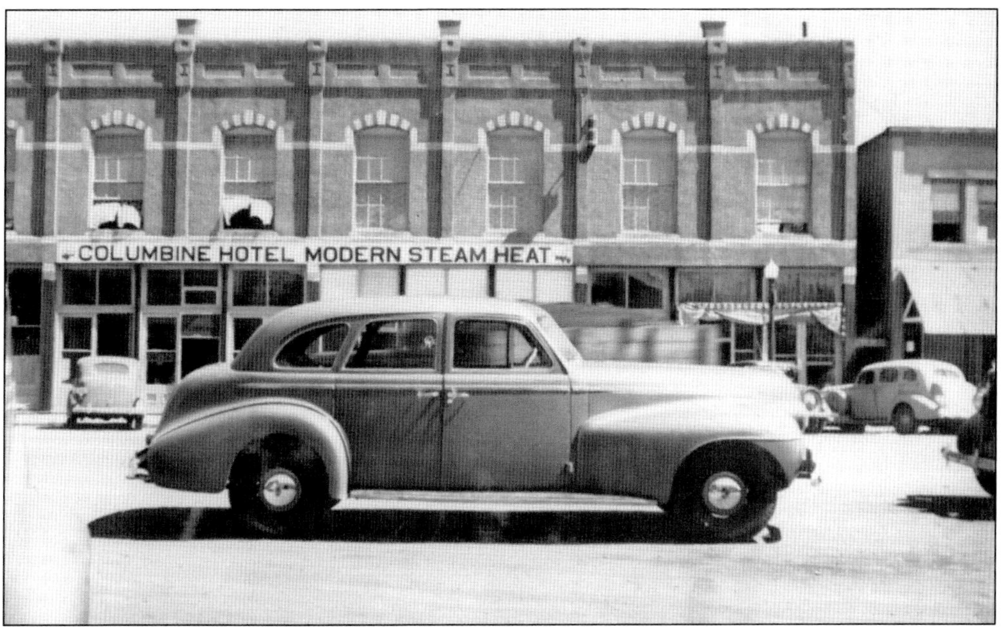

The Columbine. Built in the 1880s, the Columbine Hotel was one of Gunnison's earliest hotels, and it still exists today. This 1930s photograph shows the hotel at a time during the Great Depression when it was simply trying to survive.

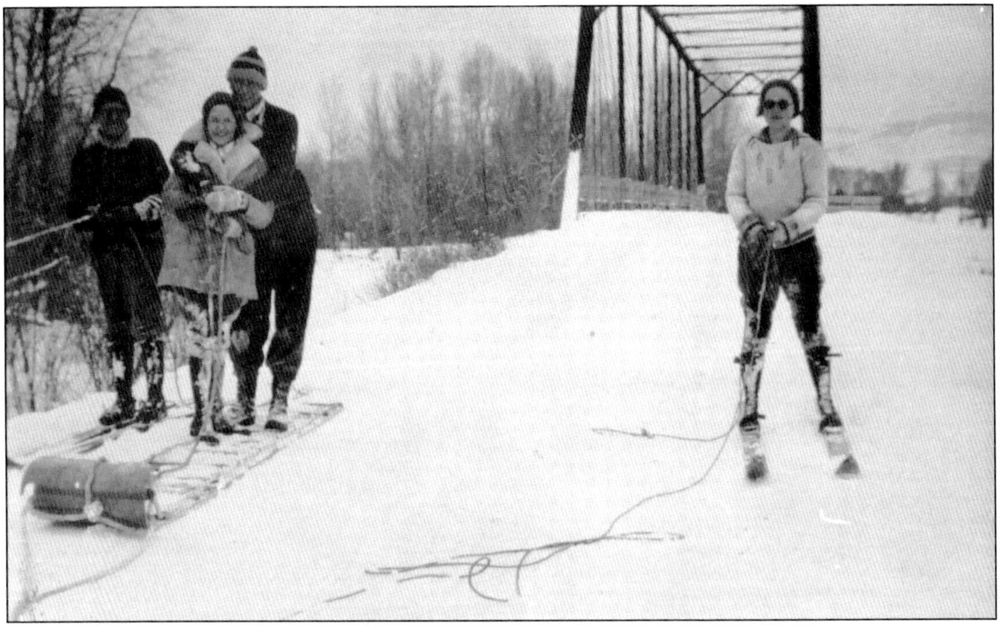

Winter Fun. Western State College students enjoy winter at the Twin Bridges just west of Gunnison in 1931. Two of the students are on skis, and two others are on top of a toboggan as they are pulled by a car along the road. This was exciting, as speeds got up to 20 miles an hour.

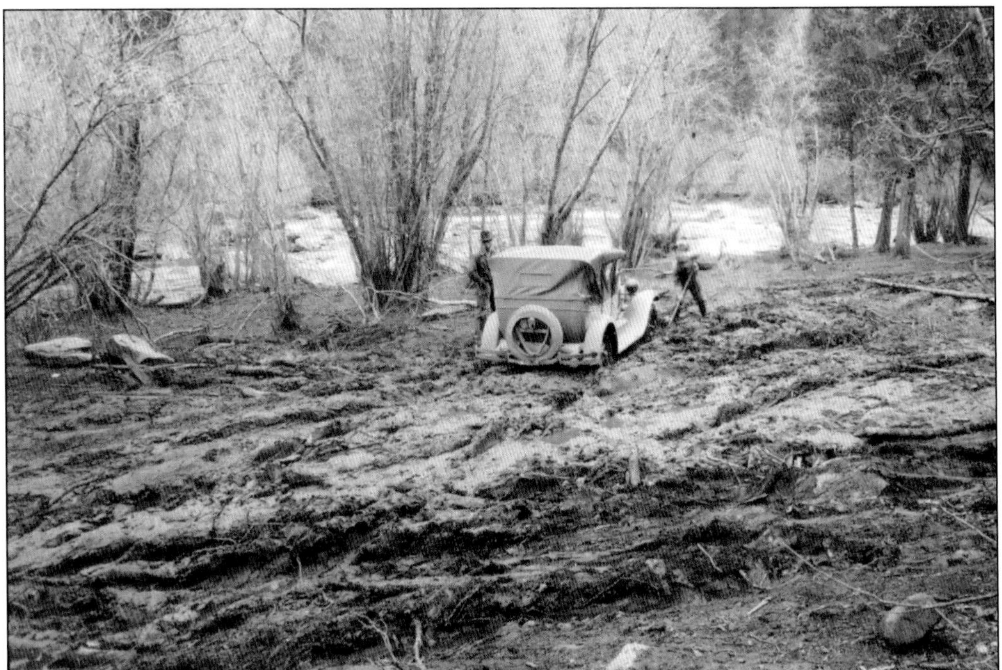

Trouble in the Mud. In the spring of the year before better, higher, and blacktop roads were built, travel in the Gunnison Country was a horror. On May 7, 1935, for seven miles from Almont and along the Taylor River, the road was a quagmire, and the car seen here is hopelessly stuck. Why the driver attempted to go through this section of road is a mystery.

1931 Football. Coach Tefler Mead of the Western State football team poses with three of his top players in front of the wooden stands at the college in 1931. The players are, from left to right, (first row) Maurice Kyffin and William McCool; (second row) Lewis Michaels. (WSCU.)

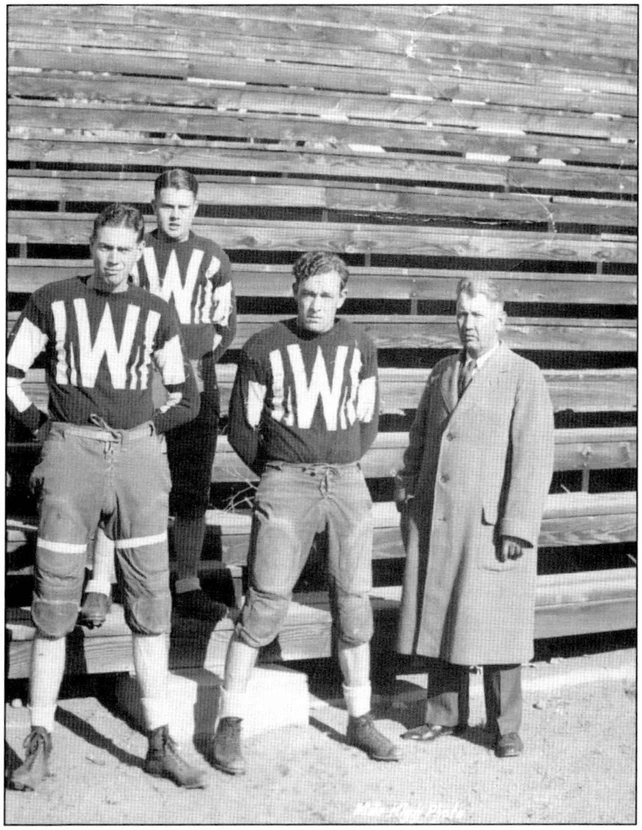

The Skaters. Young boys and girls pose for a photograph at the skating pond on the Western State campus in 1934. Taylor and Ute Halls are in the background. Skating was a popular pastime during the tough days of the Depression, and the rink was always crowded on weekends.

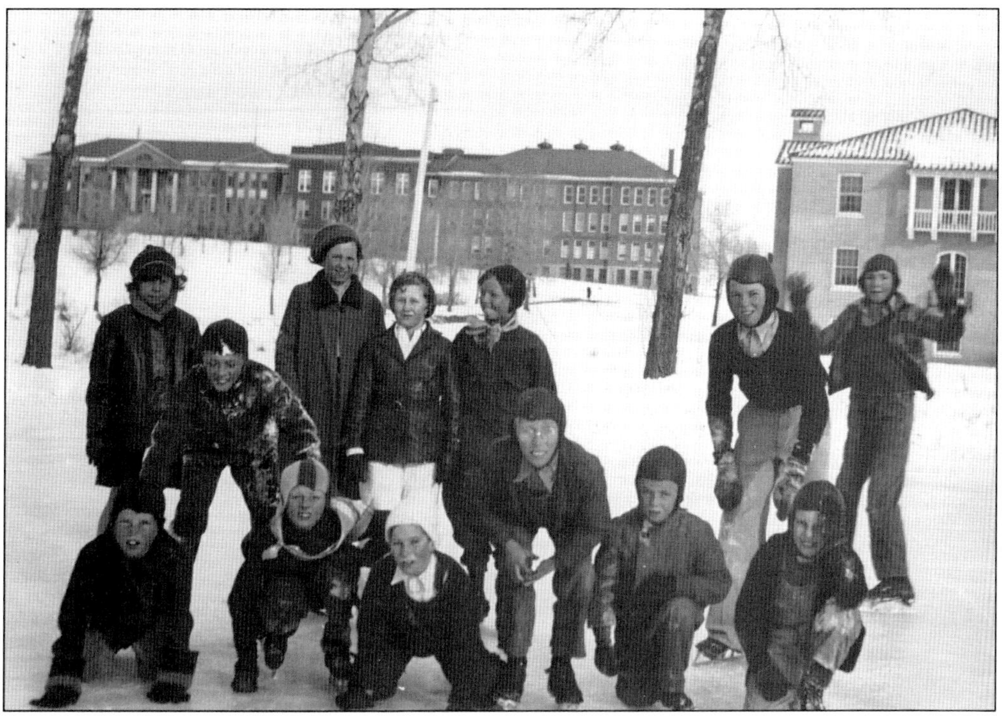

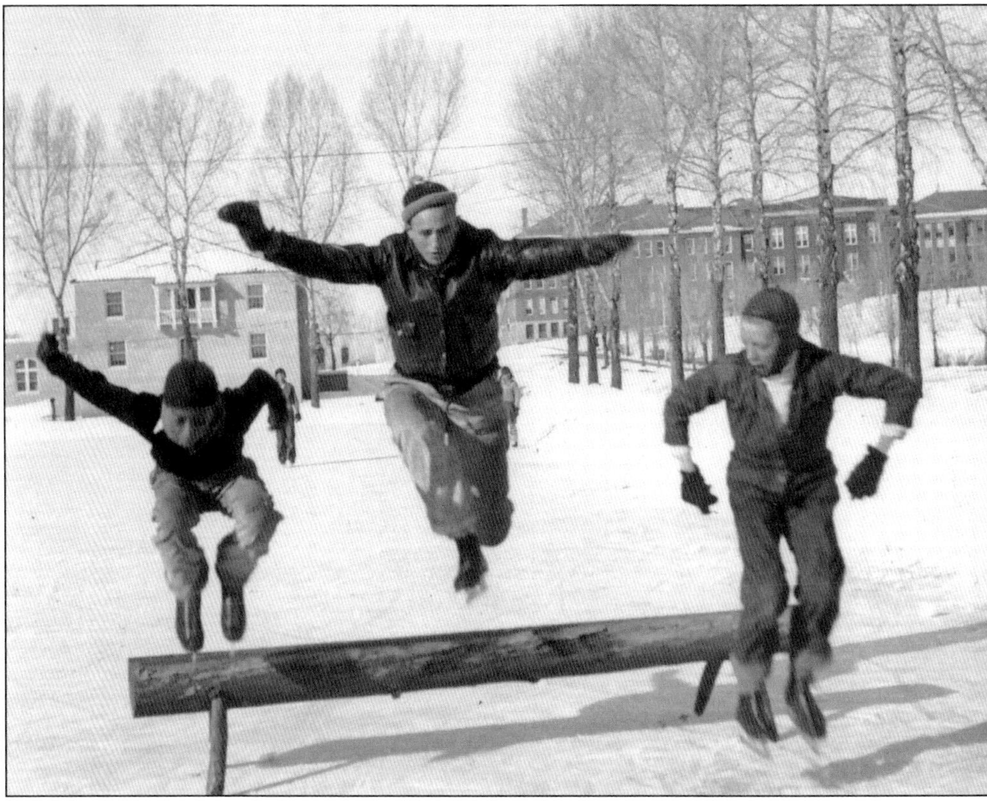

KEITH FRY. Western State student Keith Fry is in full flight along with two younger friends at the Western State skating rink in the mid-1930s. Fry went on to become a prominent citizen in Gunnison and one of its top fly fishermen.

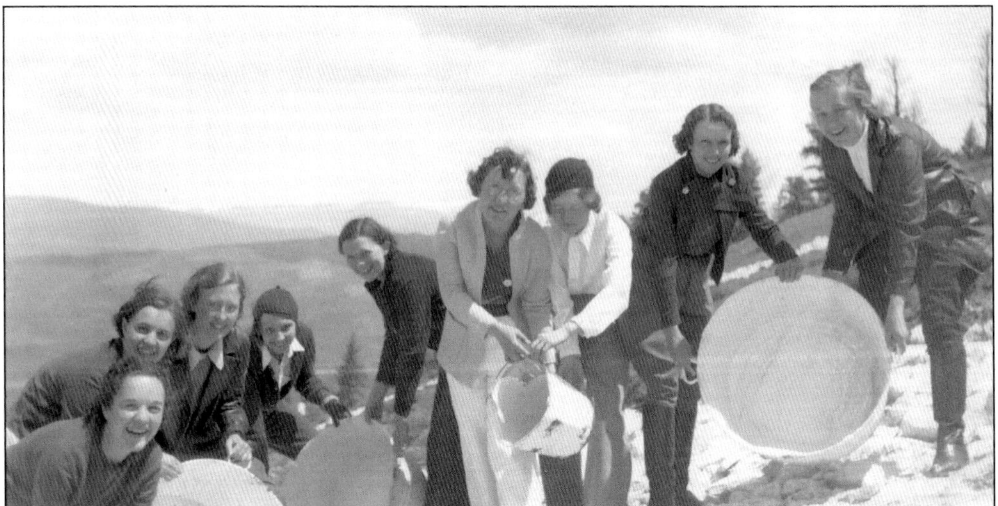

WHITEWASHING THE "W." Western State coeds make up the bucket brigade in the spring of 1935 as they whitewash the "W" on Tenderfoot Mountain. W Day, a huge day with the entire student body, involved melting snow, mixing lime, passing buckets, and making the "W" look good. (WSCU.)

CAPTAINS. Standing before a 1930s auto on the Western State campus, two unidentified captains of the tennis team are decked out in their colorful letter sweaters. Tennis did not have the popularity of football or basketball, but matches were well attended. (WSCU.)

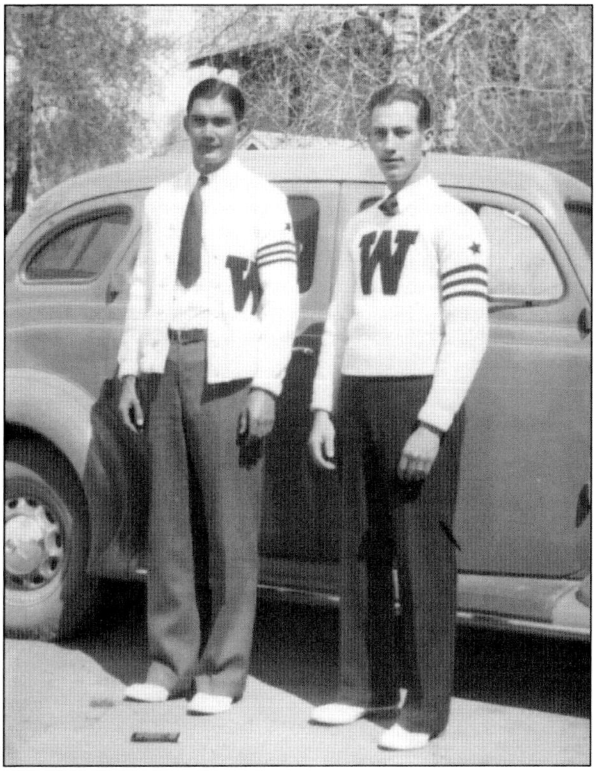

TWIRLERS. Western State College music camp twirlers go through their practice routines during the summer of 1939 on the college campus. With over 500 in the band camps every year, Gunnison and WSC got a huge economic lift. (WSCU.)

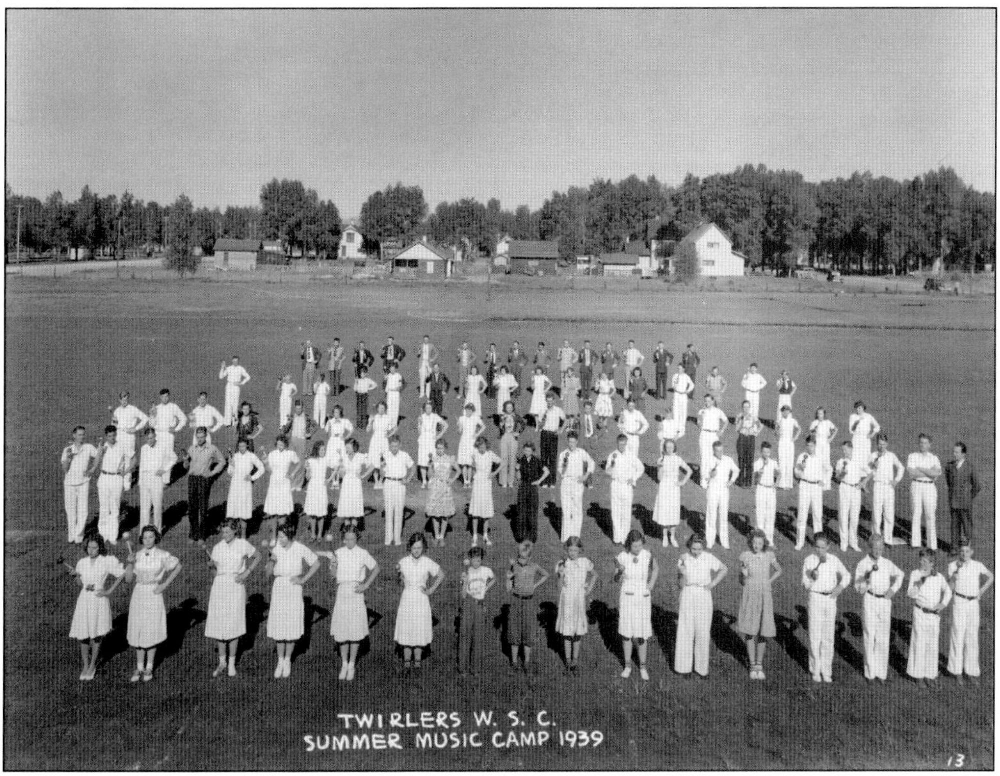

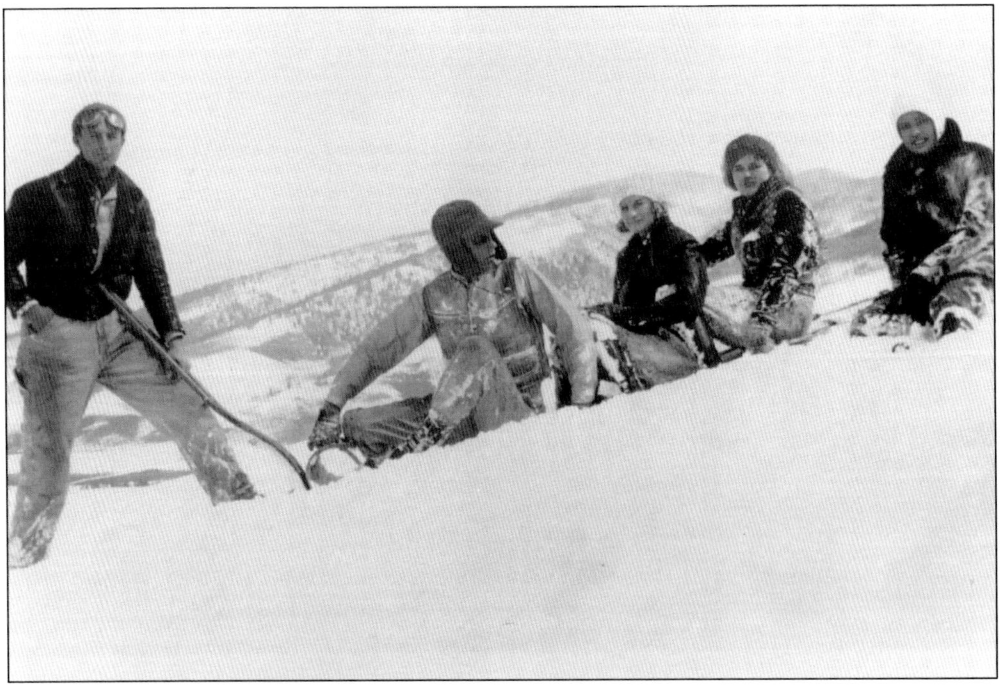

Tobogganing. Four Western State College students are ready to ride a toboggan on Quick's Hill in 1932. The hill dropped 400 feet and was very steep. Some of the students built a jump to make the ride even more exciting. Over 200 inches of snow fell yearly on the hill near Crested Butte. WSC student Fred Brand is on the left.

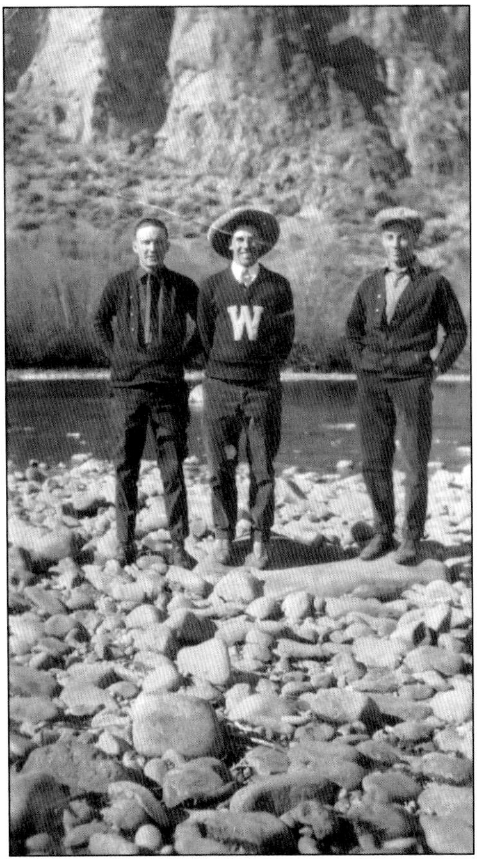

In the Black Canyon. Three Western State students have a day off in the Black Canyon on a fall day in 1934. The canyon was a popular spot for Western students who had much fun climbing, fishing, or boating. Some of Western's students, such as Jim Newberry of Cimarron, pioneered new climbing routes on the canyon walls.

Three

GUNNISON

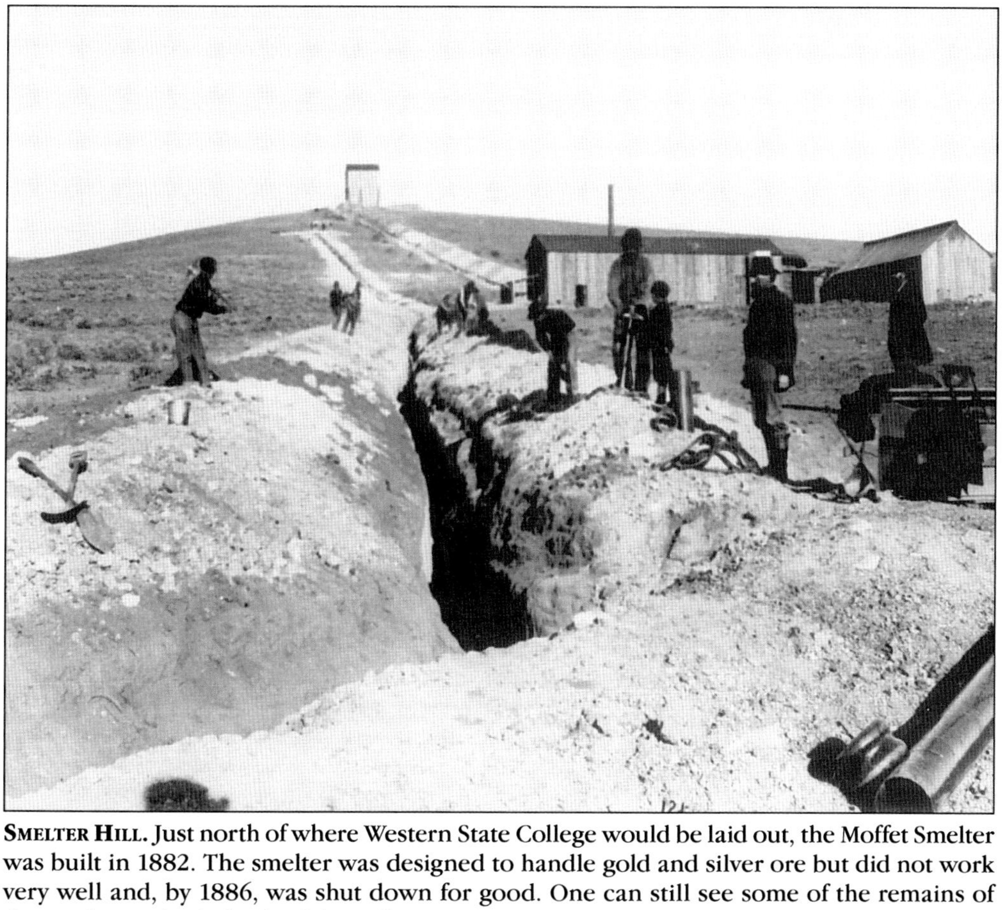

SMELTER HILL. Just north of where Western State College would be laid out, the Moffet Smelter was built in 1882. The smelter was designed to handle gold and silver ore but did not work very well and, by 1886, was shut down for good. One can still see some of the remains of the smelter today in back of the college.

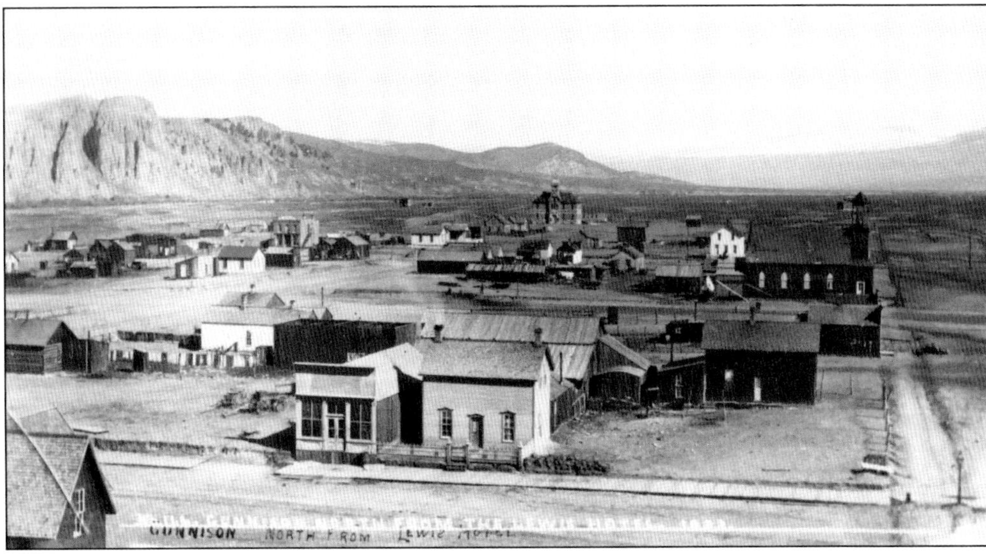

Gunnison, 1883. Viewed from the top of the La Veta Hotel, also called the Lewis House, Gunnison is shown in 1883. The famed Palisades, a rock formation named for the palisades on the Hudson River, and with an early Gunnison school can be seen in the background. (GPM.)

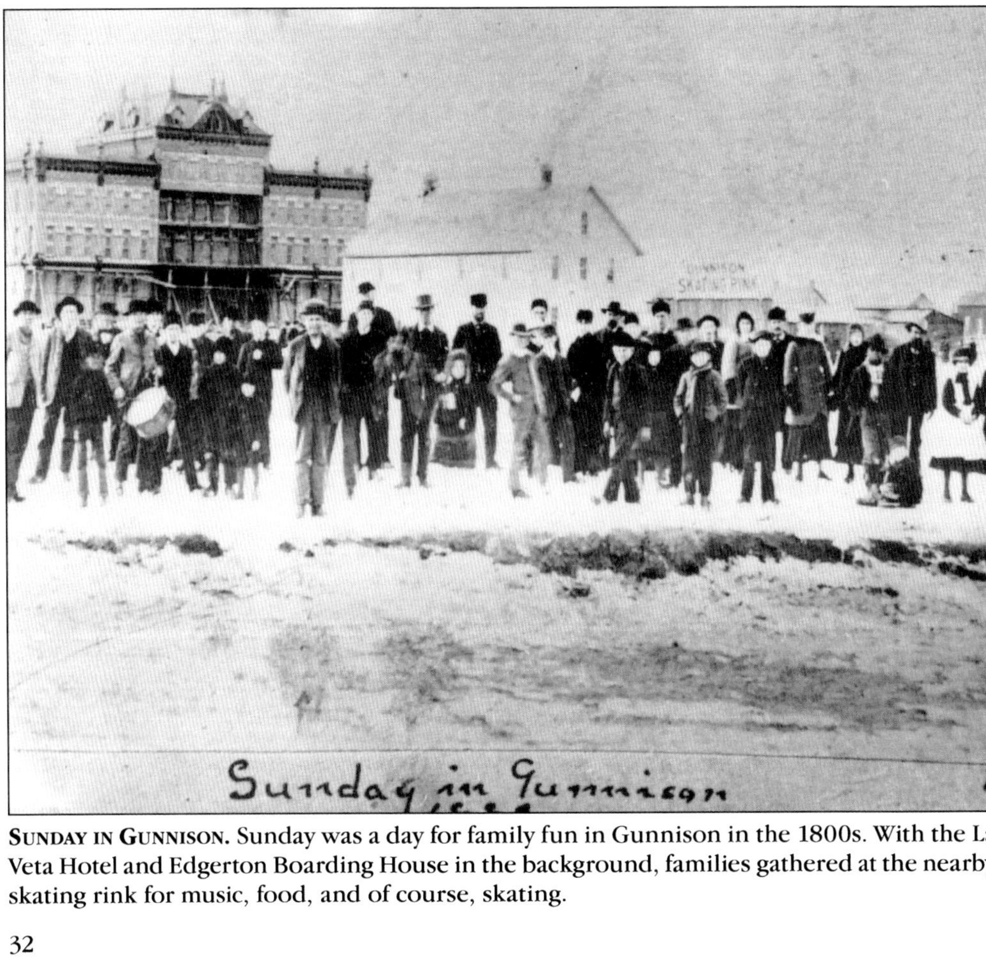

Sunday in Gunnison. Sunday was a day for family fun in Gunnison in the 1800s. With the La Veta Hotel and Edgerton Boarding House in the background, families gathered at the nearby skating rink for music, food, and of course, skating.

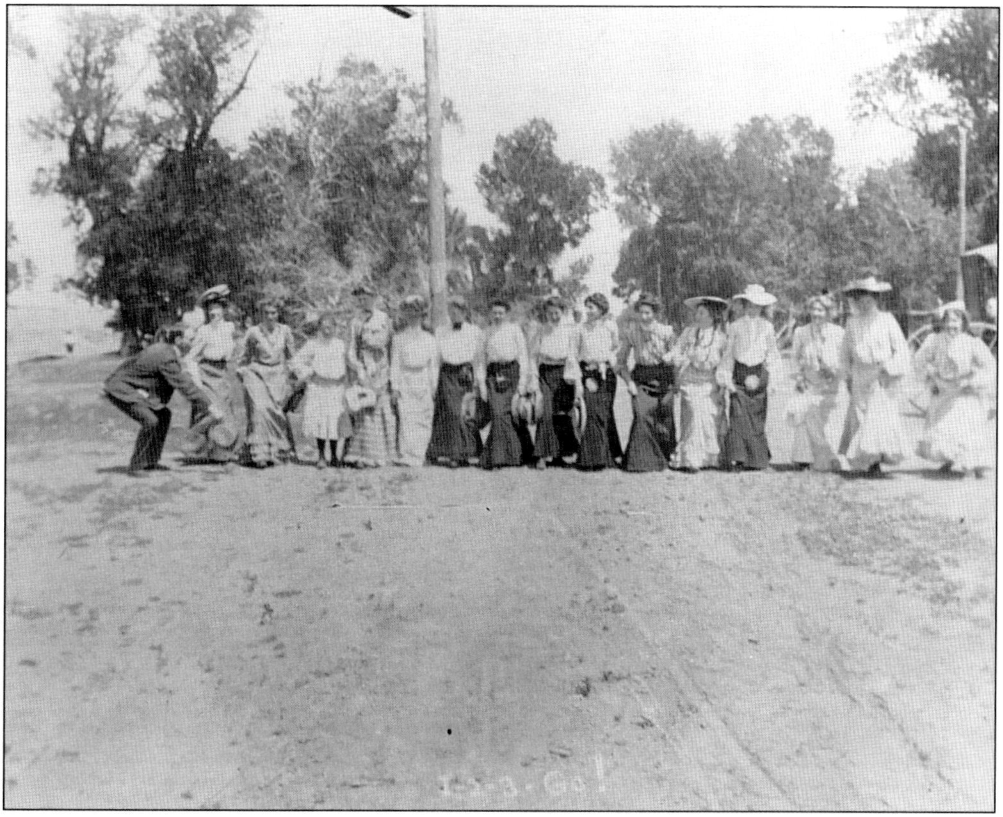

FOOTRACE. Local Gunnison women gather for a 50-yard race in Gunnison in 1894. The women were all decked out because it was July 4. With the type of dresses they were wearing, the race could not have been very fast.

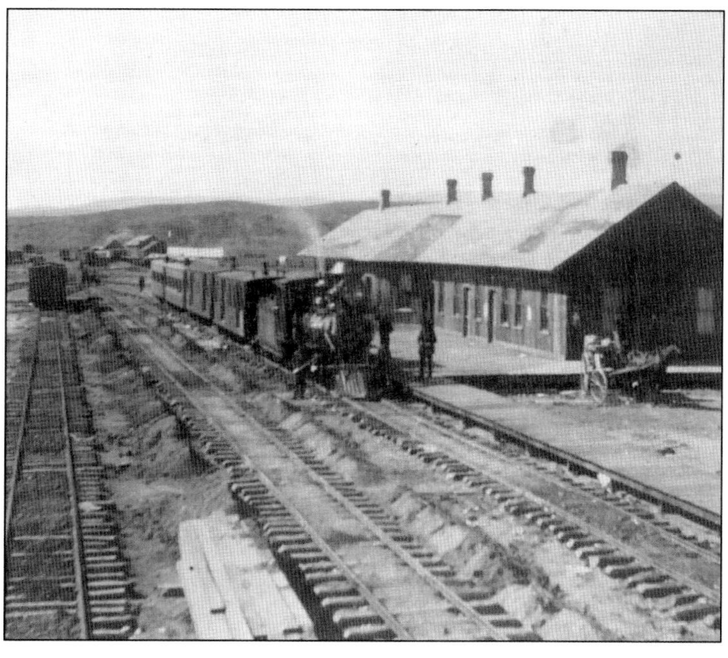

D&RG DEPOT. After the beginning of Colorado State Normal School in 1911, all non-local students came to Gunnison by Denver & Rio Grande narrow-gauge train. The train ran from Denver over 200 miles west to Gunnison and also ran from Ouray and Grand Junction east to Colorado State Normal.

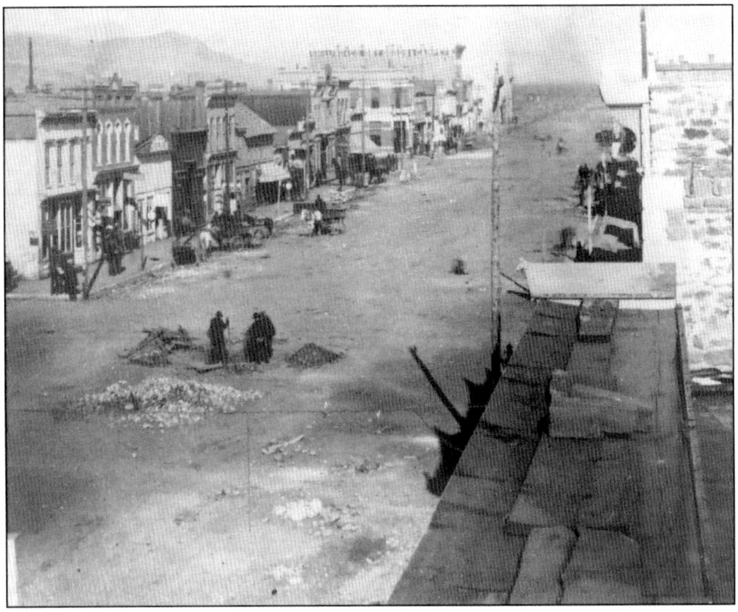

Early-day Gunnison. Gunnison was in the midst of a boom in 1882. Main Street was filled with new buildings and hundreds of people a day coming to the new Eldorado. The town had a railroad, smelter, and rich investors—the future looked bright.

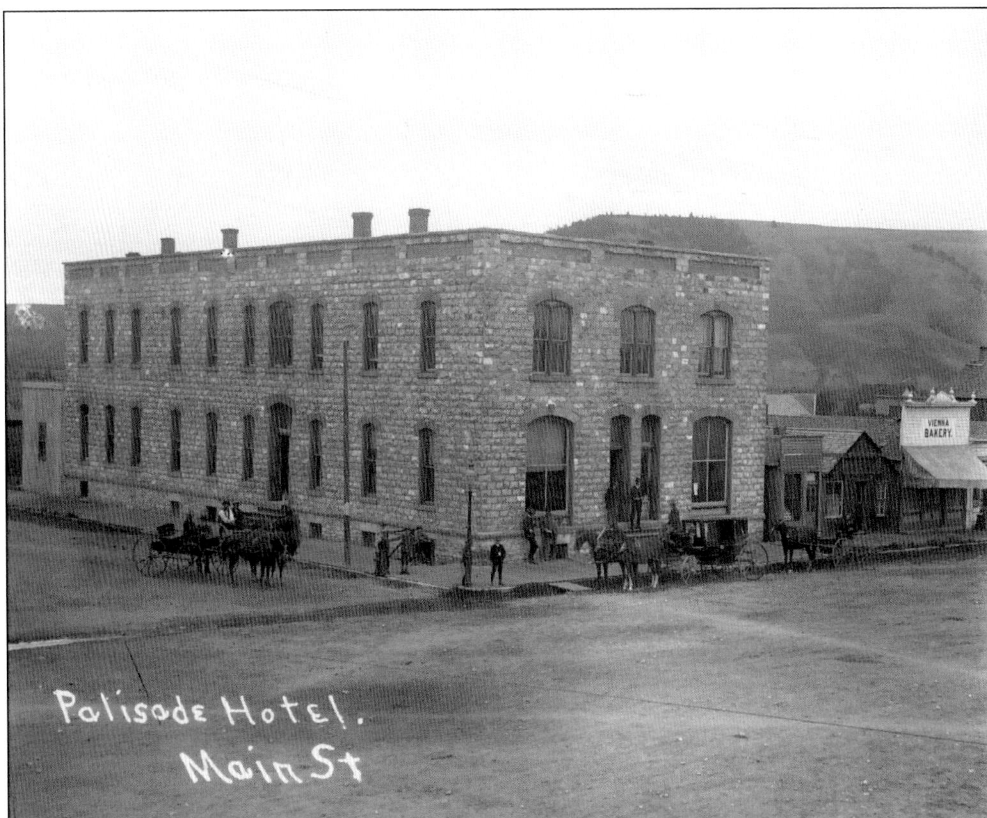

Palisade Hotel. The Palisade Hotel on Gunnison's Main Street was one of the finest in the early 1880s. Originally known as the Tabor House, the hotel was built in 1881 for $27,000. The hotel had 27 rooms and fed 110 to 140 customers per day. (GPM.)

Colorado Street School. Built in the 1880s, the Colorado Street School stood alone just as Gunnison was beginning to prosper. The Moffet Smelter is in the background. The school was built out of brick and one of the finest of its kind in Western Colorado. (GPM.)

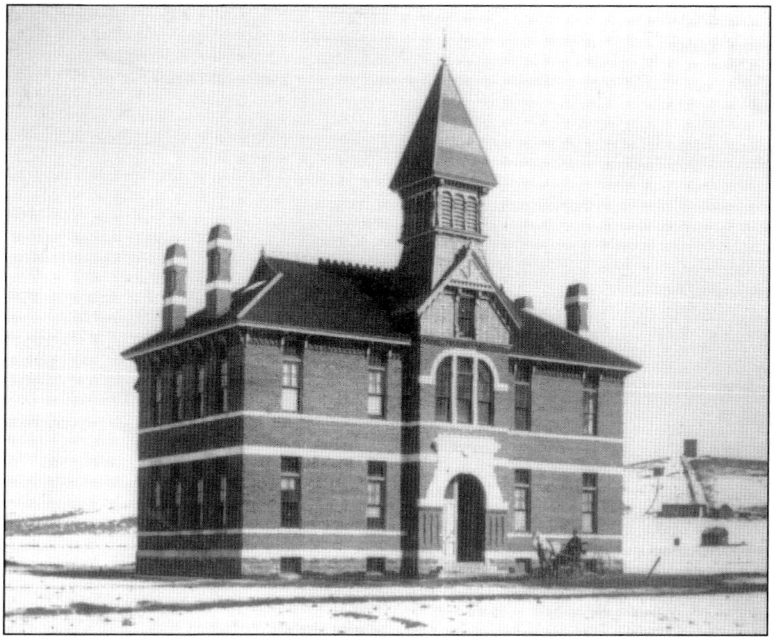

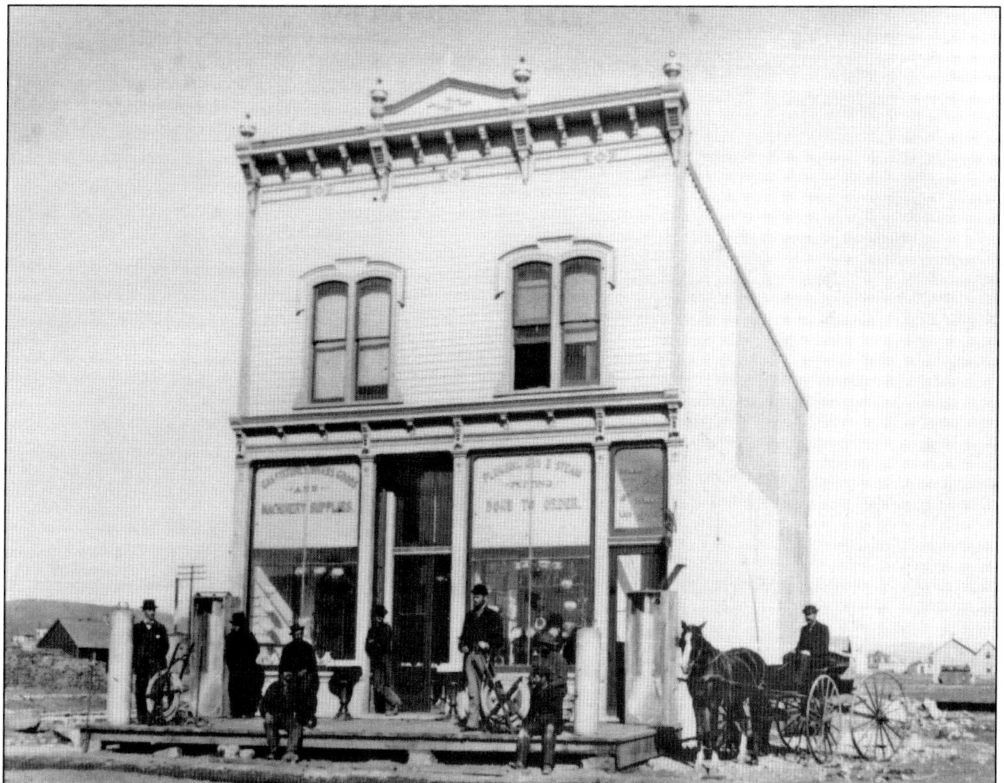

Lonely Sentinel. A gas, plumbing, and machinery store sits alone in the middle of Gunnison in 1881. The town was growing rapidly, and by the following year, the store was surrounded by many others on Tomichi Avenue. (GPM.)

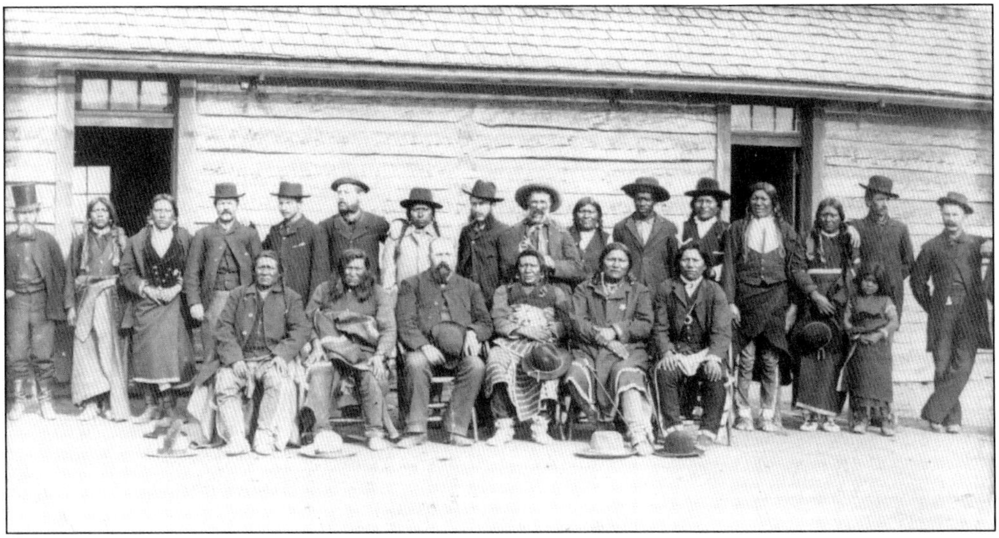

Los Pinos. The Los Pinos Ute Indian Agency was located approximately 35 miles southeast of Gunnison and operated from 1868 to 1875. Government officials and a group of Utes pose for a picture in 1871. A cow camp, which supplied the Utes with food, was centered where Gunnison eventually would be established.

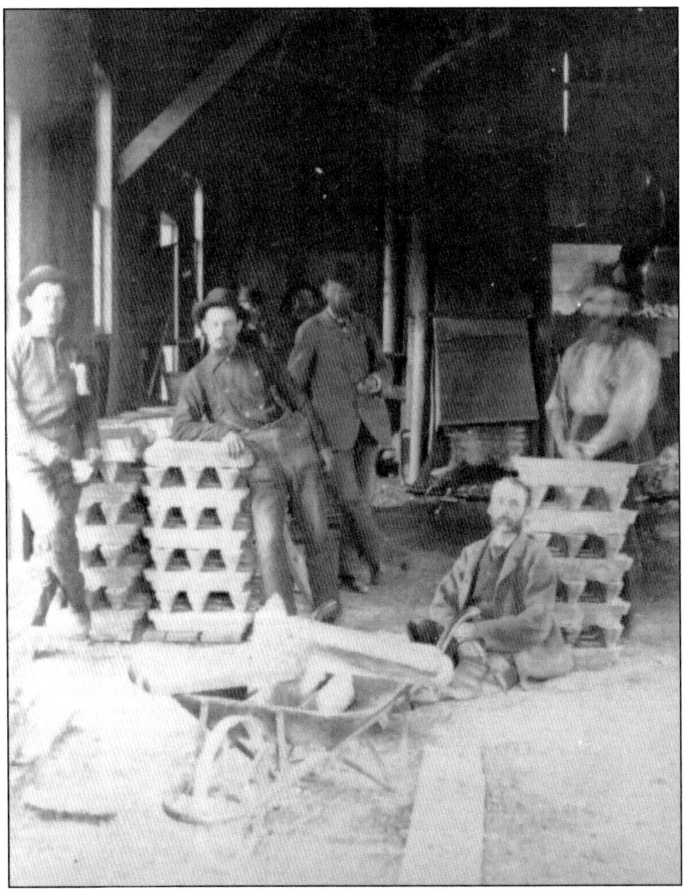

Silver Ore. Silver bars produced by miners from nearby Gothic, Pitkin, White Pine, Tin Cup, and Irwin are shown here at the Moffet Smelter. The smelter has separated the silver from all its impurities. Silver sold for $1 an ounce in the early 1880s but soon fell to 58¢, forcing the closure of all silver mines.

"THE BOY ORATOR OF THE PLATTE." The famed and legendary William Jennings Bryan was in Gunnison in 1908 as he ran for president for a third time. Bryan was an advocate of the silver standard and the leader of Populist and Democrats nationwide. He lost the 1908 election to William Howard Taft. (GPM.)

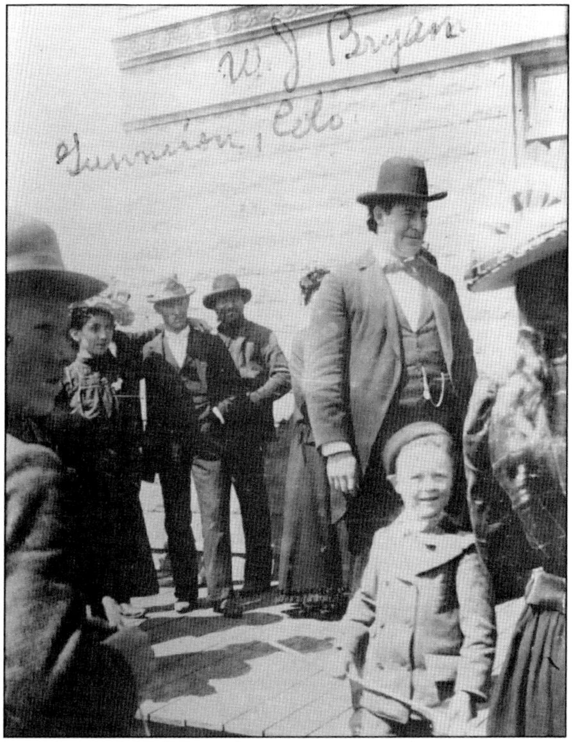

CORNET BAND. Music was very important in the early days of Gunnison with many groups forming bands. Competition was fierce, and all bands aspired to be called the best. The Gunnison Cornet Band in 1880 achieved that honor in a vote of town leaders. (GPM.)

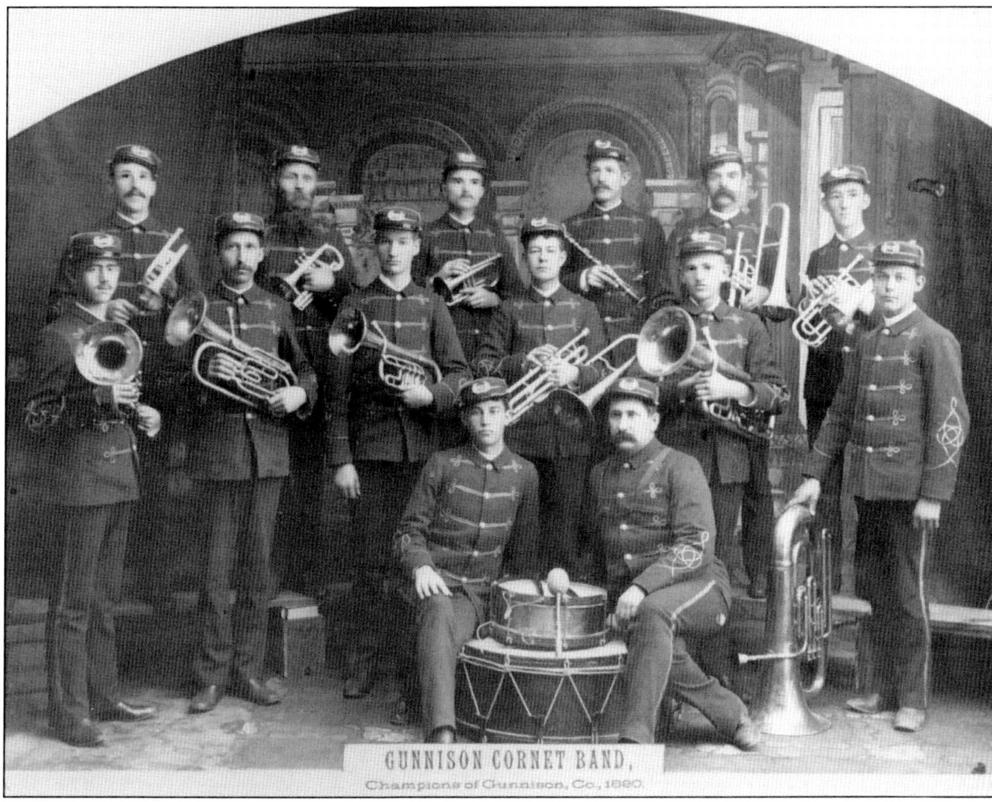

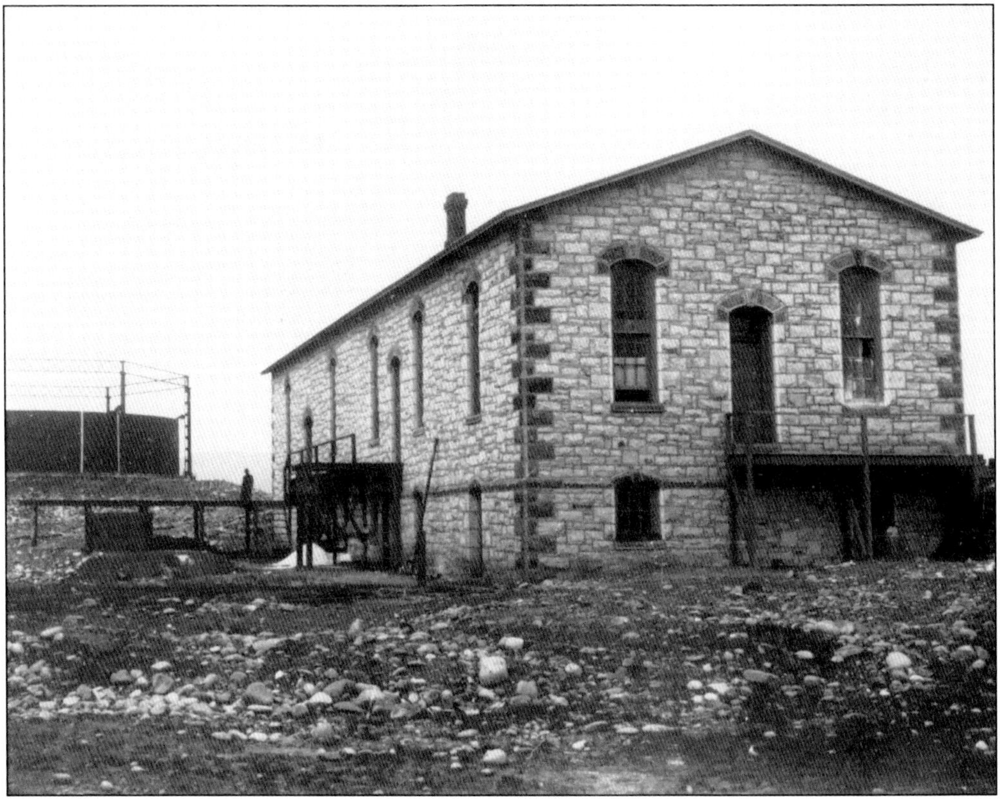

GUNNISON GAS AND WATERWORKS. D.J. McCanne, a top engineer, was chosen to construct and manage the new gas and waterworks in Gunnison in 1882. The waterworks began operating in June and the gasworks in August. No enterprise in Gunnison did more to ensure the town's future.

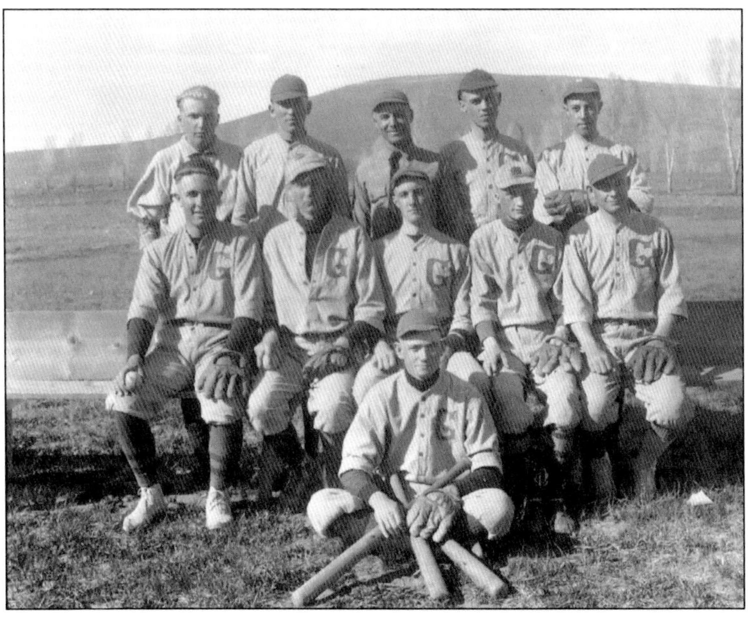

GUNNISON BASEBALL. Baseball was the major game played in Colorado prior to World War I. The Gunnison baseball team played games all over the Western Slope and, in 1900, was considered one of the finest. (GPM.)

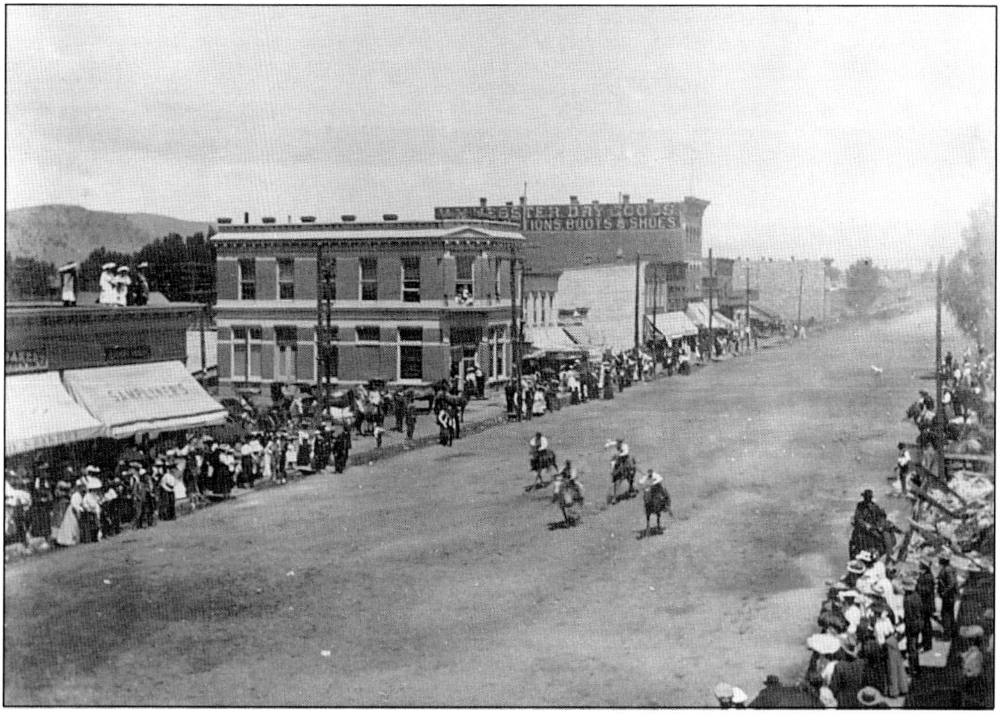

Horse Race. Before the start of Cattleman's Days, ranchers of the Gunnison Country had a major celebration on July 4. One of the highlights was a rodeo, but close behind came the exciting horse races featuring ranchers riding their fastest horses in a race down Main Street.

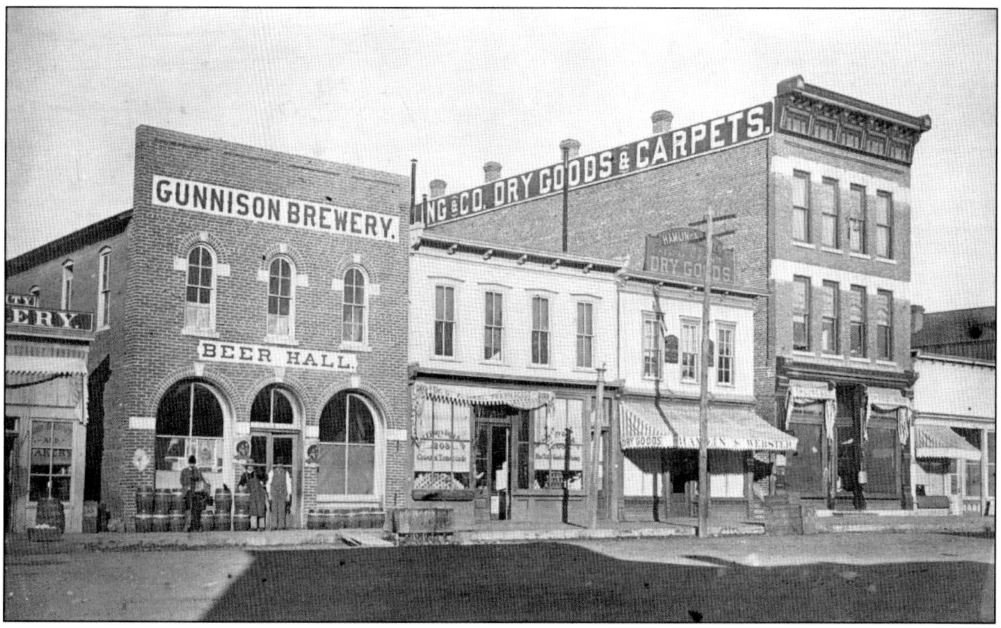

Gunnison Brewery. In the booming early 1880s, Gunnison had two breweries, and they were both kept busy. The Gunnison Brewery was on Main Street. The Dry Goods & Carpets Building still exists in 2013.

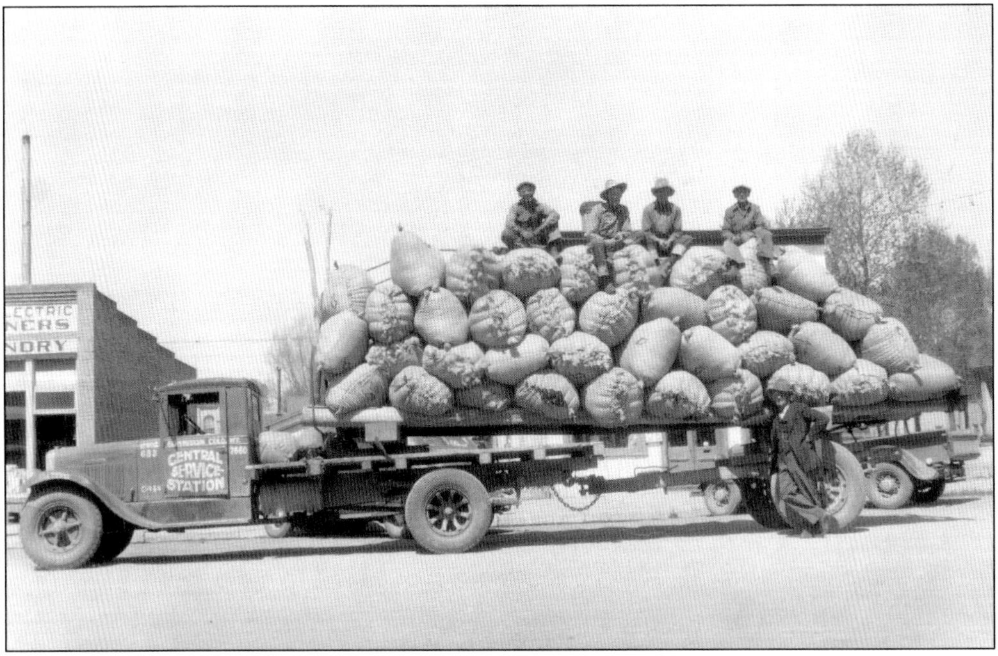

Woolies. The Gunnison Country is famous for its well-bred cattle along with cattle-sheep wars that went on for over 50 years. Some sheep, however, grazed on the federal range. Here, in 1936 in Gunnison, sheepman Otis Moore takes a large quantity of wool to the railroad.

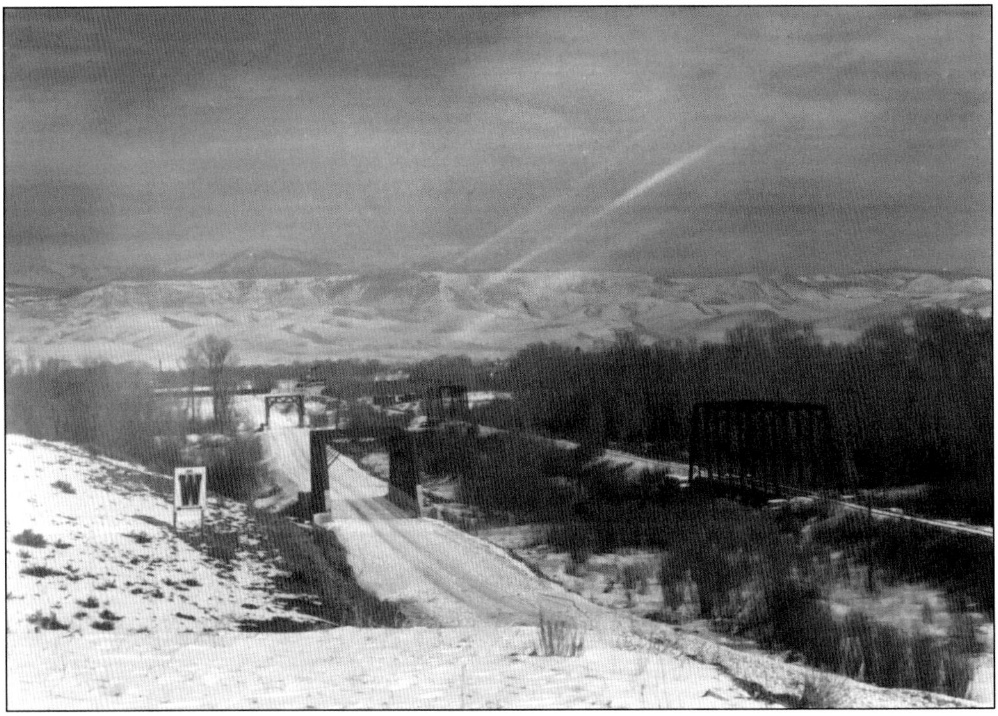

Twin Bridges. West of Gunnison, twin bridges allowed for both the Denver & Rio Grande Railroad and auto traffic in the 1930s. The sign with the "W" provided advertising for Western State and caught the eye of anyone headed east along Highway 50.

Four

The 1940s and 1950s

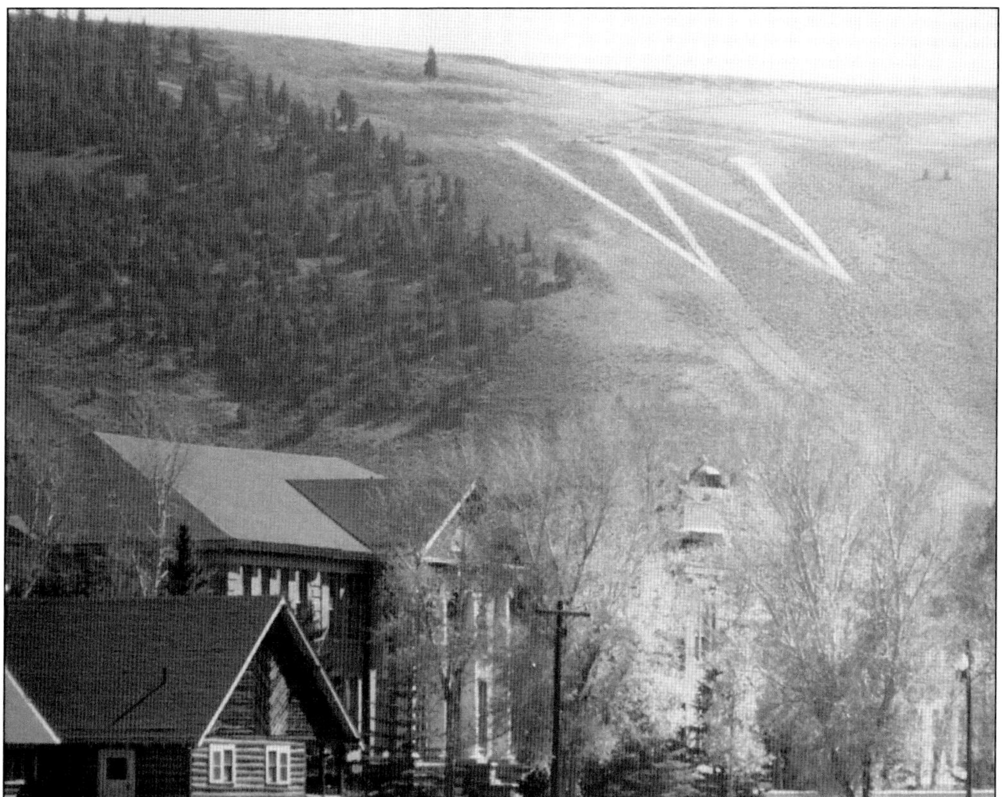

Magnificent Splendor. Taylor Hall and the Western State Clubhouse highlight this view in 1955. In the background is the "W," the largest college letter in the nation. The "W" was built out of rocks on Tenderfoot Mountain in 1923 and extends over 400 feet up and down.

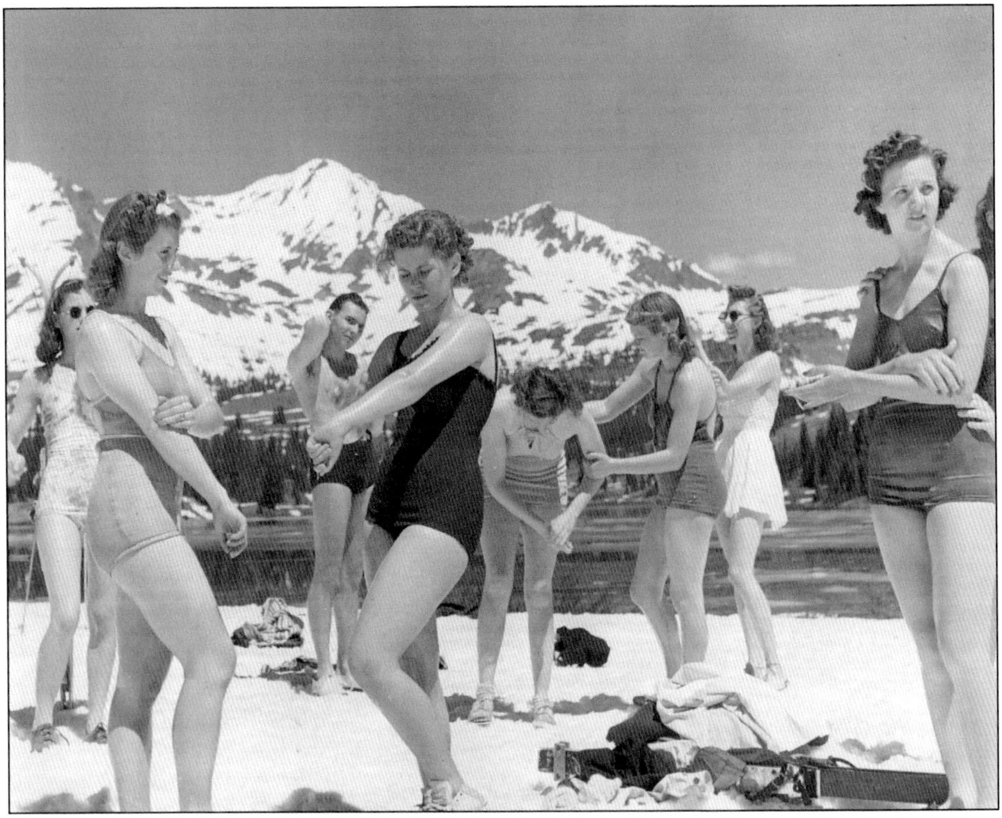

Springtime in the Rockies. One year before Pearl Harbor, Western State attempted to dispel views concerning the cold climate of the Gunnison Country. Students were taken to 10,000-foot-high Lake Irwin, 30 miles north of Gunnison, to sunbath with the Ruby Mountains forming the backdrop. They rafted, fished, and threw snowballs, and some even got into the lake for a short swim. (WSCU.)

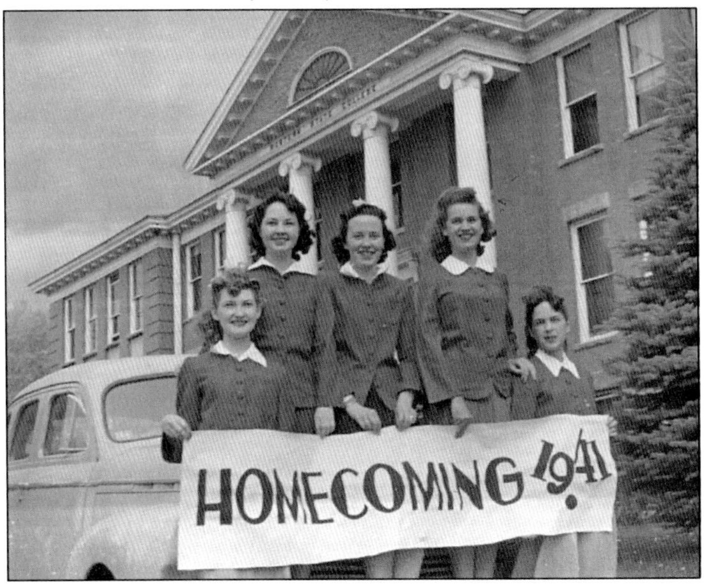

The Fateful Year. Five Western State coeds have homecoming on their minds in front of Taylor Hall in October 1941. Pearl Harbor was two months away, and after December 7, their lives would be changed forever. (WSCU.)

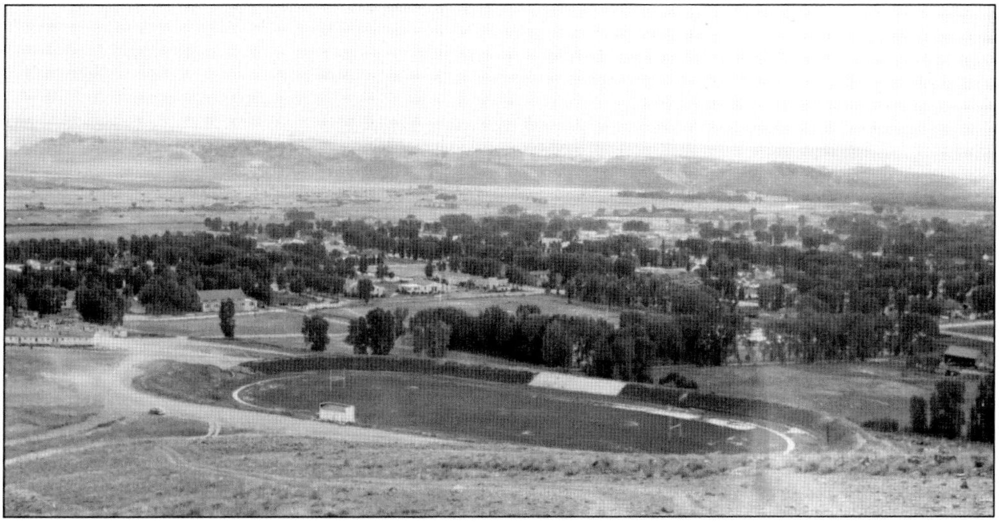

Mountaineer Bowl. Built in 1948, Mountaineer Bowl was a football stadium with seating for 3,000. A tremendous amount of rock was blasted out to create the field. Explosions could be heard all over the Gunnison Country, and some of the rocks landed 40 to 50 yards away.

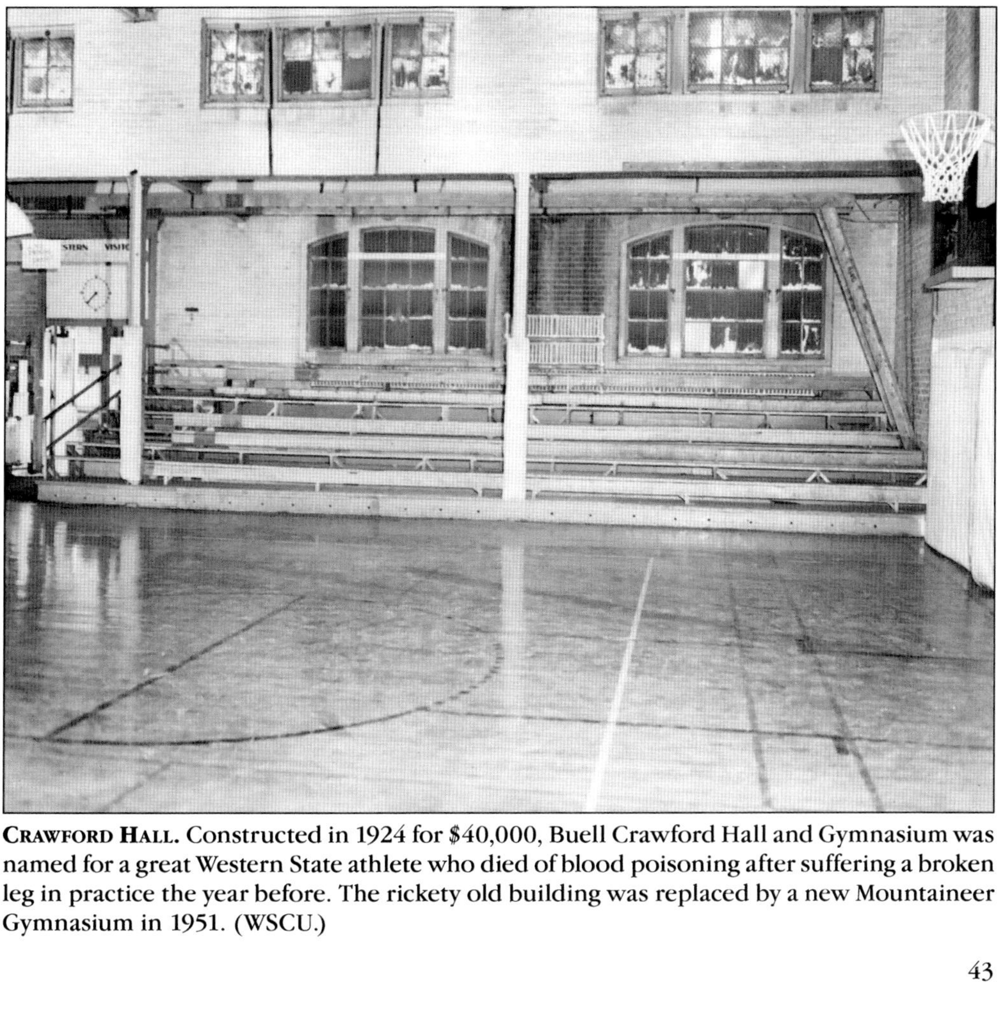

Crawford Hall. Constructed in 1924 for $40,000, Buell Crawford Hall and Gymnasium was named for a great Western State athlete who died of blood poisoning after suffering a broken leg in practice the year before. The rickety old building was replaced by a new Mountaineer Gymnasium in 1951. (WSCU.)

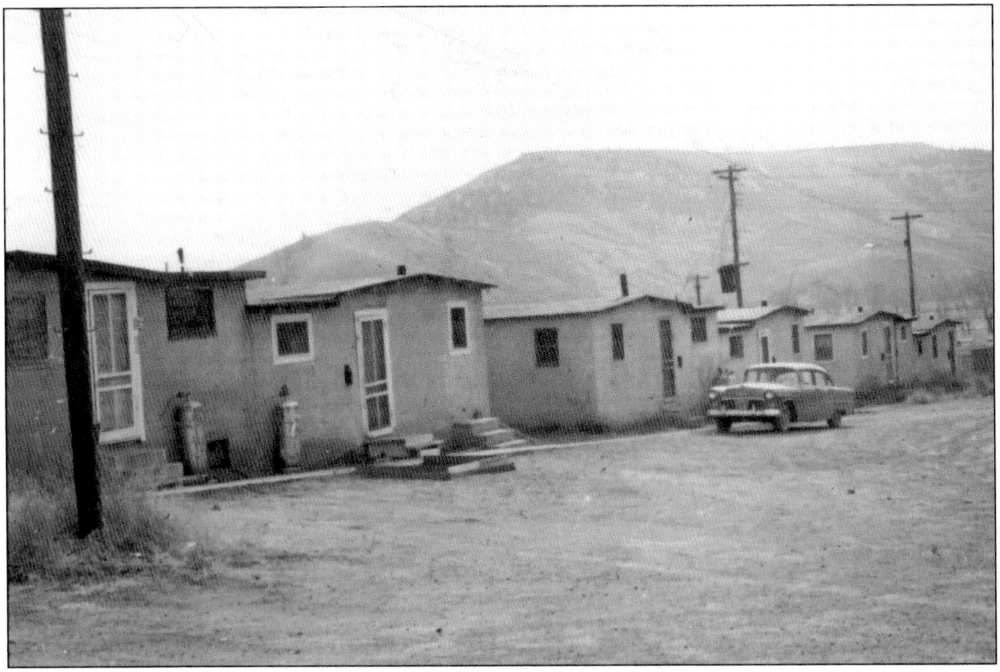

Highland Village. Built in 1922 with money coming from Western faculty and Gunnison citizens, Highland Village was north of Taylor Hall. Thirty cabins were built for $150 each and were rented to students for $4 a week. In 1923, ten more units were built. The village had its own mayor and government. (WSCU.)

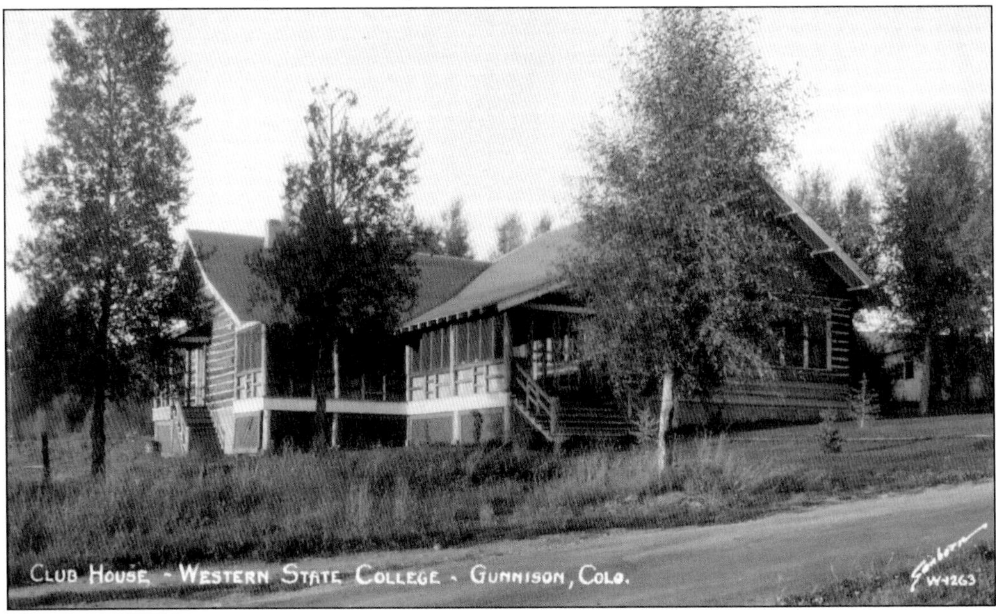

Western's Clubhouse. Built in the 1920s, the Western Clubhouse burned down in 1933. Within a few months, a new log structure was built with insurance funds and money from students and alumni. The clubhouse was the social center of the campus. This photograph shows it in the 1940s. In 1962, it was moved off campus and became the Last Chance, a bar which hosted many WSC students.

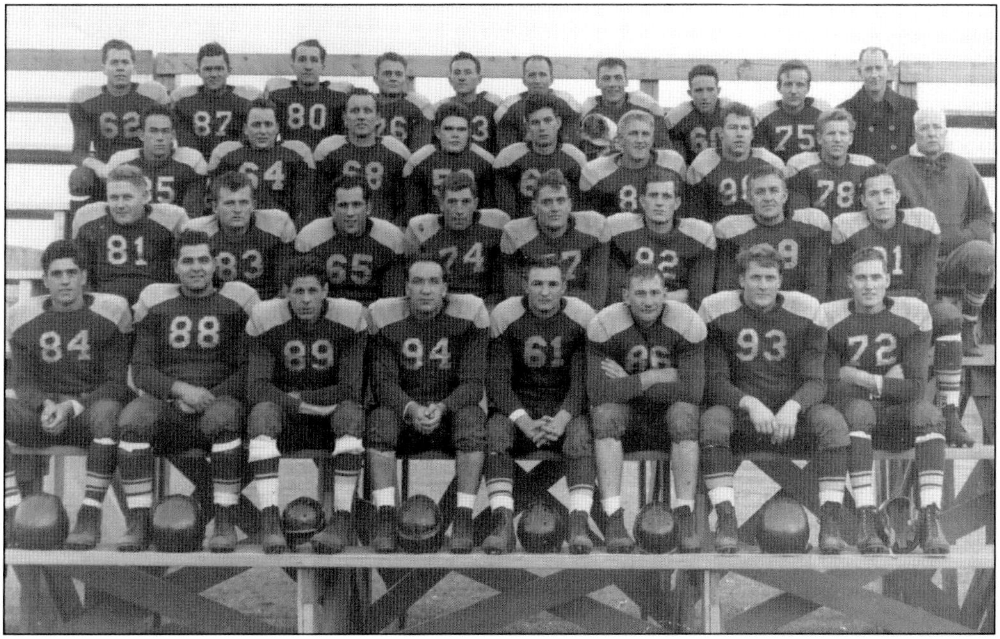

Football Team, 1948. With the end of World War II, football once again became popular and important at Western State. The 1948 team was coached by Paul Wright (far right in the third row) with Wayne Weare (far right in the fourth row) as his assistant. (WSCU.)

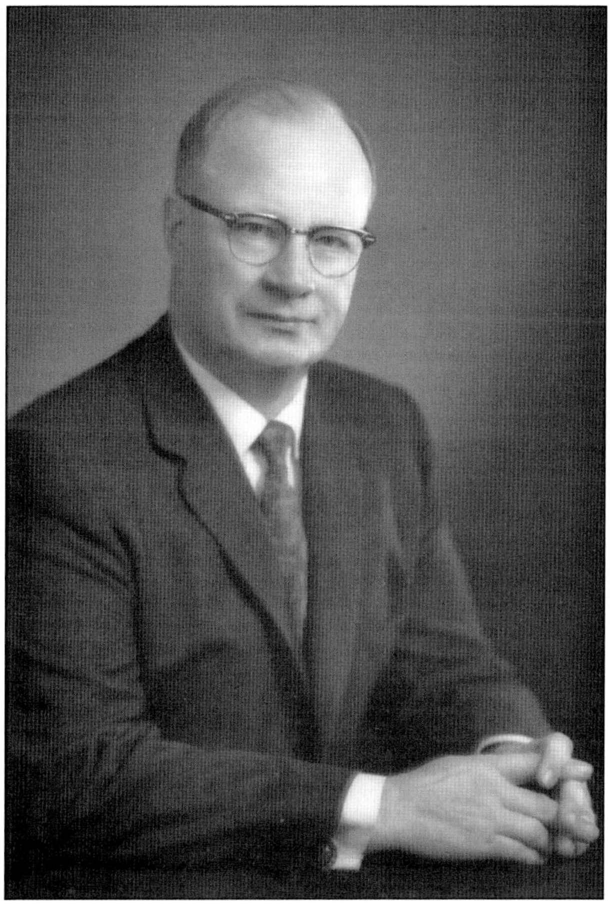

Peter P. Mickelson. Forty-two-year-old Peter Mickelson became Western State president in 1946. Mickelson had a tremendous relationship with the Gunnison community, doubled campus buildings, markedly improved the college's athletic programs, and greatly increased enrollment. He is generally regarded as the greatest president in Western's history.

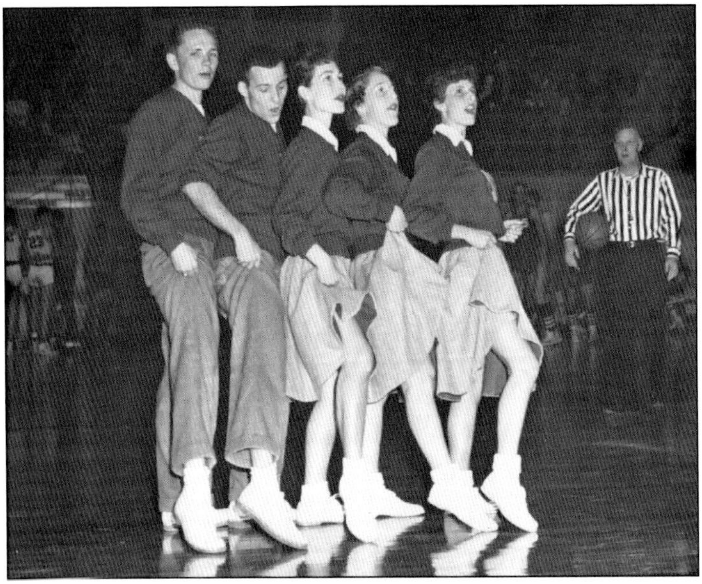

Cheerleaders. From left to right, Western State cheerleaders Clyde Rader, Bunny Culesco, Suzie Hect, Mable Littlefield, and Ethel Mae Houesin strut their stuff during a timeout at a 1950s basketball game in the college gymnasium. (WSCU.)

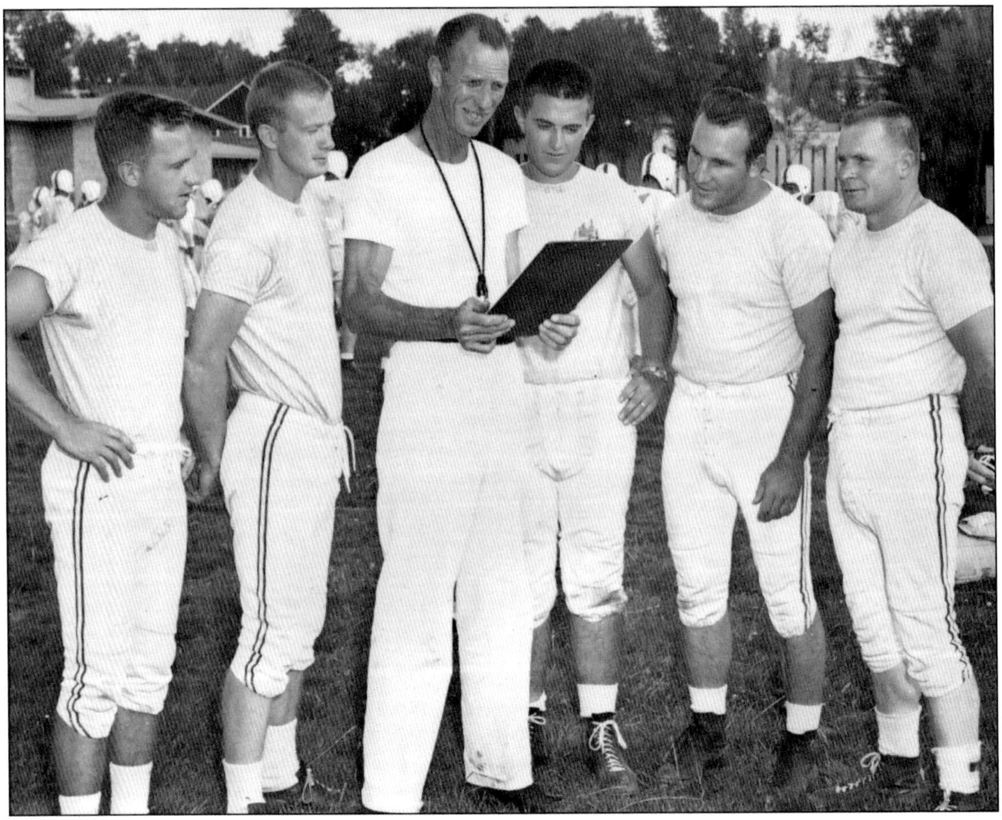

Pete Pederson. The head football coach in the 1950s, Pete Pederson was the greatest athlete in Western State history. He had a great career in basketball and football and was the heavyweight boxing champion of Colorado. Pederson exhibited great bravery in World War II as a frogman. Flanking him in this 1950s photograph are assistant coaches Frank Zanatell (second from right) and Tracy Borah (far right). (WSCU.)

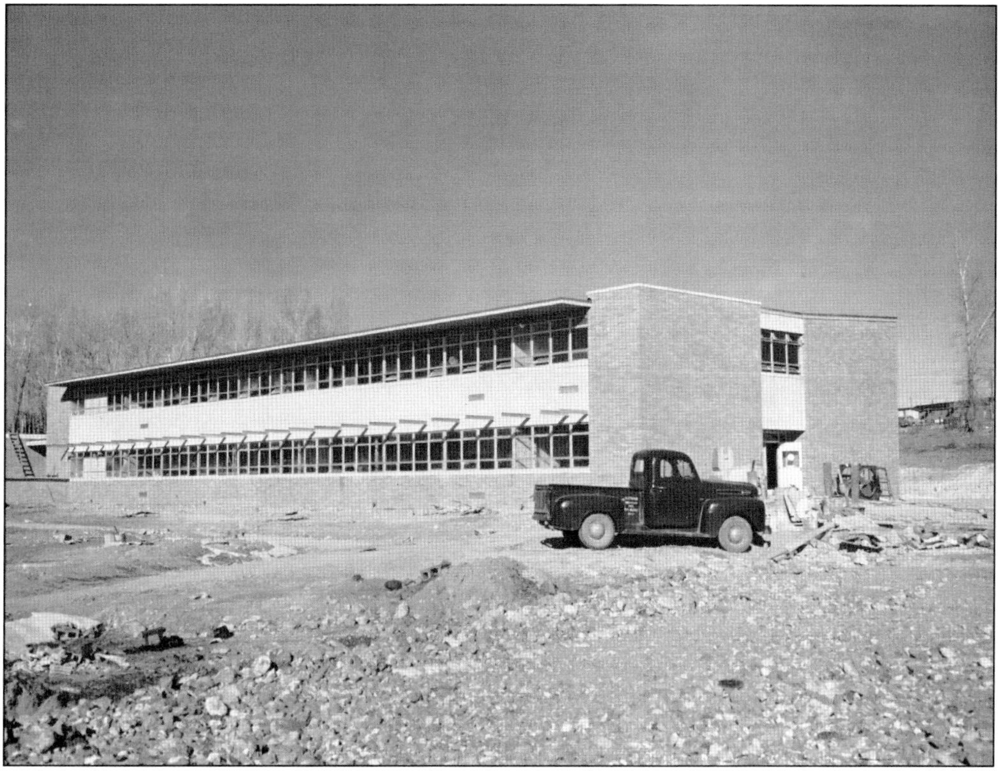

Kelley Hall. In 1956, work began on a new building that would house the education department on the first floor and the social science department on the second. Kelley Hall was just east of Taylor Hall. Kelley was completely renovated at a cost of $6 million in 2008. (WSCU.)

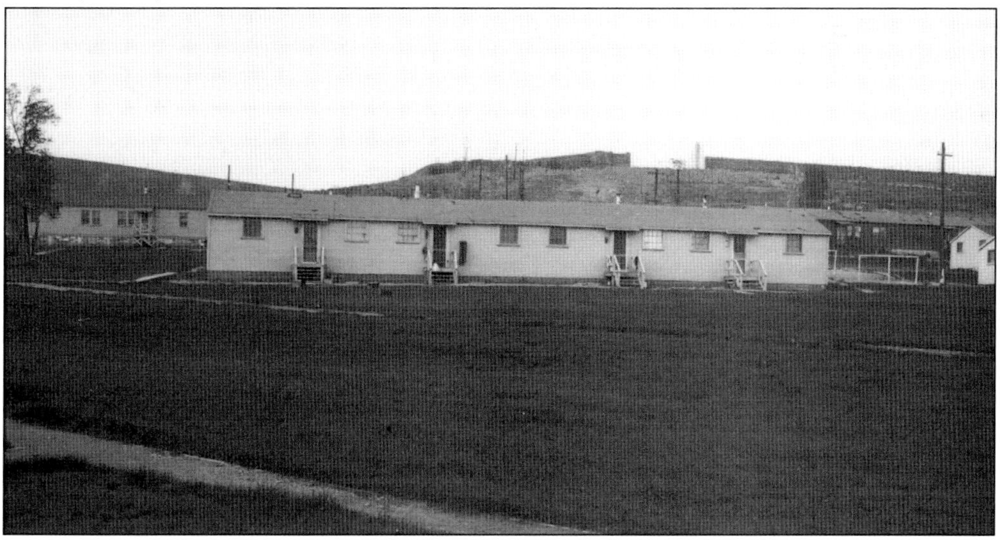

Escalante Heights. Because of increased enrollment caused by veterans returning from World War II, Western bought surplus army buildings and started Escalante Heights in 1947. The college converted the army buildings into 31 student apartments and put them above Highland Village on College Hill. All were used by veterans. (WSCU.)

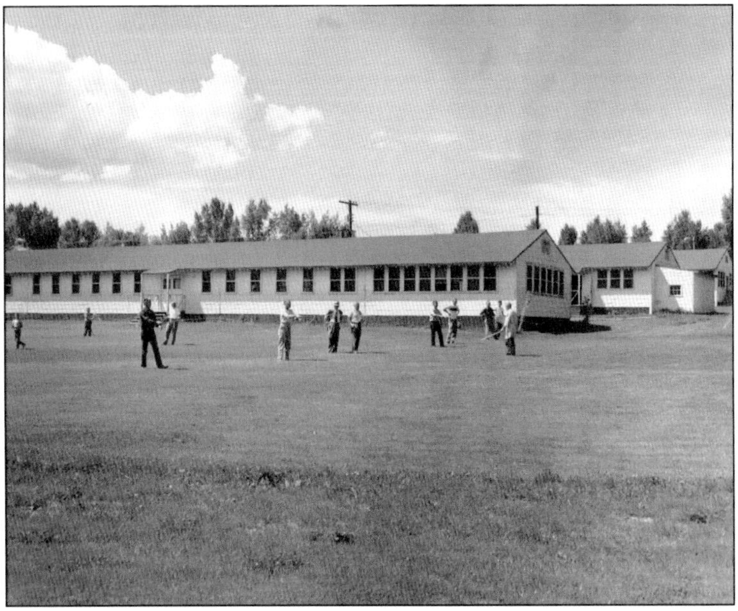

Fly Fishing Class. Ralph Walker's fly fishing class practices technique in the 1950s. Behind the class are barracks acquired from the Army after World War II to serve as classrooms as college enrollment greatly increased. (WSCU.)

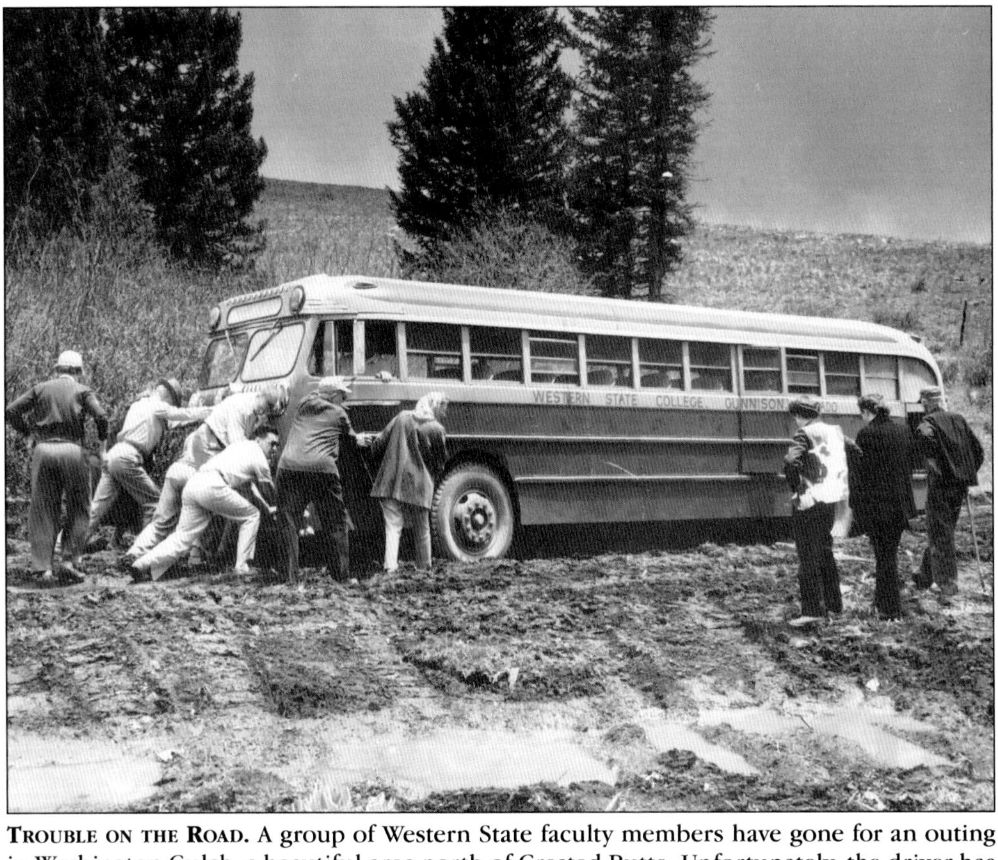

Trouble on the Road. A group of Western State faculty members have gone for an outing in Washington Gulch, a beautiful area north of Crested Butte. Unfortunately, the driver has made a mistake in thinking he could get through the mud hole. After much work, the bus was freed from its calamity. (WSCU.)

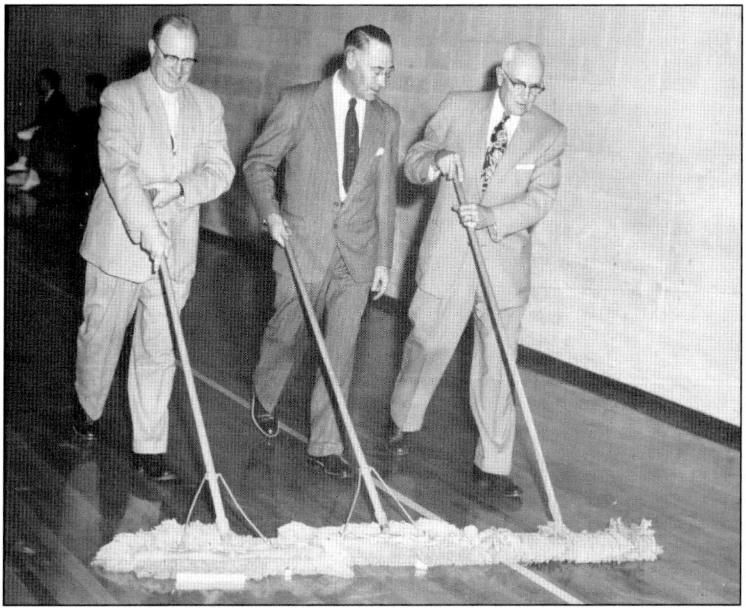

SWEEPING UP MONEY. Three prominent Gunnison citizens, from left to right, Western State president Peter Mickelson, First National Bank president Pete Eastman, and coach Paul Wright, sweep up money from a March of Dimes fundraiser in 1955. (WSCU.)

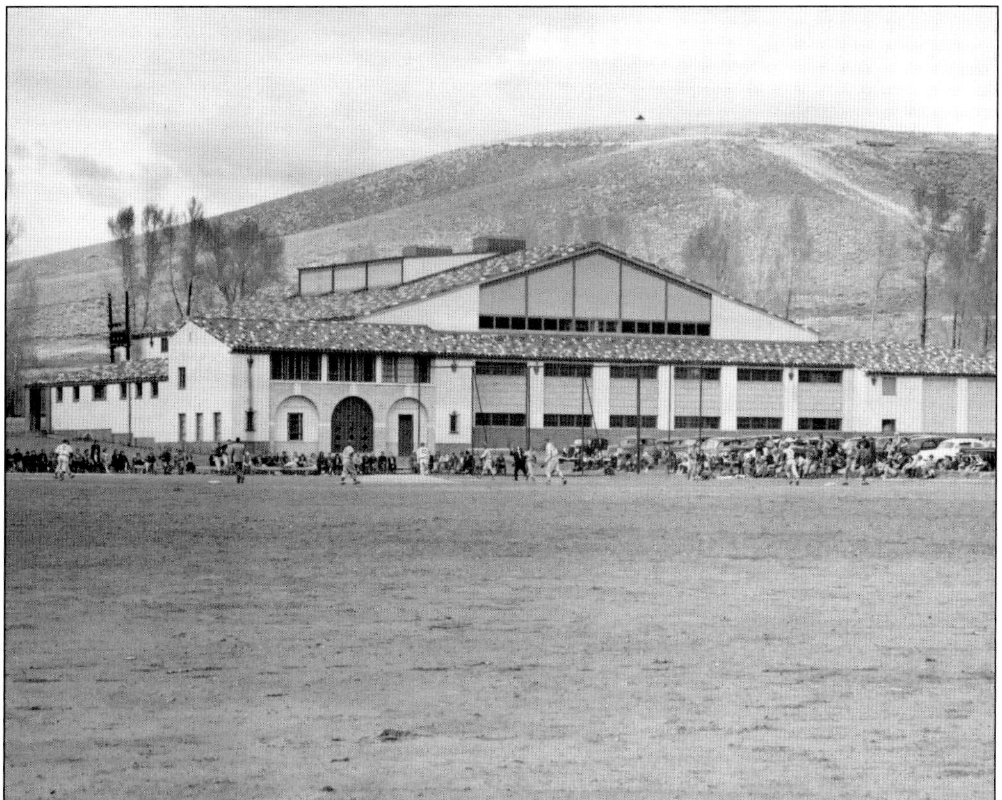

NEW MOUNTAINEER GYMNASIUM. Built in 1951, the new physical education building, which included a new gym, dwarfed the tiny Crawford Hall athletic building. Gunnison governor Dan Thornton spoke at the dedication. Crawford Hall became the music building on campus. In this 1951 photograph, the Mountaineer baseball team is in action.

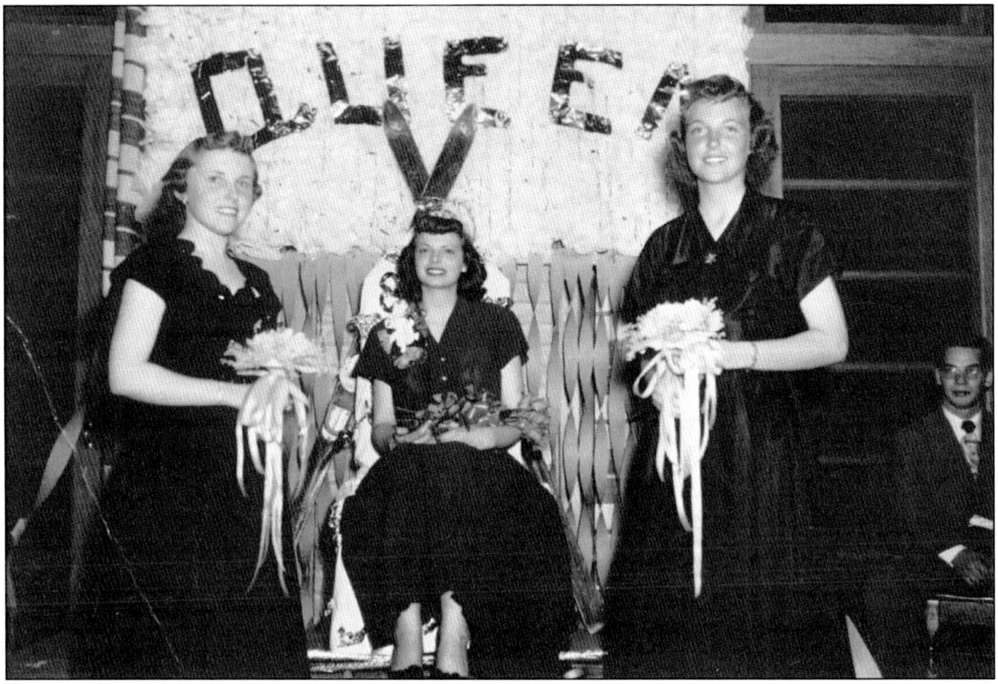

WINTER CARNIVAL ROYALTY. The 1951 queen and her attendants are crowned at Western State's Winter Carnival. On the right is Carol Baird, who was a top skier and the only woman on Sven Wiik's team. Baird came close to making the US Olympic team and was also a great tennis player and golfer and taught scuba diving. She was one of the great female athletes in WSC history.

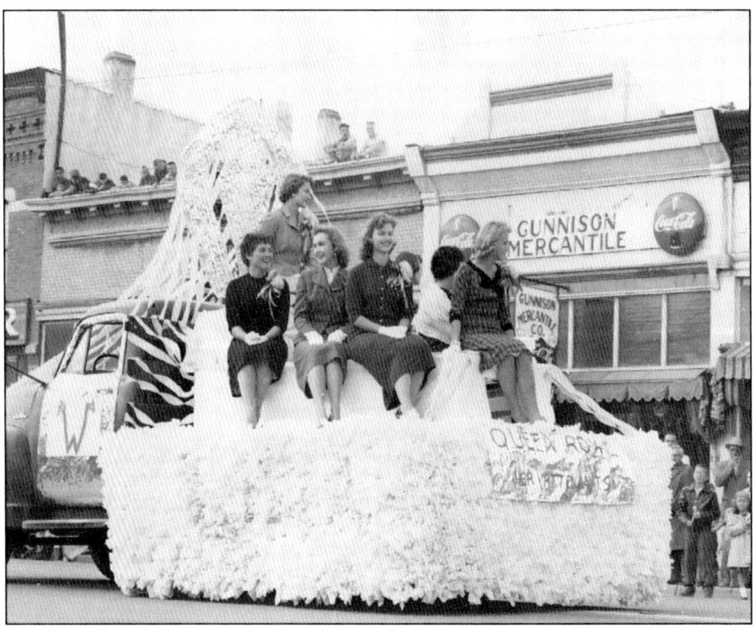

QUEEN ROXY. A 1957 homecoming float with queen Roxy Lake and her attendants moves past the Gunnison Mercantile Store. Lake was the daughter of Rial Lake, whose grandfather was an original pioneer of the Gunnison Country. (WSCU.)

Posing for Cattleman's Days. Local beauty Ellen McCartney sits on top of a loading chute in the 1950s in a promotional shot for Cattleman's Days. She was supposed to resemble a "rootin', tootin' cowgirl." (WSCU.)

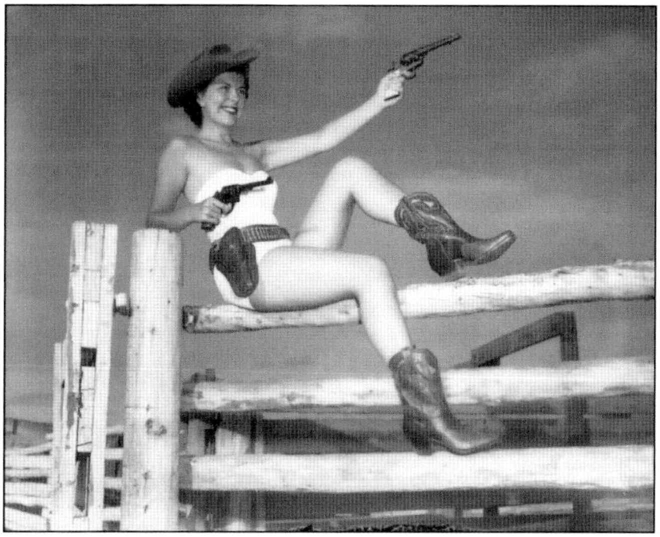

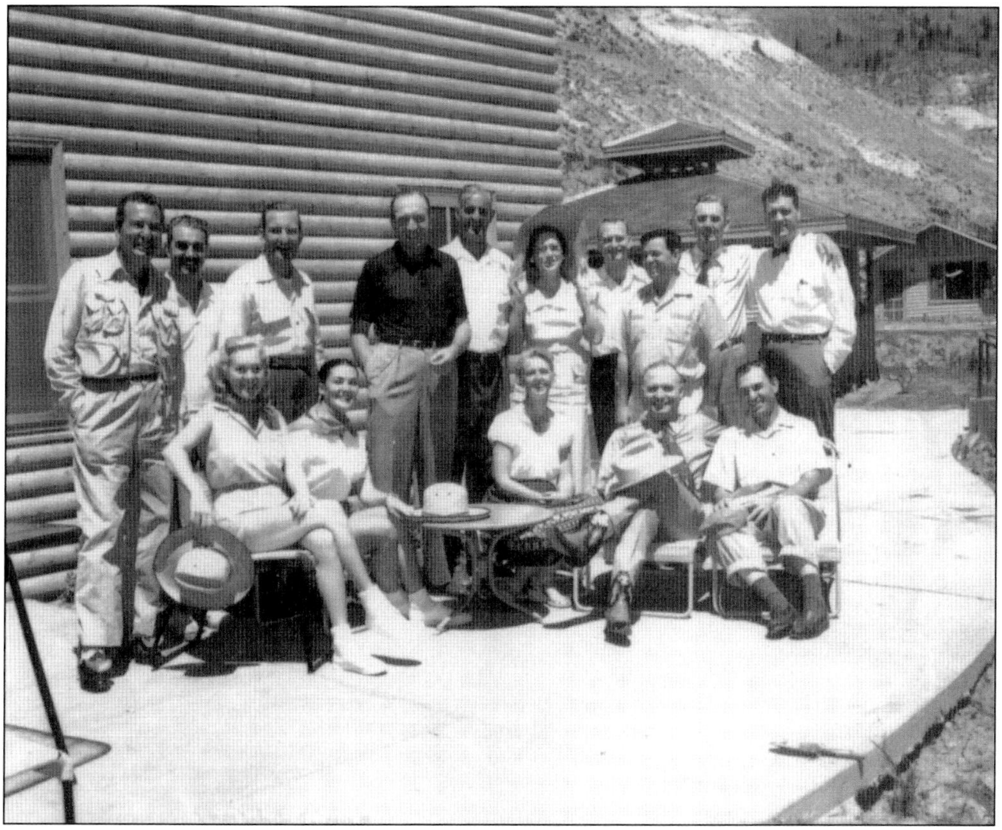

Moncrief's. Sixteen miles west of Gunnison, Texas oil man Tex Moncrief had a beautiful resort along the Gunnison River. Moncrief often hosted many famous people who came to fish and relax. On the left in back is comedian Phil Harris, and sitting in front of him is wife, Alice Faye. The three people sitting down on the right are Jessie Thornton, governor of Colorado Dan Thornton (with the hat), and famed golfer Ben Hogan. The photograph was taken in the 1950s.

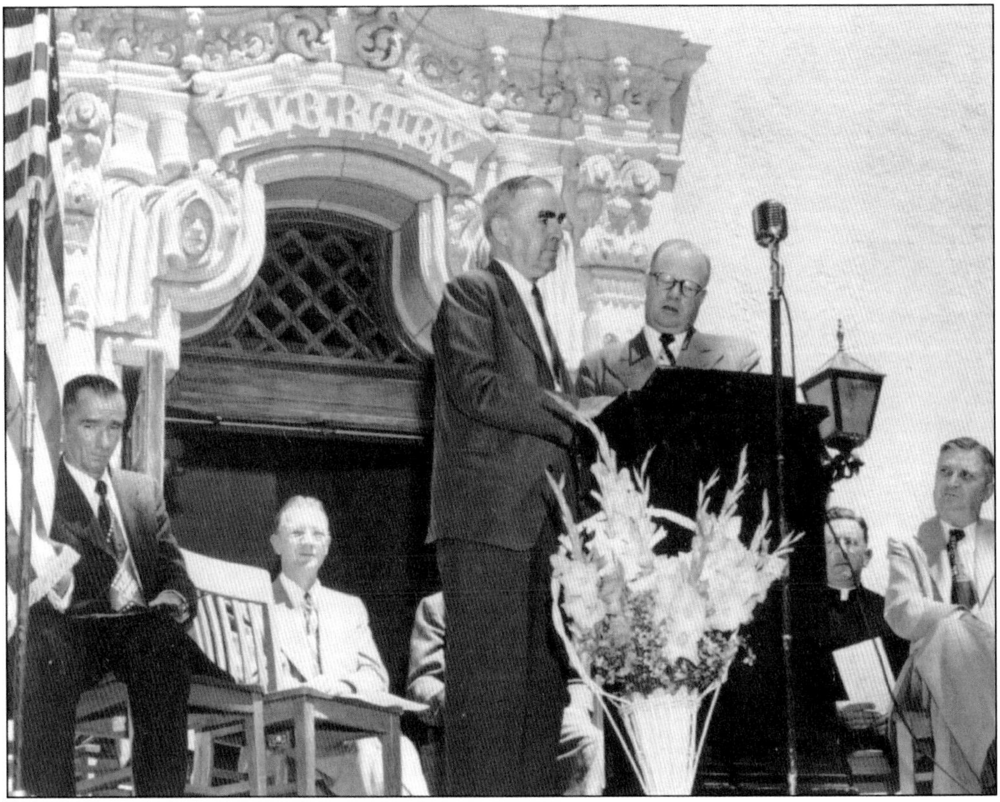

Savage Library Dedication. Board of trustees member Leslie Savage stands next to Western State president Peter Mickelson (with glasses) in 1951 during the dedication of Savage Library. Savage had been instrumental in getting funding for many college buildings. Dean of faculty D.H. Cummins (far left) and dean of students Olaf Kjosness are on the left. (WSCU.)

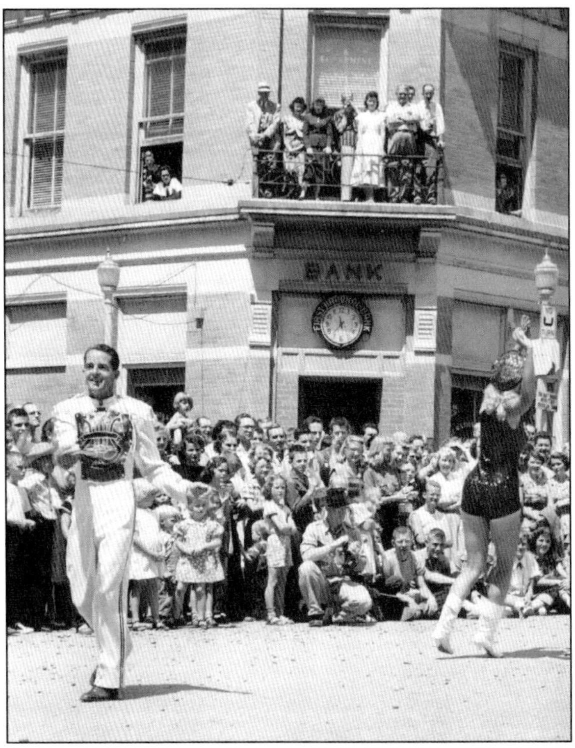

Twirlers. A huge crowd gathers during a Fourth of July parade on Main Street in Gunnison in the 1950s. Two twirling instructors from the Western State College music camp wow the crowd as they parade by the First National Bank building. (WSCU.)

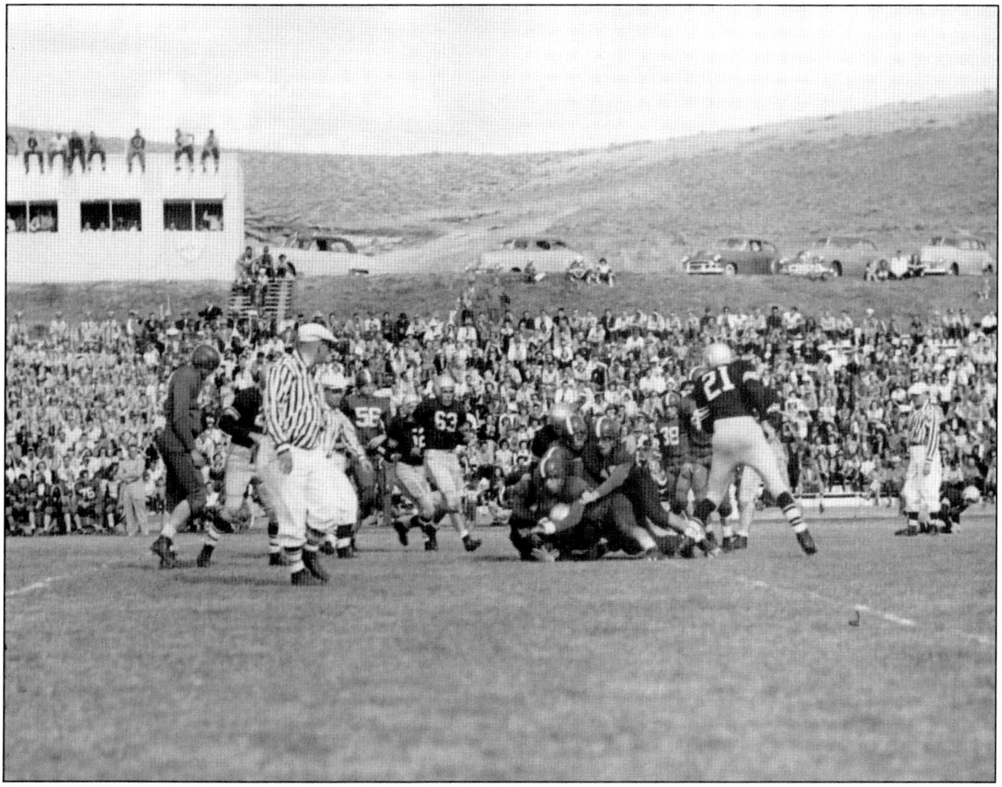

Football, 1955. The 1955 football team was one of the finest in Western State history, going undefeated. The stands are packed for this home game in Mountaineer Bowl. The team was led by All-American running back Bill Rhodes.

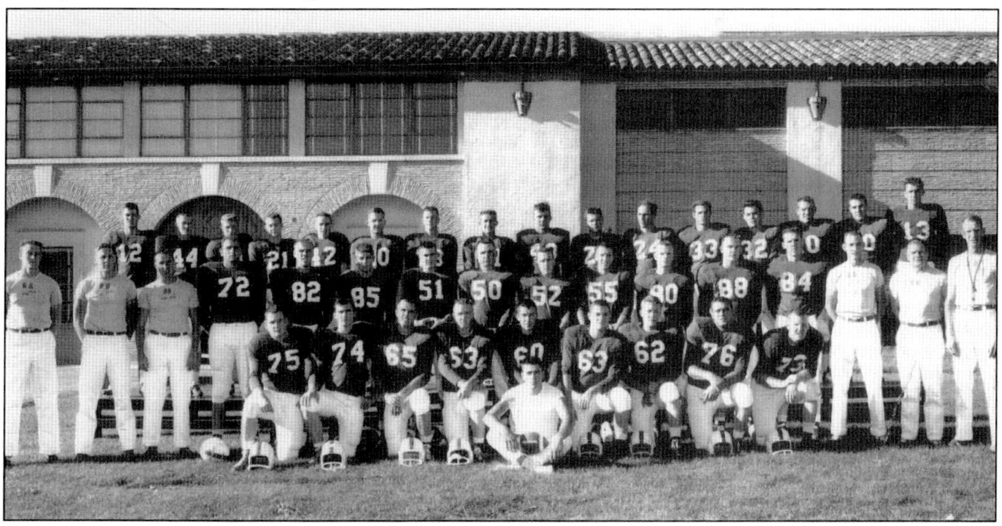

Glory Years Gone. The 1959 Western State football team won one game, a far cry from the glory years of the early and mid-1950s. Coach Pete Pederson would leave after the following year, replaced by one of the most successful coaches in Western history, O.K. Dalton. From left to right, coaches Tom Muhic, Tracy Borah, and Pederson are the three men standing on the right of the front row.

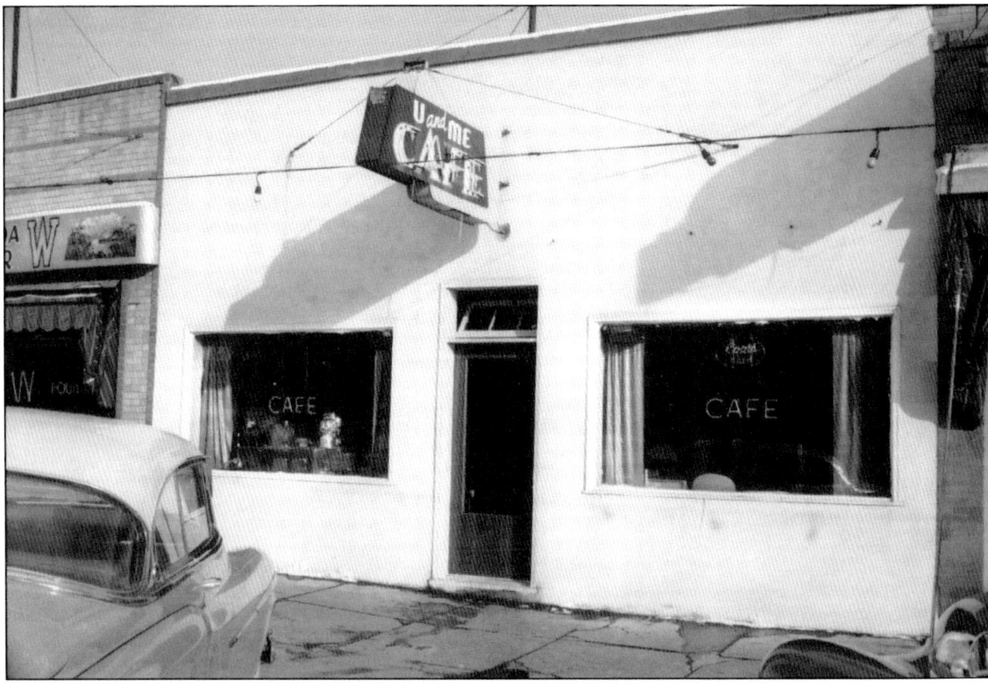

U and Me. Located on Gunnison's Main Street, the uniquely named U and Me Café was a favorite hangout for Western State students in the 1950s. The simply built café served fine food, and many alumni looked forward to returning to one of their favorite haunts.

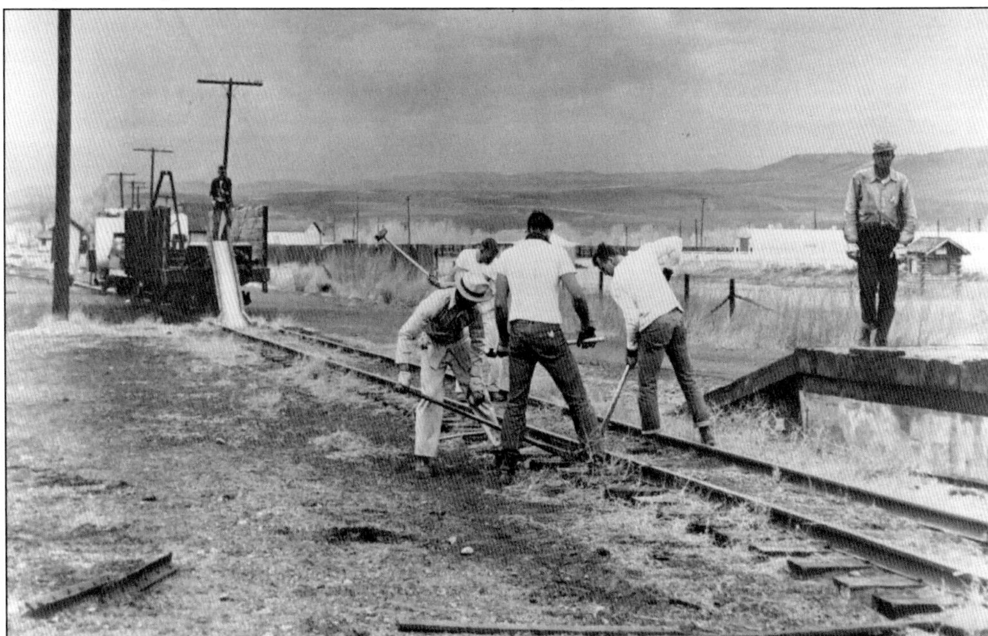

Pulling Up the Tracks. It was a sad day in the Gunnison Country in 1955 when Denver & Rio Grande Railroad tracks were removed. The railroad had been in the Gunnison Country for 74 years. Paul Brinkerhof of Salida supervised the pulling of the tracks, and Western State College students provided the labor.

Five

GREATNESS ON SKIS

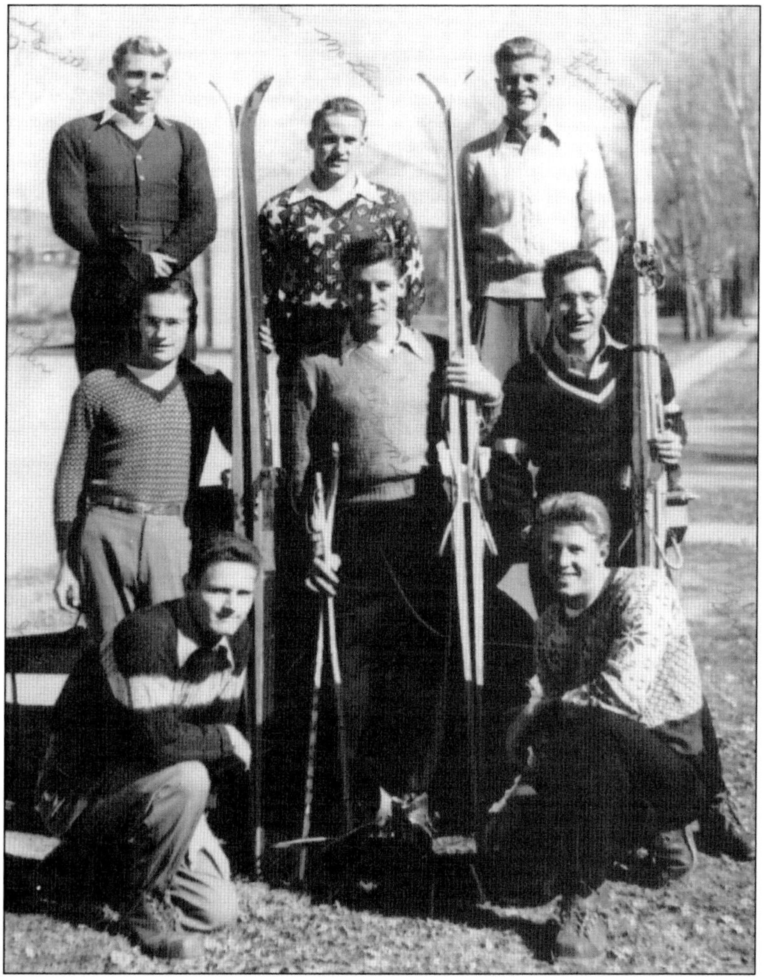

EARLY SKI TEAM. The second ski team in Western State's history poses for an on-campus photograph in the spring of 1948. From left to right are (first row) Fred Pearce and Bill Gorsuch; (second row) Hubert Snyder, Glenn McLean, and Dick Wellington; (third row) Crosby Perry-Smith, Len McLean, and Thor Groswold. This team began a great tradition in intercollegiate skiing and turned out Olympic coach Sven Wiik and many Olympic skiers.

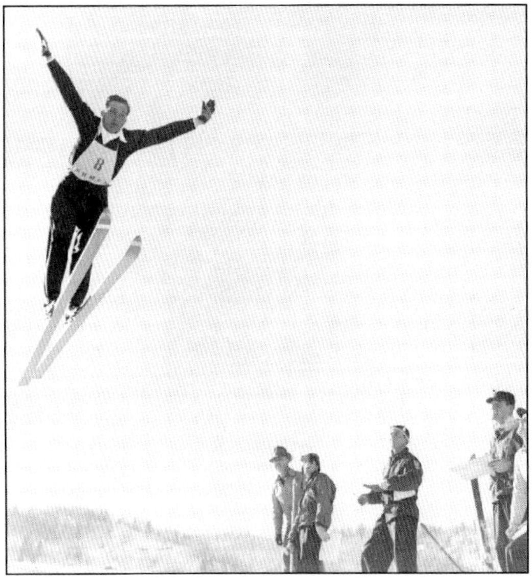

Crosby Perry-Smith. Perry-Smith was one of the greatest skiers in Western State history. Crosby was part of the famed 10th Mountain Ski Division in World War II and was instrumental in starting WSC's first ski team during the winter of 1946–1947. He made the 1952 Olympic team but, because of an injury, did not compete. Crosby set many jumping records on the ski hills across the nation.

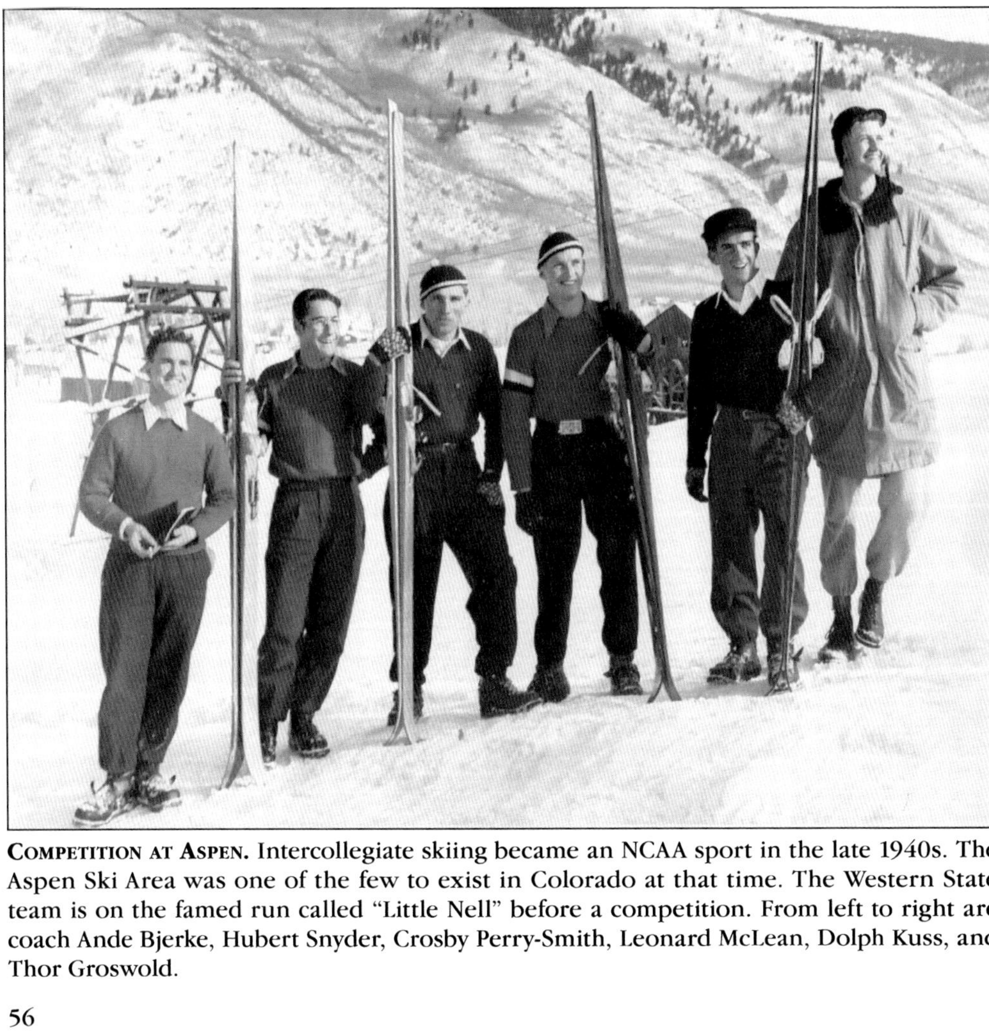

Competition at Aspen. Intercollegiate skiing became an NCAA sport in the late 1940s. The Aspen Ski Area was one of the few to exist in Colorado at that time. The Western State team is on the famed run called "Little Nell" before a competition. From left to right are coach Ande Bjerke, Hubert Snyder, Crosby Perry-Smith, Leonard McLean, Dolph Kuss, and Thor Groswold.

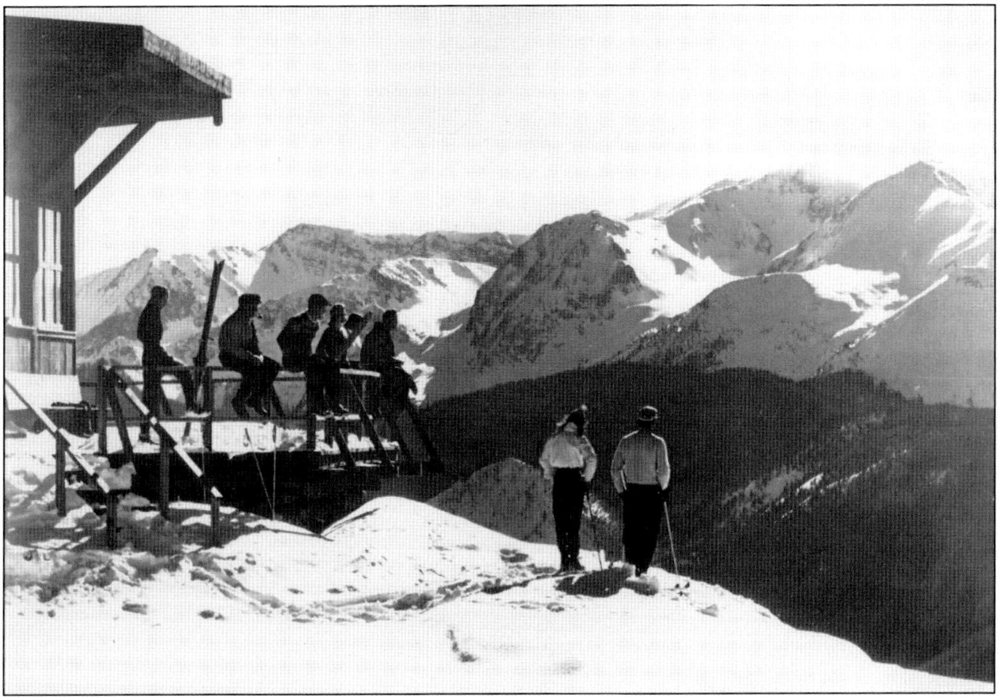

Aspen Mountain. The great ski town of Aspen is only 25 miles away from Crested Butte as the crow flies. Many locals walk over East Maroon (11,800 feet) or Western Maroon Pass (12,400 feet) through beautiful flower fields in the summer. This photograph shows the Sun Deck at the Aspen Ski Area with a stunning panorama of 14 towering peaks, all over 13,000 feet.

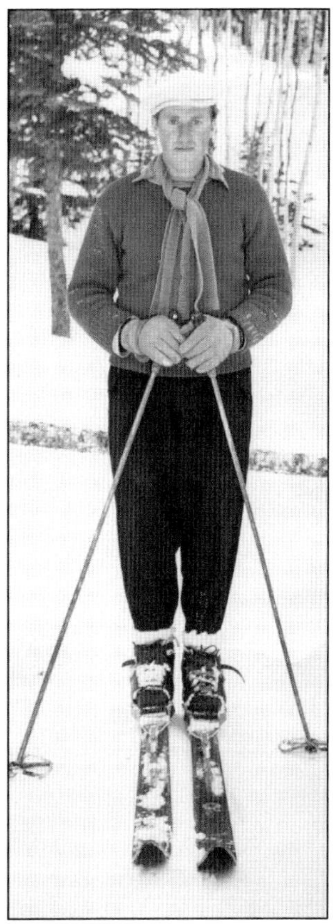

Sven Wiik. Sven Wiik was the Western State College ski coach from 1949 to 1967. From Sweden, Wiik soon became the father of Nordic skiing in the United States. He participated in three Olympic games, once in 1948 as part of a gymnastics demonstration team and twice as the US Nordic coach. Now 91 years old and living in Steamboat Springs, Wiik still skis nearly every day during the winter.

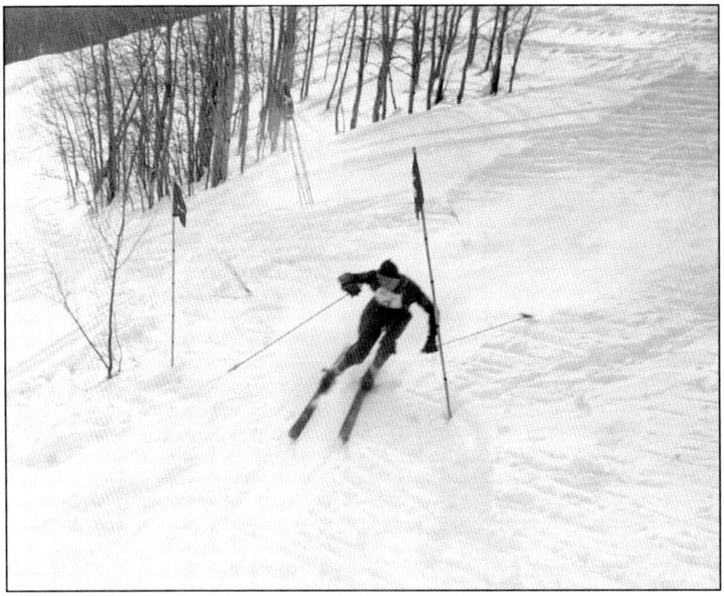

Rozman Hill Run. Rozman Hill's runs were steep and narrow with the downhill competition fast and dangerous. Trees were on both sides of the run as racers hit speeds of over 50 miles an hour. Unlike today's alpine races, there were bamboo poles for gates and very few safety features on the downhill course. Western State's Mac Miller is on the course in 1951.

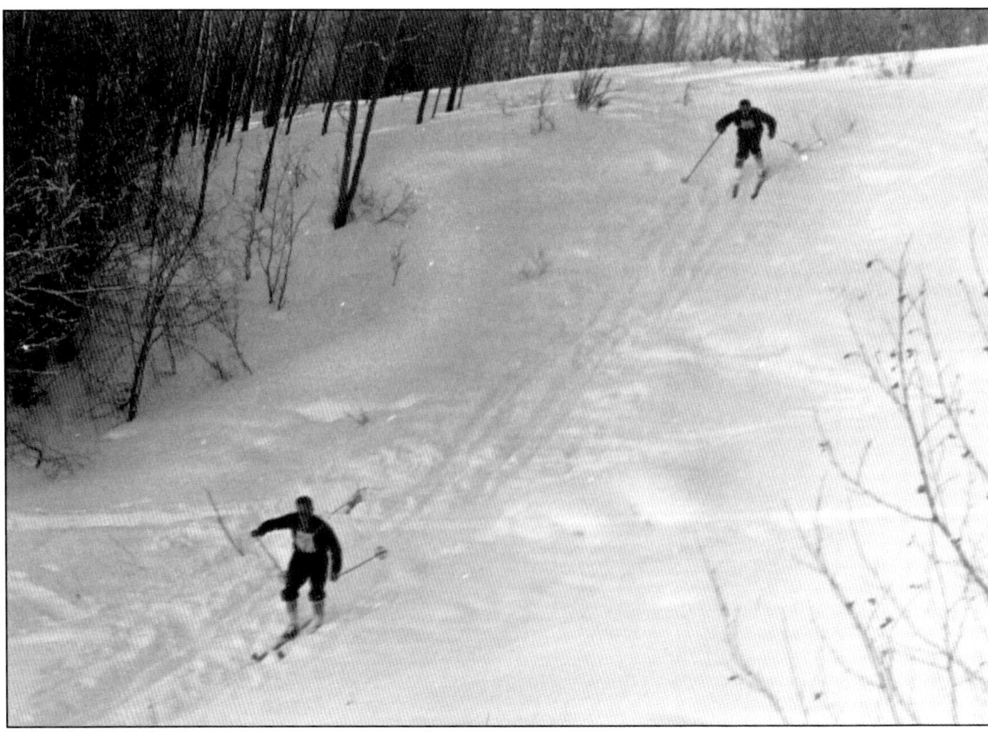

Cross-Country at Rozman. Two cross-country skiers are flying down a steep hill at the Rozman Hill Ski Area during an intercollegiate race in 1953. The early cross-country tracks set for the racers were very rough, and the steep hills were very difficult to survive standing up.

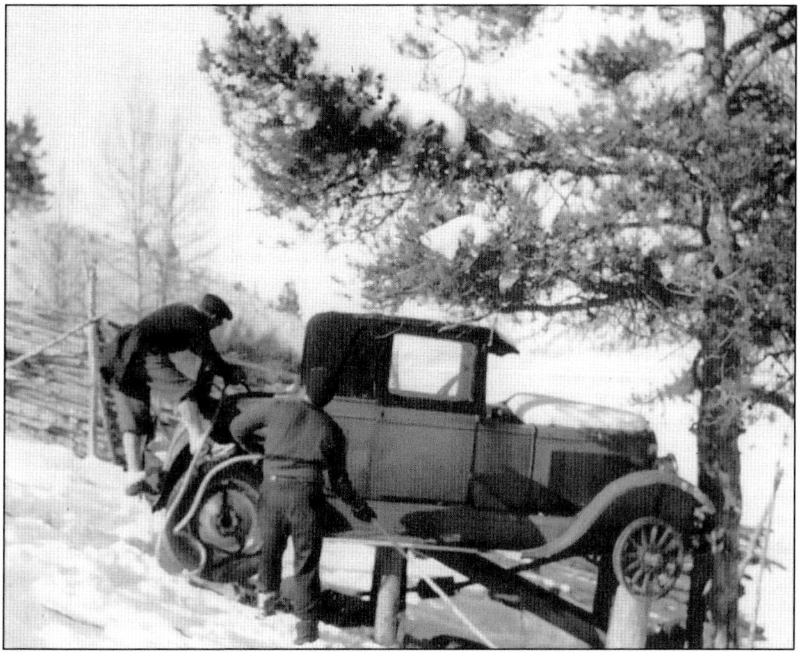

Auto-powered Rope Tow. The Western State ski team started the Rozman Hill Ski Area, eight miles south of Crested Butte, during the winter of 1950–1951. The initial rope tow was powered by an old automobile at the base of the hill.

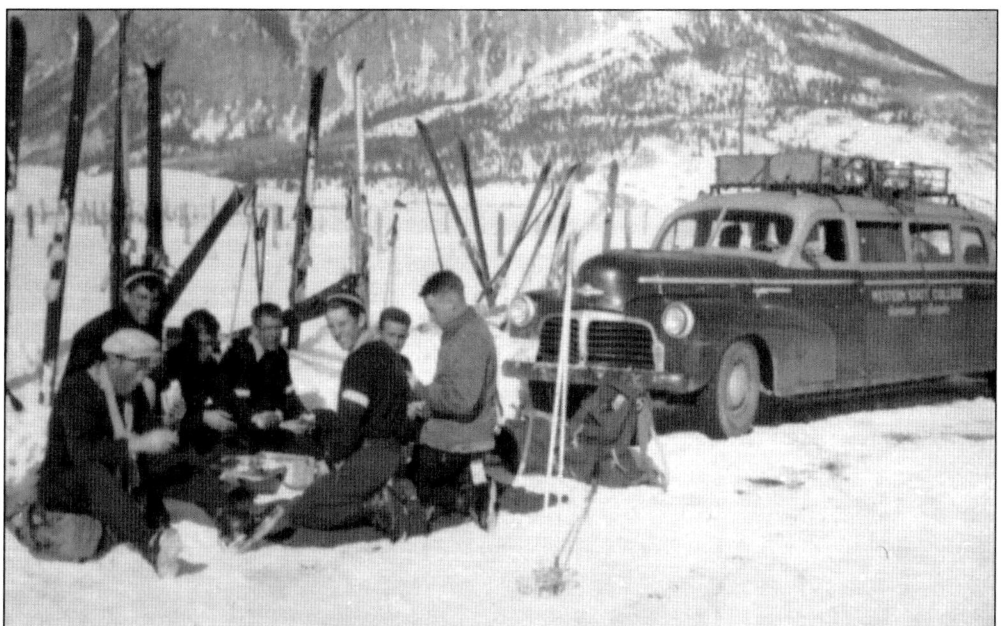

Lunch Break. Sven Wiik and Western State skiers break for lunch next to their "weenie wagon" with Crested Butte Mountain in the background in the 1950s. Most of the skiers were jumpers who had spent the morning practicing on Rozman Hill.

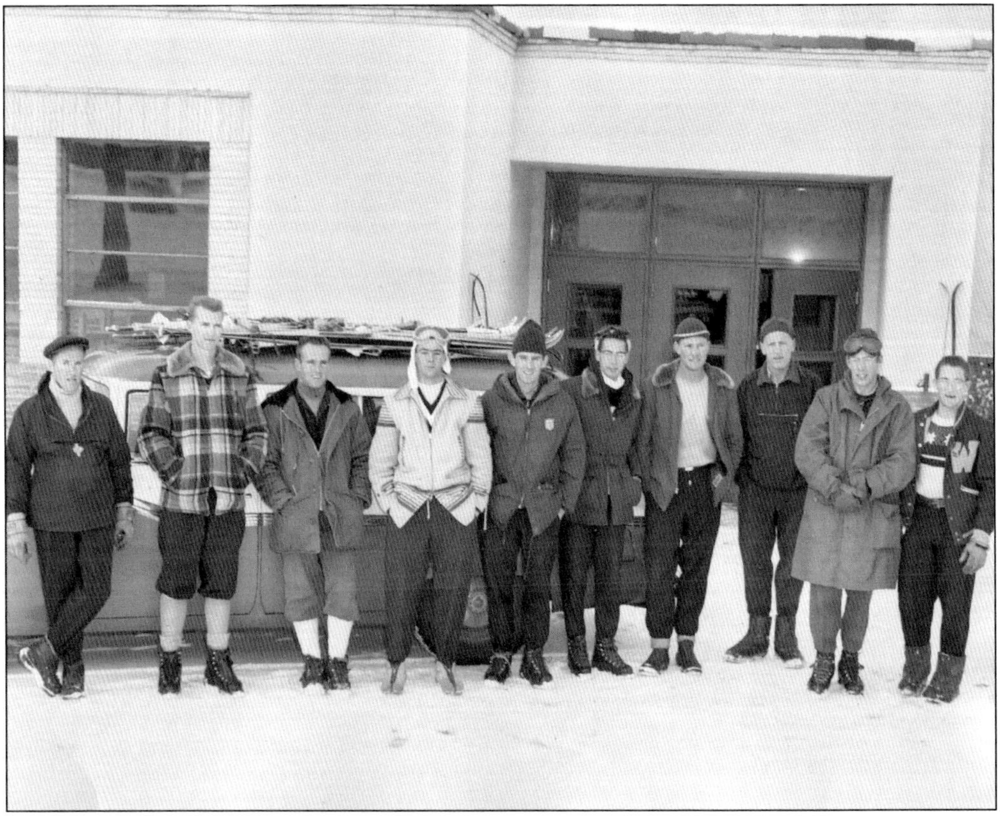

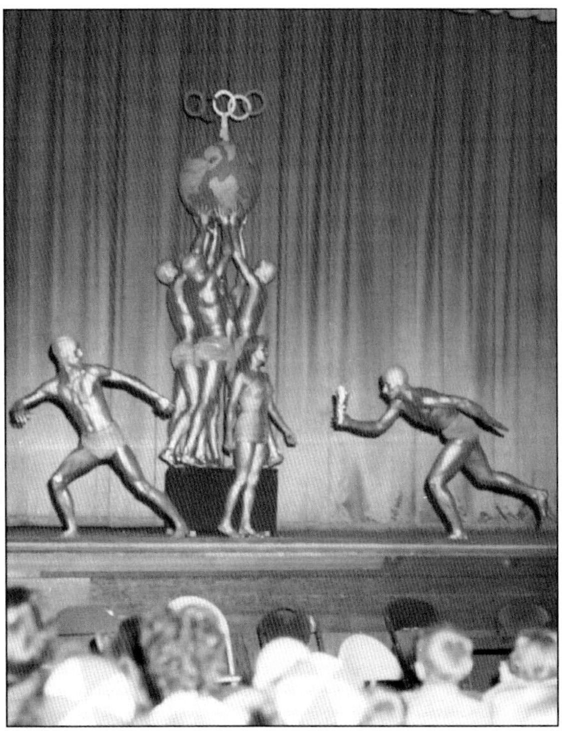

READY TO TRAVEL. Sven Wiik and ski team members pose for a picture before leaving for a ski meet in the early 1950s. The ski team competed in various Rocky Mountain resorts such as Winter Park, Aspen; Alta, Utah; and Sun Valley, Idaho.

MOUNTAIN DEWINS SKIT. A highlight of "Mountain Dewins," a series of skits performed during homecoming, was the Western State ski team's exhibition. Painted in gold, the skiers performed with jumps and tumbling and also formed tableaux that were stunning. This performance took place in 1954.

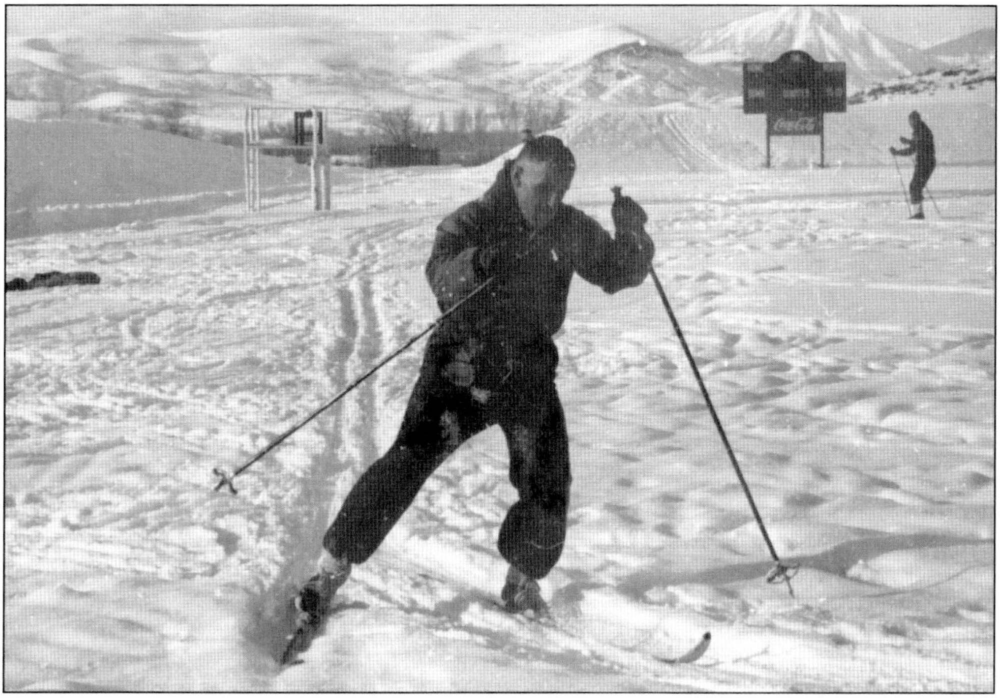

Mountaineer Bowl. Some of the intercollegiate ski races were held on the Western State campus. Here, two skiers are warming up, skiing through Mountaineer Bowl and the college football field. Carbon Peak, over 12,000 feet high, forms the backdrop.

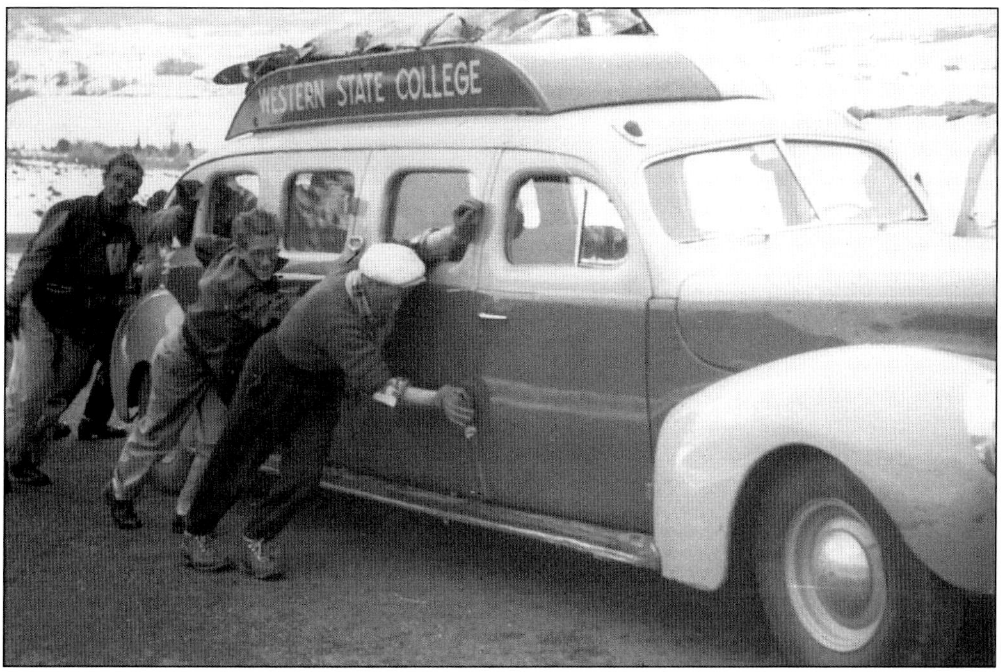

Out of Gas. The famous Western State College weenie wagon is out of gas, and Sven Wiik and his skiers are pushing it to the side of the road in the 1950s. The weenie wagon seated 12 people and always drew surprised stares from out-of-towners because of its uniqueness.

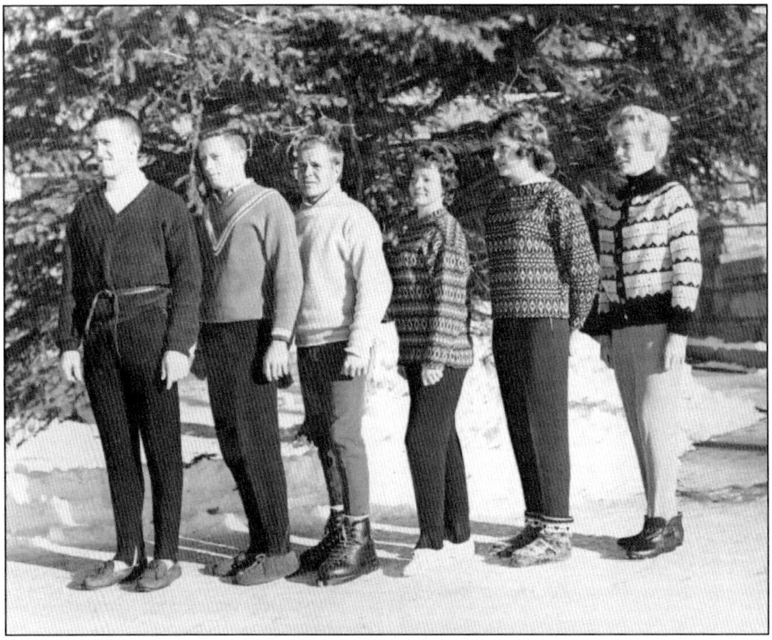

Ski Royalty in the 1960s. Winter Carnival was one of the major events at Western State with a king and queen being crowned. The royalty during the winter of 1961–1962 included, from left to right, Jim Bombard, Jennings Cress, Jim Mattson, Sara Squires, Judy Mitchell, and Dee Ann Kiklas.

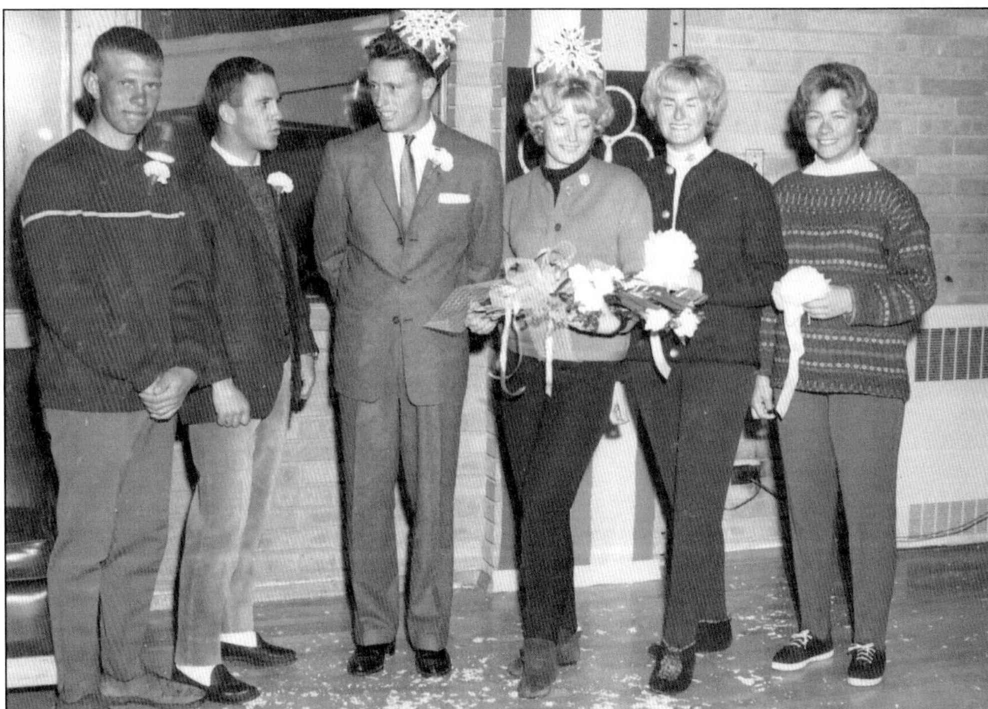

Royalty in 1965. Western State royalty for the Winter Carnival of 1965 included, from left to right, Jim Burkholder, Loris Werner (brother of legendary alpine skier Buddy Werner, killed in an avalanche in Europe in 1964), Jennings Cress, Dee Ann Kiklas, unidentified, and Barbara Strawn. The Winter Carnival was the major event of the winter.

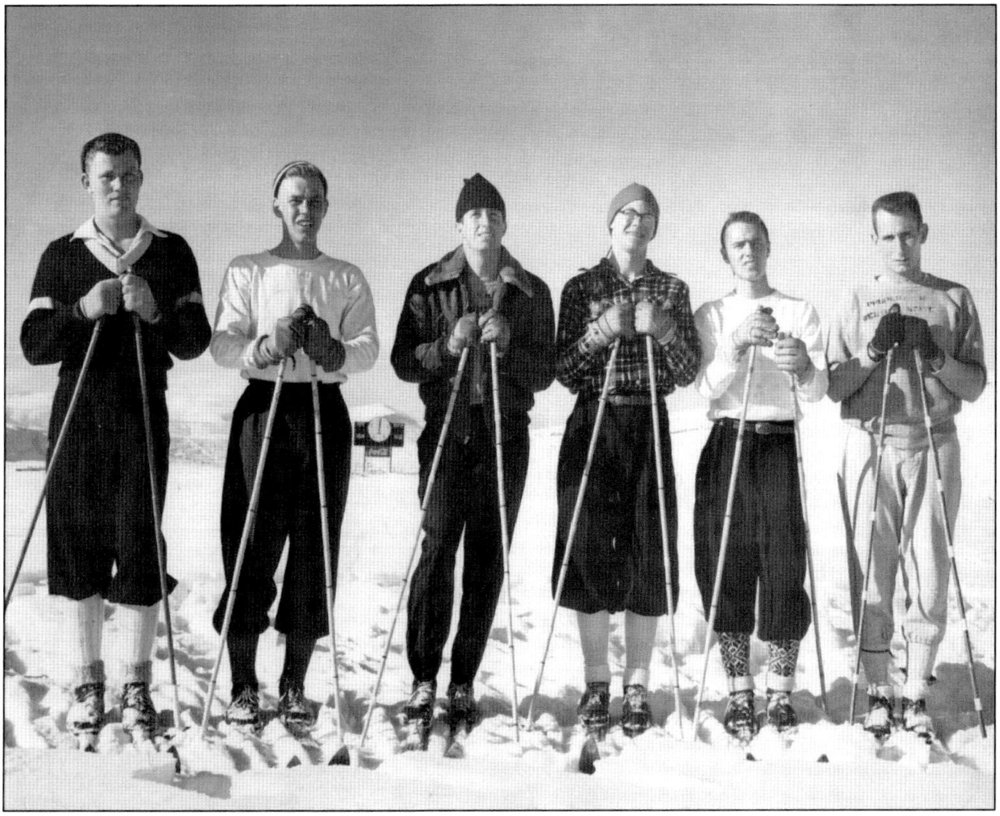

NORDIC TEAM, 1950s. The Western State Nordic ski team is in Mountaineer Bowl in the 1950s. Pictured from left to right are John Burritt, Jim Gibson, Ken MacLennan (later the coach of the Mountaineers after Sven Wiik's departure in 1967), Walter Jackson, Dick Mize, and Jim Mahaffey. The Mountaineer Nordic team was always one of the best teams in the nation and turned out several Olympians.

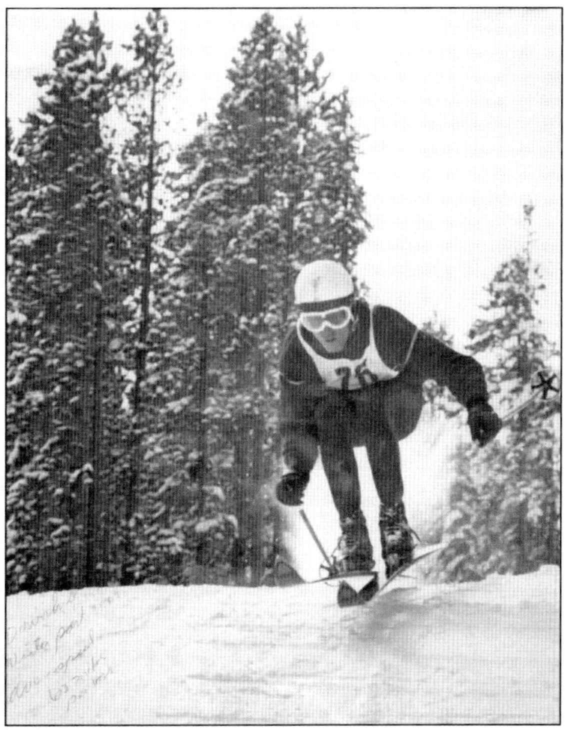

JENNINGS CRESS AT WINTER PARK. From Granby in Colorado's Middle Park, Cress was one of the great all-around US skiers in the 1960s. He won the NCAA Skimiester award, given to the top skier in four combined alpine and Nordic events: downhill, slalom, cross-country, and jumping.

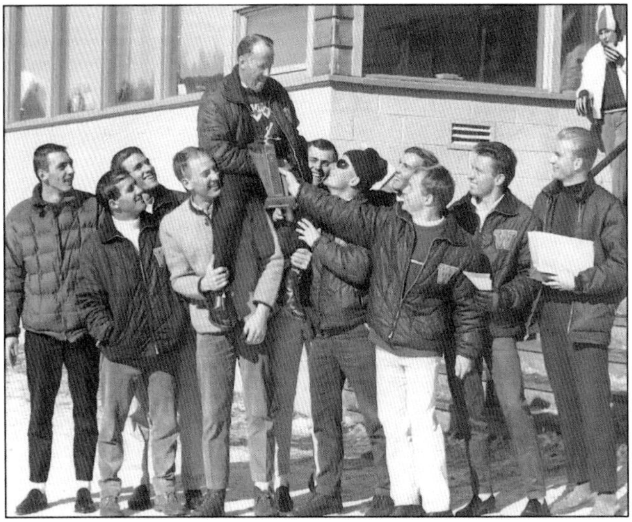

The Greatest. Perhaps the greatest among many great Western State ski teams was the 1963 team, which finished very high in the NCAA Championships. After the meet, coach Sven Wiik was given a ride by team members. From left to right are Danny New, Loris Werner, unidentified, Dave Gorsuch, Ken Phelps, Jim Balfanz, Bill Sweitzer, Jim Mattson, Jennings Cress, and Rod Bell.

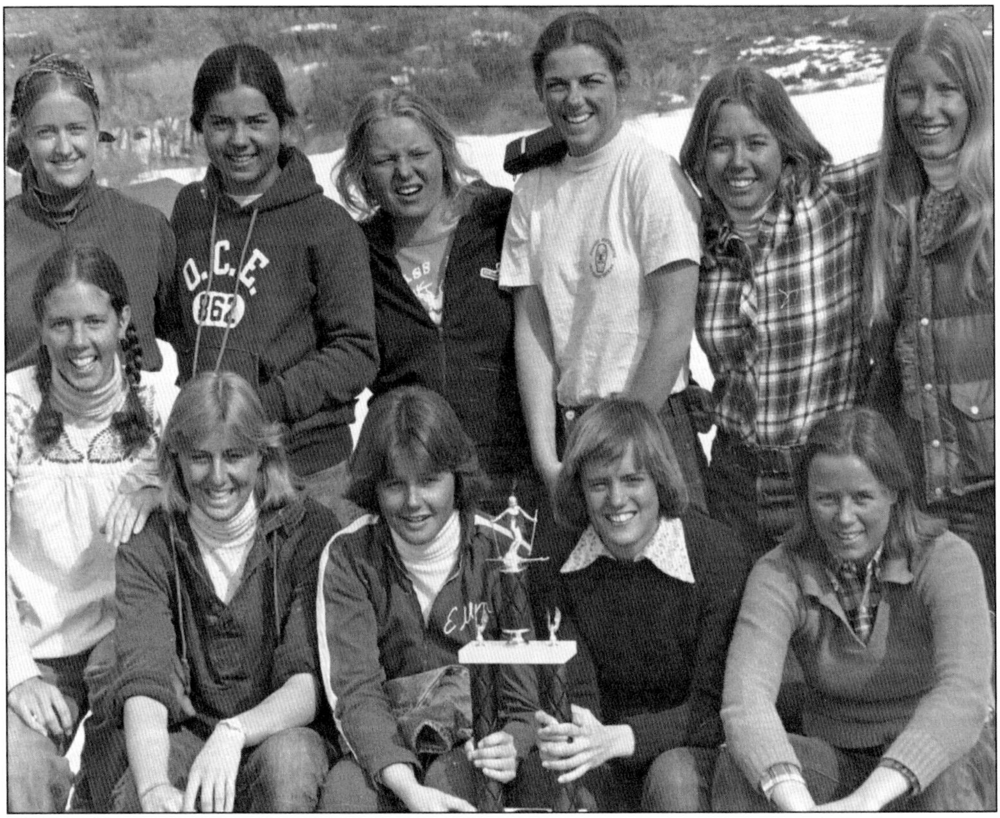

Women's Ski Team. The Western State women's team began in the early 1960s. In the absence of a national organization, the women competed in Rocky Mountain races and usually won. The 1978 team competed in the Association for Intercollegiate Athletics for Women (AIAW) National Championships at Red River, New Mexico, and finished fourth. Pictured from left to right are (first row) Mary Thalofer, Donna Terrill, Ellen Shick, Sally Owen, and Dana Temple; (second row) coach Brigitta Wiik, Maria McClain, Karen Dorris, Shere Kuss, Kim England, and Kim McNeill.

Six

THE GUNNISON COUNTRY

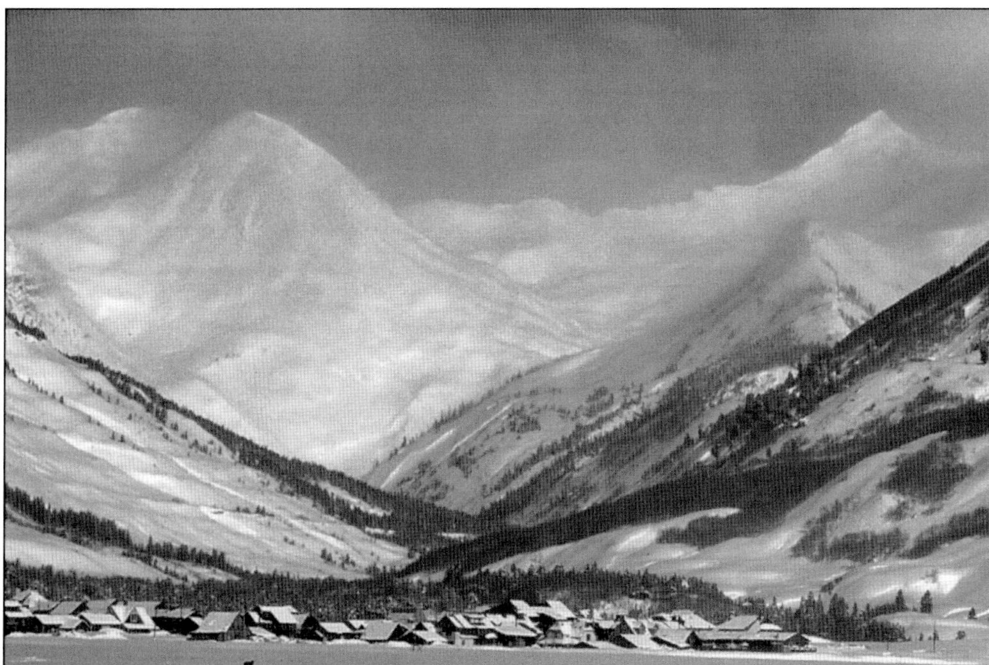

CRESTED BUTTE. One of the most beautiful towns in the nation, Crested Butte is 8,885 feet high with the majestic Elk Mountains as a backdrop. Most of its residents came from southeastern Europe: Italy, Austria, and Serbia. Western State College students flocked to the town because of the nearby ski area. (CBMHM.)

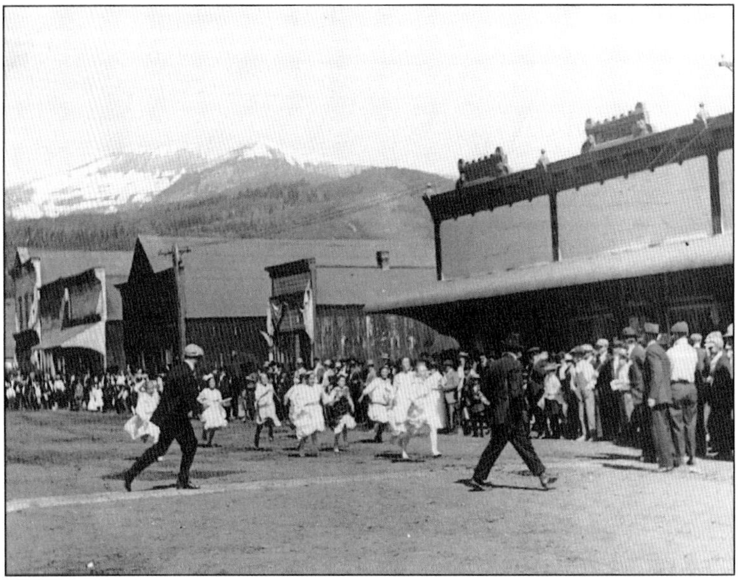

FOURTH OF JULY RACE. The largest celebration in the Gunnison Country is Fourth of July in Crested Butte, where 10,000 or more people gather. An eight-mile race, parade, music, polka dance, and contests are only some of the activities. This 1930s celebration included a girls' 100-yard dash on Elk Avenue.

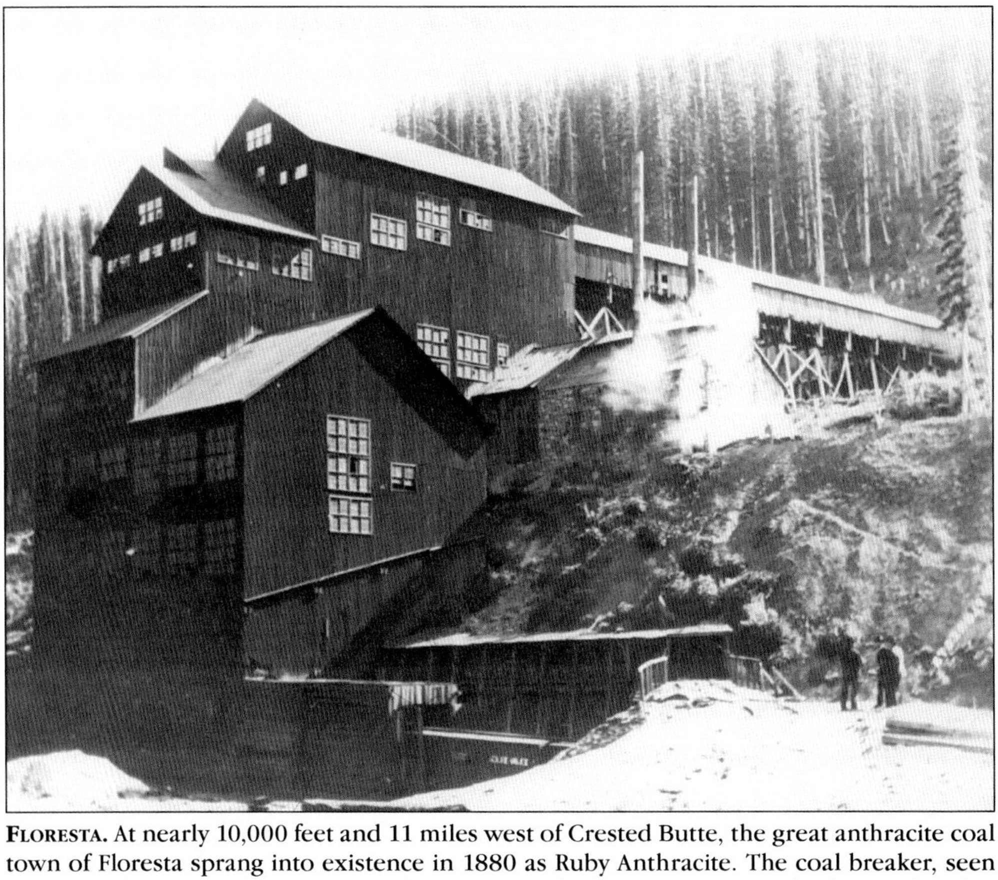

FLORESTA. At nearly 10,000 feet and 11 miles west of Crested Butte, the great anthracite coal town of Floresta sprang into existence in 1880 as Ruby Anthracite. The coal breaker, seen here, was five stories high and was built in 1898 for $100,000; it was the largest breaker west of Pennsylvania. Here, early geology students of Western State studied the nuances of anthracite coal.

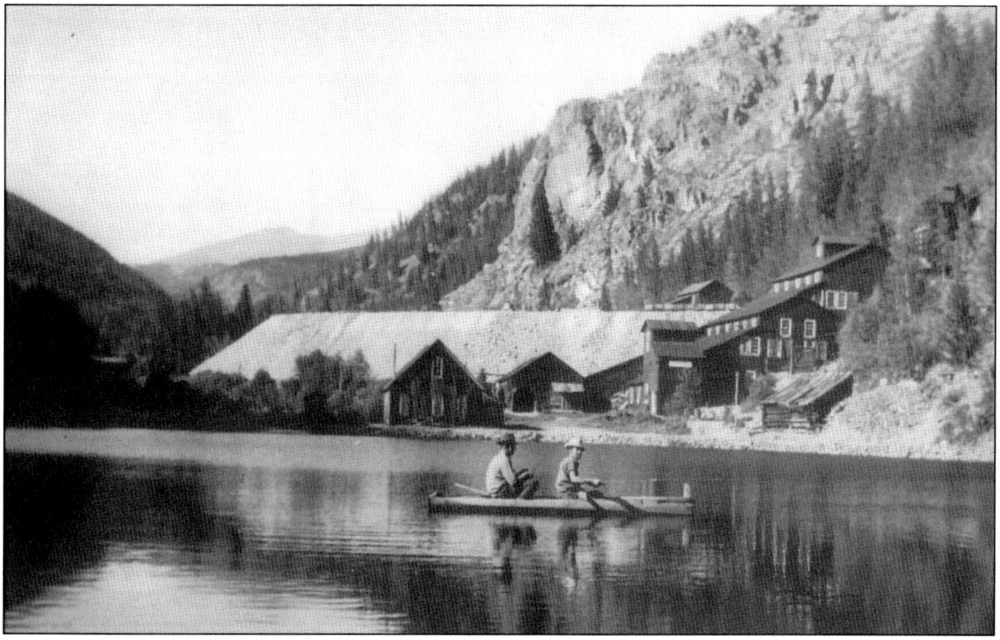

Lake San Cristobal. With the Ute-Ulay Mine as a backdrop, two fishermen hope for good luck on Lake Cristobal at nearly 9,000 feet outside of the mining camp of Lake City in the 1930s. The lake was formed around 700 years earlier by the Slumgullion landslide and is visited by geology students from Western State and all over the nation. (GPM.)

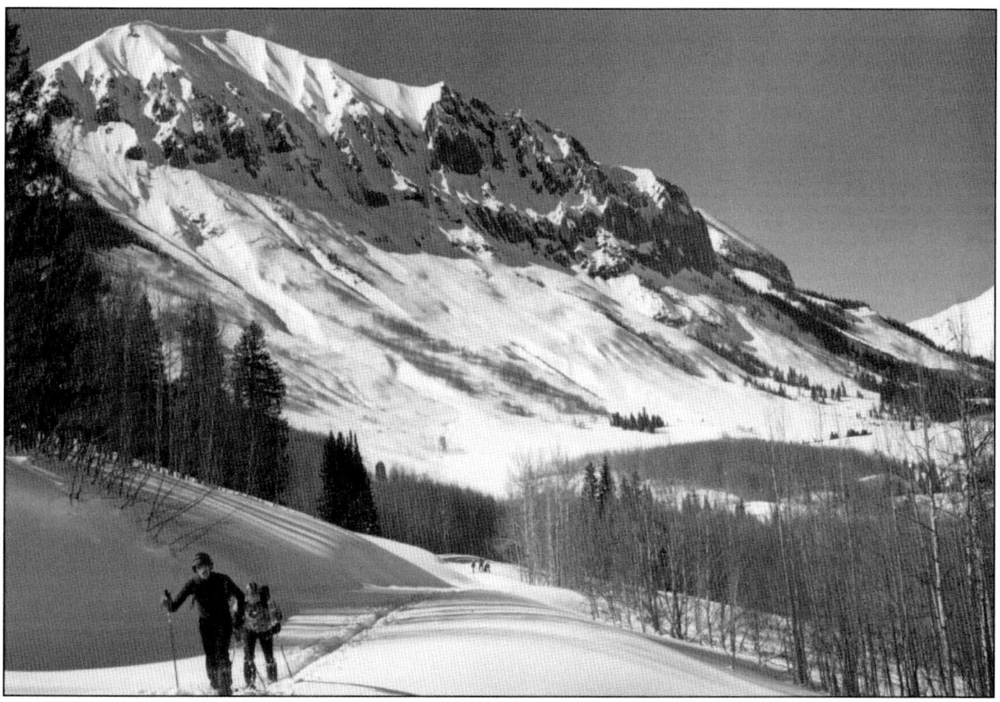

Gothic Mountain. With beautiful 12,500-foot-high Gothic Mountain in the background, Western State College students ski toward the Crested Butte Ski Area, located five miles away. Over a foot of new snow has fallen. (CBMHM.)

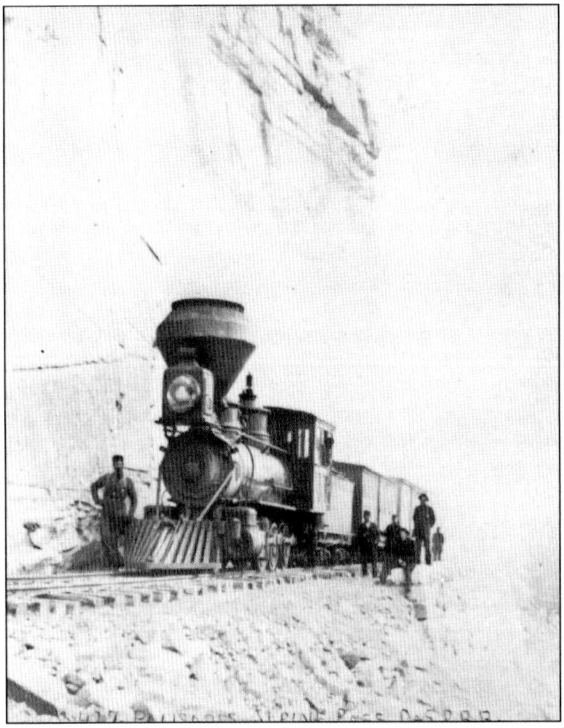

Denver South Park Railroad. Forty miles northeast of Gunnison, the famed Alpine Tunnel existed from 1882 to 1910. Denver South Park trains crawled through the 1,771-foot-long railroad tunnel, the highest in the world at 11,523 feet. The railroad and tunnel became major research topics for history students at Western State.

Marshall Pass. Until rails were removed in 1955, the major means of transportation in and out of Gunnison was the Denver & Rio Grande Railroad, which either left or entered the Gunnison Country via 10,846-foot-high Marshall Pass, 45 miles to the east. One of Western State's major problems, historically, was its inaccessibility. It took 12 hours for the D&RG to go from Gunnison to Denver.

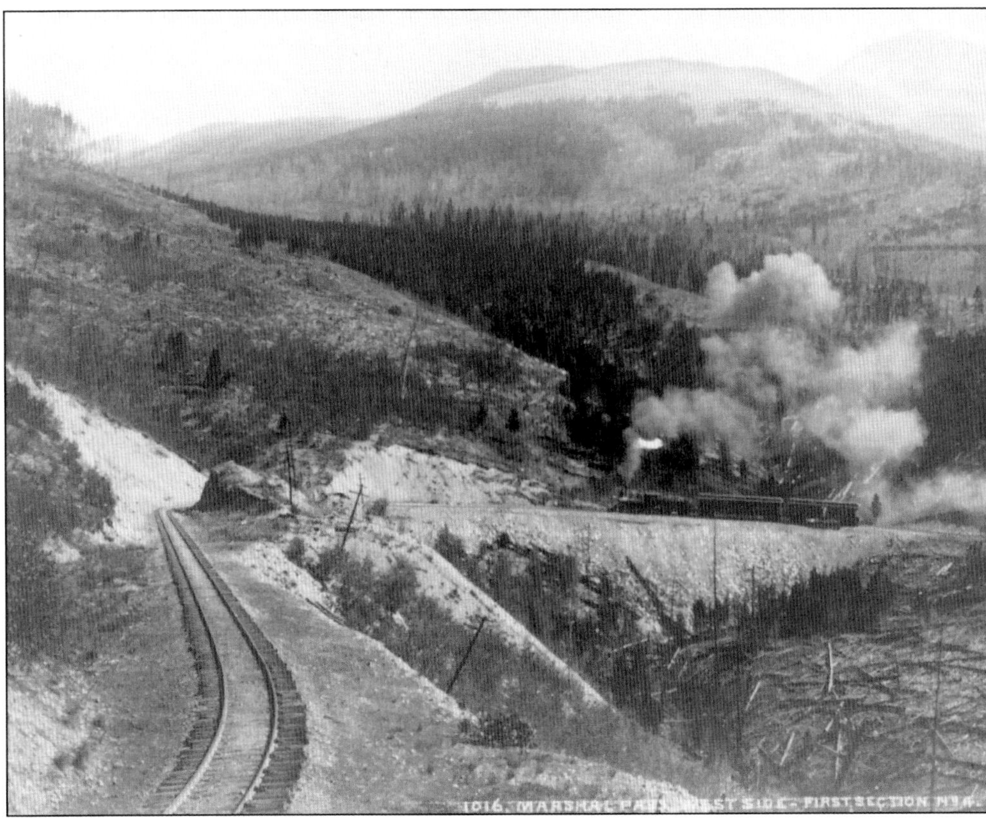

Irwin. Thirty miles from Gunnison and 10 miles from Crested Butte, the booming mining camp of Irwin sprang up in 1879. The great silver camp, at its peak, had 4,000 residents. This early 1880 photograph shows the camp in its early stages of development.

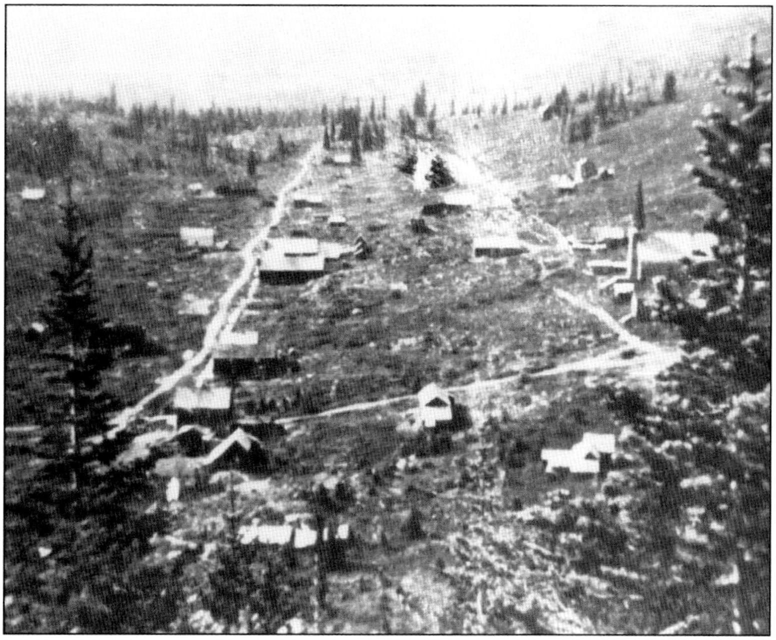

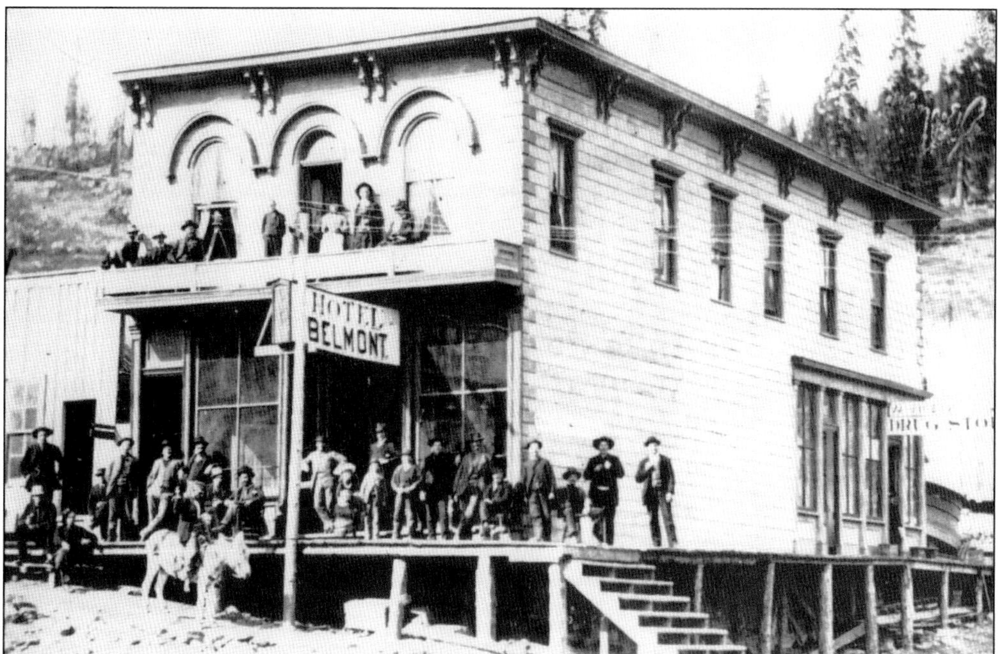

Irwin, 1882. By 1882, Irwin had great mines turning out millions of dollars of silver, a railroad headed in, stage lines operating, and frame buildings. The Hotel Belmont was one of the most pretentious in the camp and housed such dignitaries as Baron Rothschild and John D. Rockefeller, who came looking to invest in the mines.

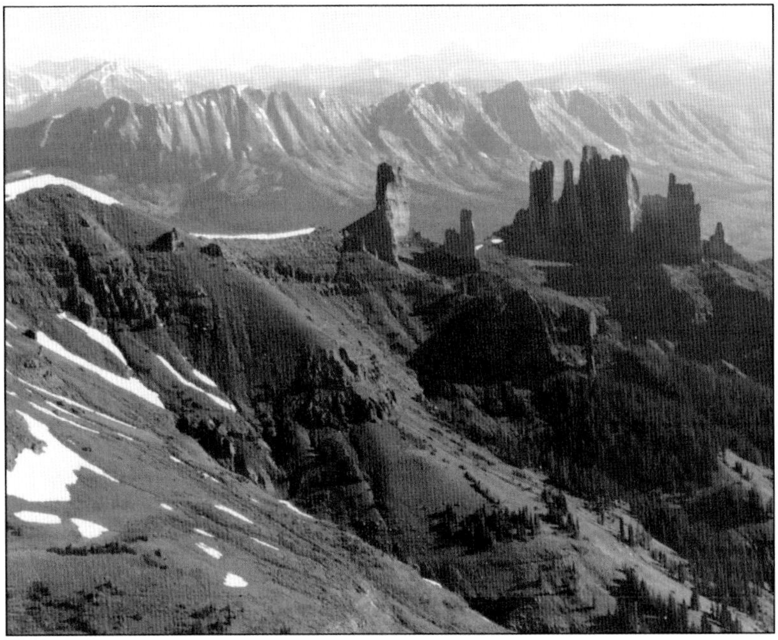

The Castles. Towering high above Castle Creek and the Ohio Creek Valley are the majestic "Castles." These rock formations, created by erosion over millions of years, are 20 miles north of Gunnison and dominate the landscape.

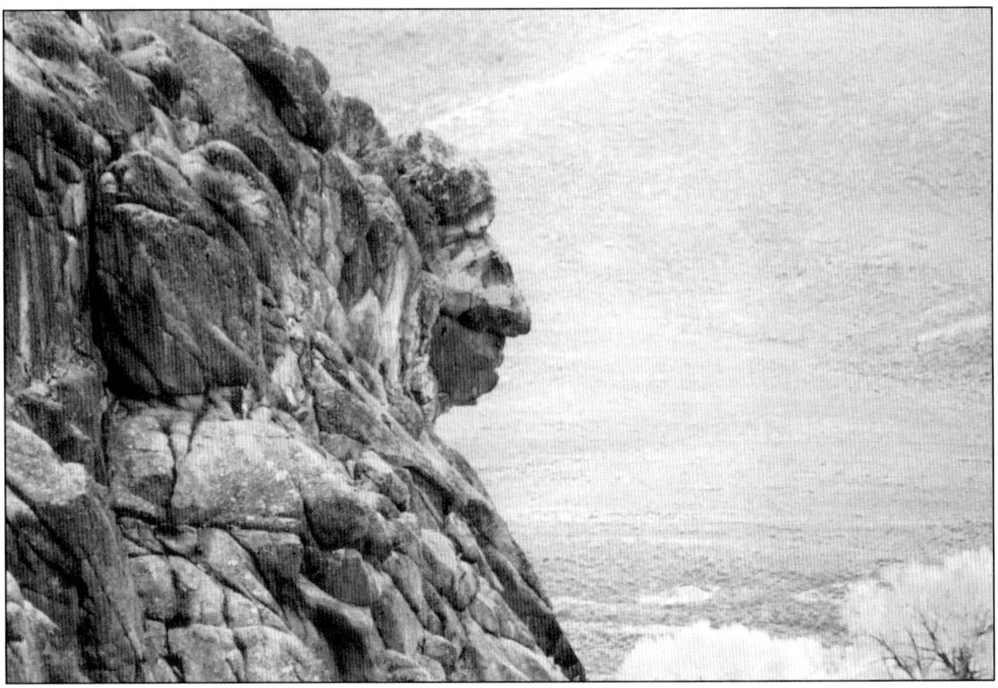

Indianhead. This perfect formation of an Indian head is located near the town of Ohio City, 19 miles east of Gunnison. Throughout the history of Western State College, the area has been a favorite hiking and photographic region for the hiking and outing club and individual students. (DC.)

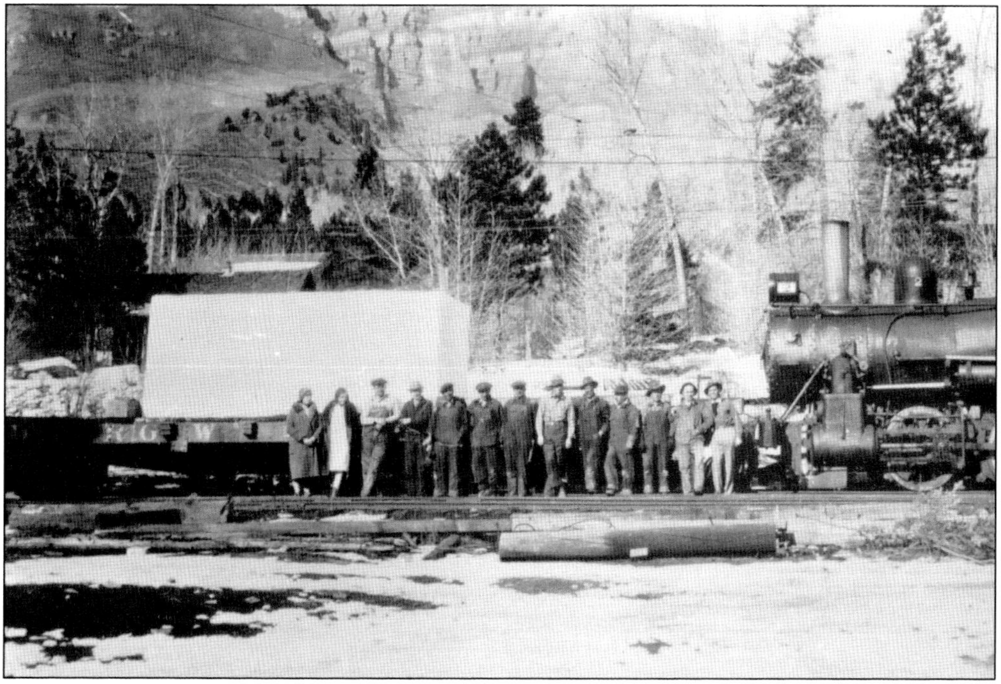

Tomb of the Unknown Soldier. Over 50 miles north of Gunnison was the town of Marble, a favorite place to visit for the Western State Hiking and Outing Club. In 1931, this huge block of pure white marble, weighing 124 tons, came out of the quarry and became the Tomb of the Unknown Soldier.

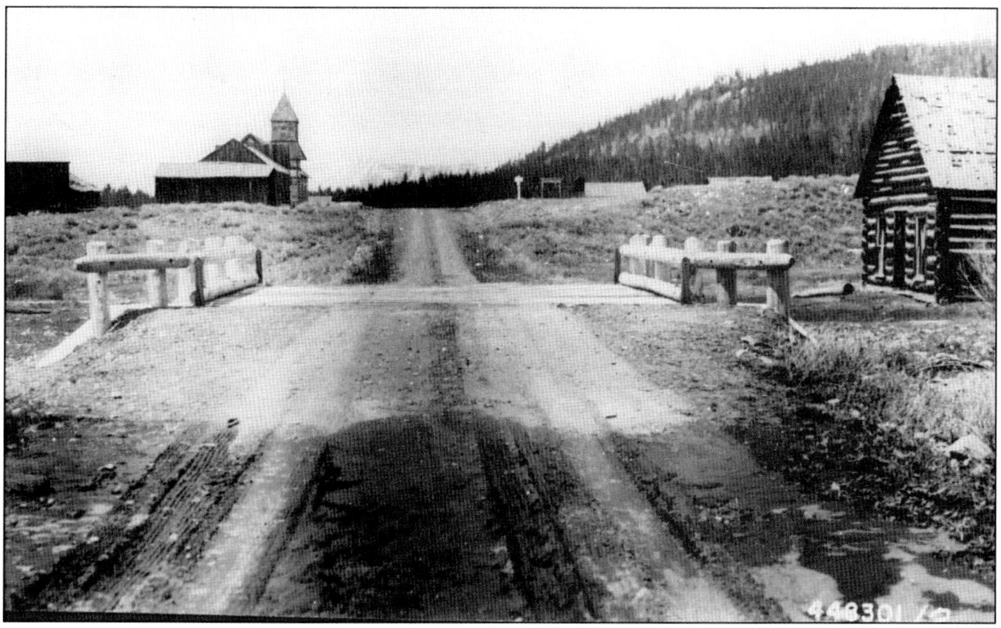

Tin Cup. A major silver camp which began in 1879, Tin Cup was named for the cup used to pan the first gold in nearby Taylor Park. The camp was close to the Taylor Reservoir, which was a favorite fishing and camping spot for Western State College students. This 1946 photograph shows the town hall and few buildings. By then, the good times were all gone.

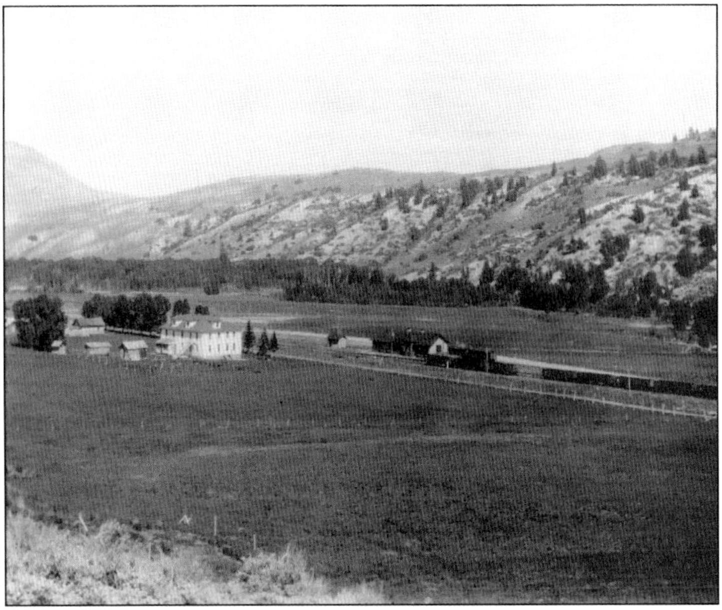

SAPINERO. This Denver & Rio Grande Railroad, resort, and ranching town, situated 26 miles west of Gunnison, began in the 1880s and lasted until the 1960s, when it was buried under 300 feet of water by the Blue Mesa Reservoir. Sapinero was at the head of the famed Black Canyon, and Western State students came there in droves to fish, climb, hike, or ride the rails through the canyon.

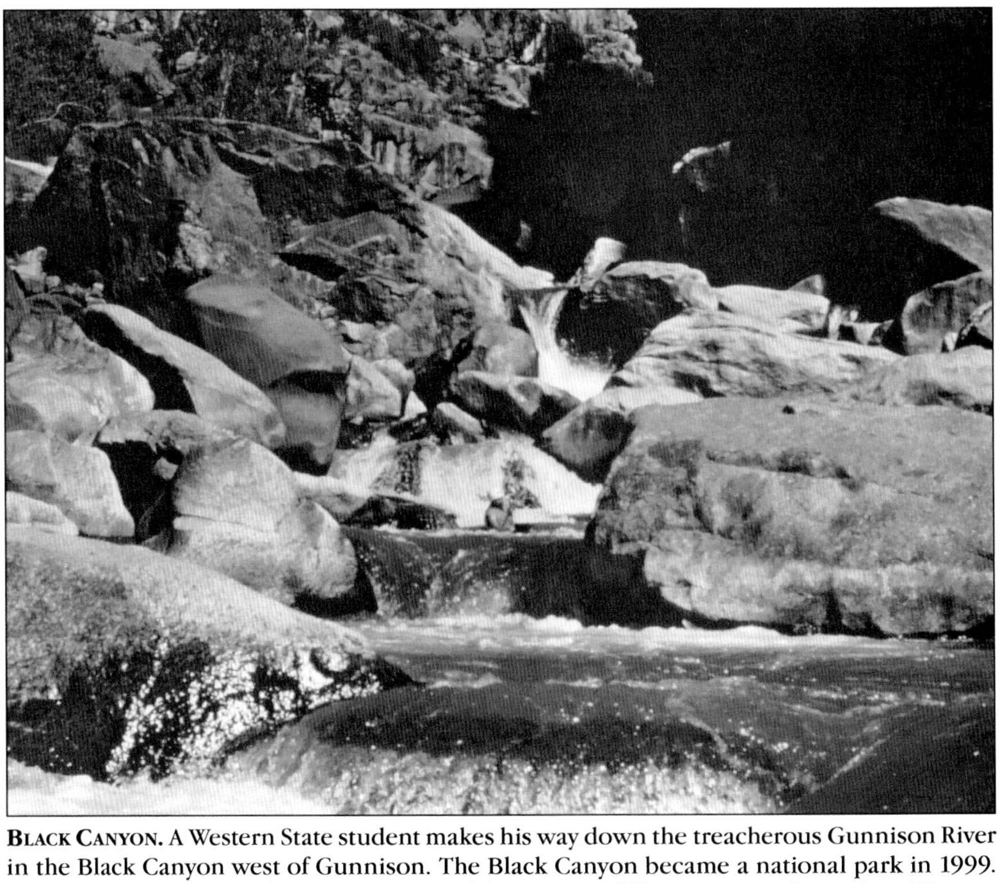

BLACK CANYON. A Western State student makes his way down the treacherous Gunnison River in the Black Canyon west of Gunnison. The Black Canyon became a national park in 1999. The Gunnison River in the canyon is one of the steepest-falling rivers in the nation. Western State students have flocked there to study geology and history.

Wendell Wilkie at Almont. In 1922, Western State College students started a tradition of having a fish fry at Almont, located 10 miles to the north. The July celebration lasted until 1940, when Republican presidential candidate Wendell Wilkie came to the fish fry and spoke to 10,000 people who came to eat and hear him speak. The sheer number of people caused the Isaak Walton League to end the fish fry.

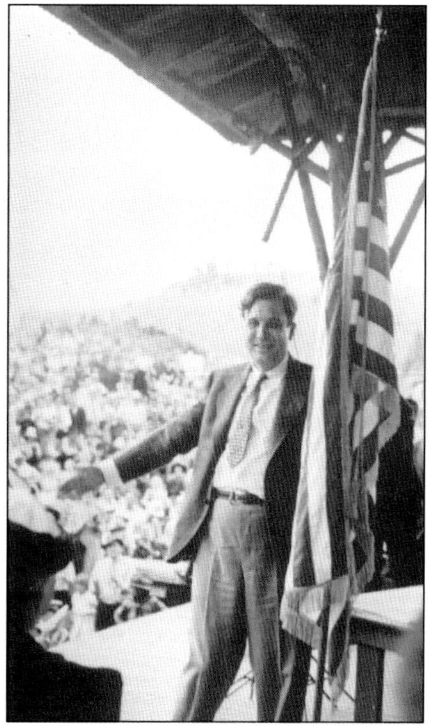

Cimarron. Forty-five miles west of Gunnison, Cimarron was a railroad center and also provided access into the Black Canyon. When the Blue Mesa Dam was built in the 1960s, it became a rip-roaring town filled with construction workers blowing off steam. Many of the workers on the dam were Western State students, including many hi-scalers. The hi-scalers hung from ropes on the walls of the Black Canyon and with steel bars and jack-hammers got rid of loose rock on the canyon walls. Following this, the hi-scalers used drills to drill holes in the rock and then inserted rock bolts, which stabilized the canyon wall.

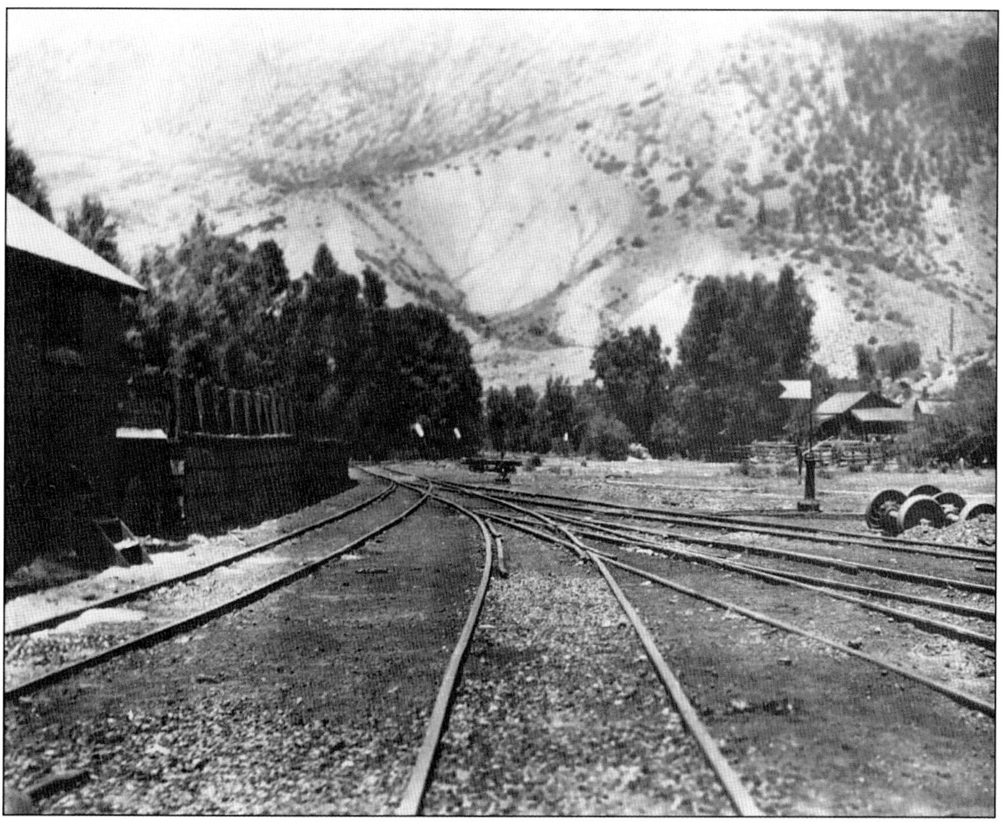

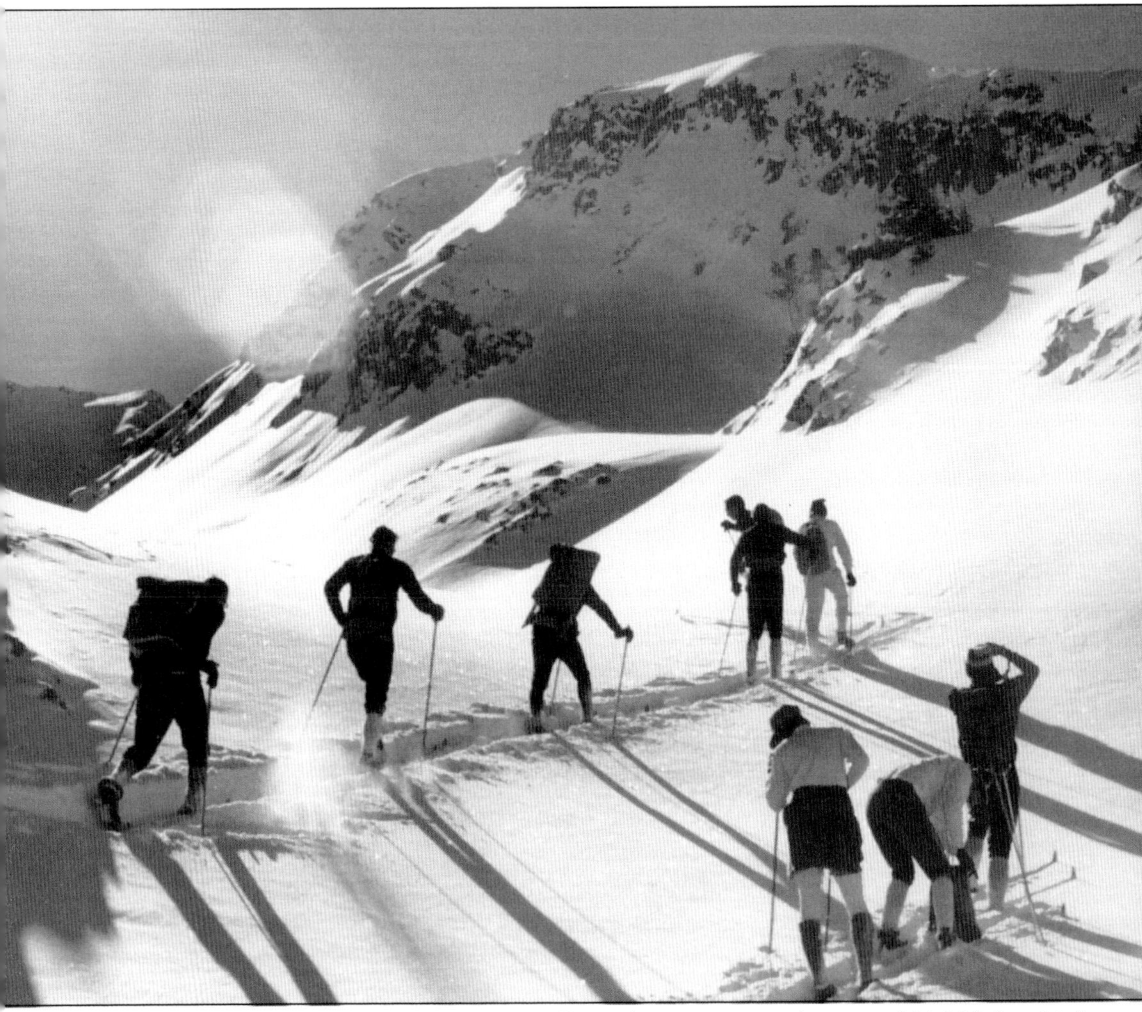

East Maroon Pass. The Western State College ski team nears the top of 11,800-foot-high East Maroon Pass en route to Aspen in the 1970s. The lead skier is carving through over a foot of new snow. The annual trip began at the Crested Butte Ski Area and concluded 20 miles later near Aspen.

Seven

The Glory Years

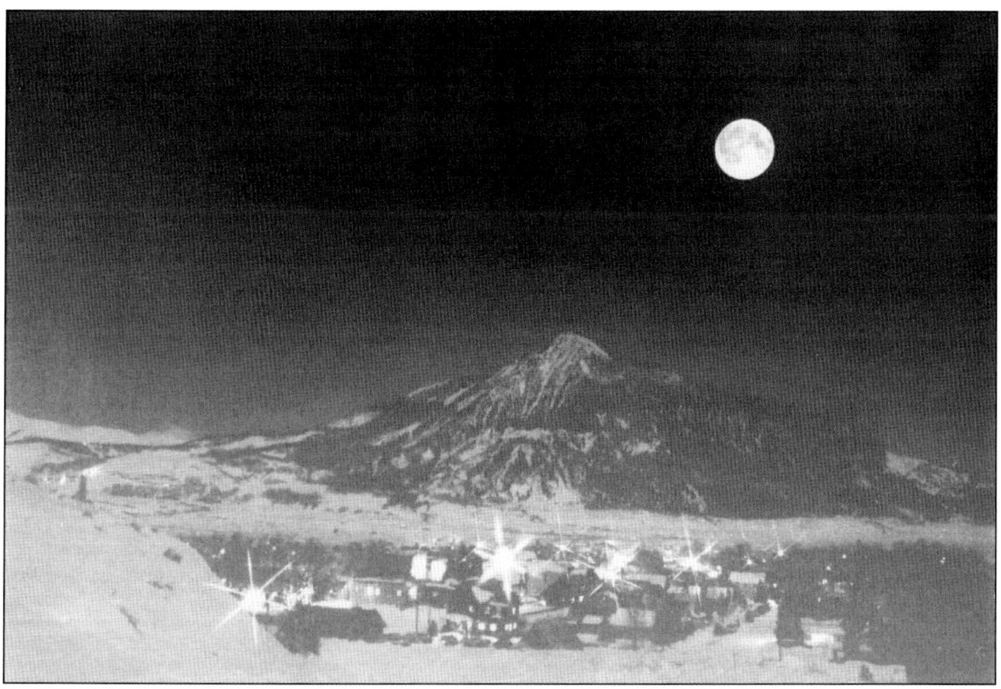

Crested Butte in the Moonlight. Twenty-eight miles north of Gunnison at the edge of the high and beautiful Elk Mountains, Crested Butte has been and is a playground for Western State students. Tremendous alpine and Nordic skiing, mountain biking, climbing, hunting, and fishing exist for both young and old alike. (WSCU.)

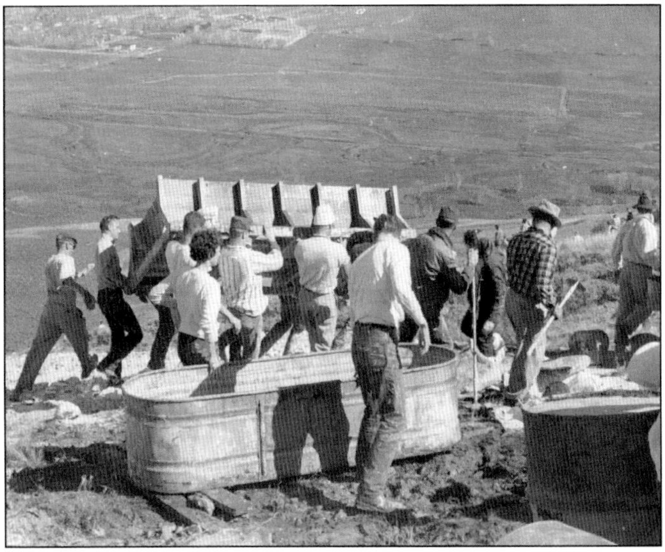

Carrying the Whitewash. A husky crew of Western State students carries a huge trough of whitewash to the top of the "W" in the 1970s. From there, a bucket brigade of hundreds of students was spaced out down the "W" and poured the whitewash onto the rocks. (WSCU.)

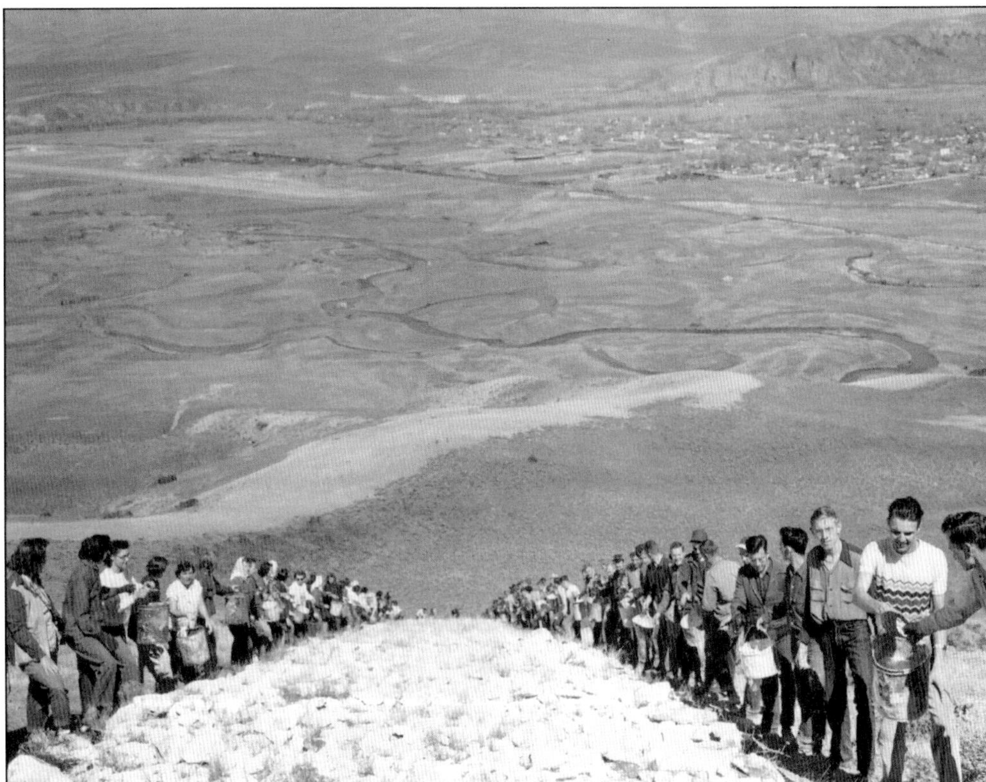

Bucket Brigade. With Gunnison and the Palisades as a backdrop, hundreds of Western State College students form a bucket brigade to whitewash the "W." This annual event was well planned, with every student or faculty member part of a well-oiled machine. In the early years, before a road was built, students walked up the face of the mountain carrying packs of lime. The students then melted snow on top of the mountain, which provided the water to mix with the lime to create the whitewash. (WSCU.)

The Winner. The year is 1962, and track and basketball player Don Spicklemier is about ready to cross the finish and win the W Mountain Race. The race began in 1951 as a fall conditioning run for Sven Wiik's skiers. Today, it is the longest-held race in Colorado. (WSCU.)

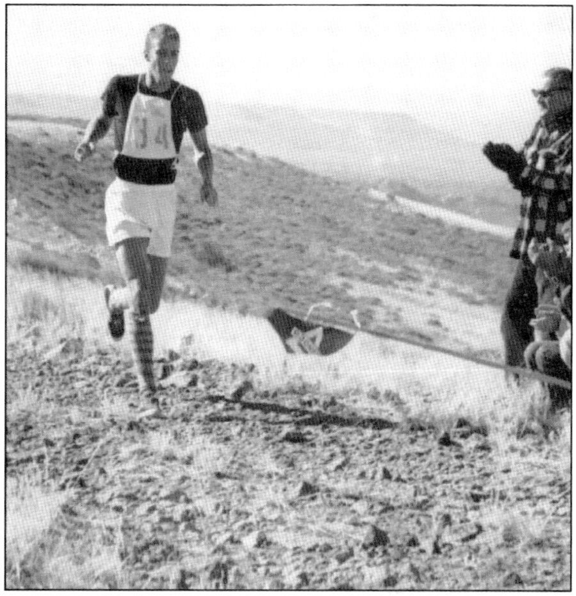

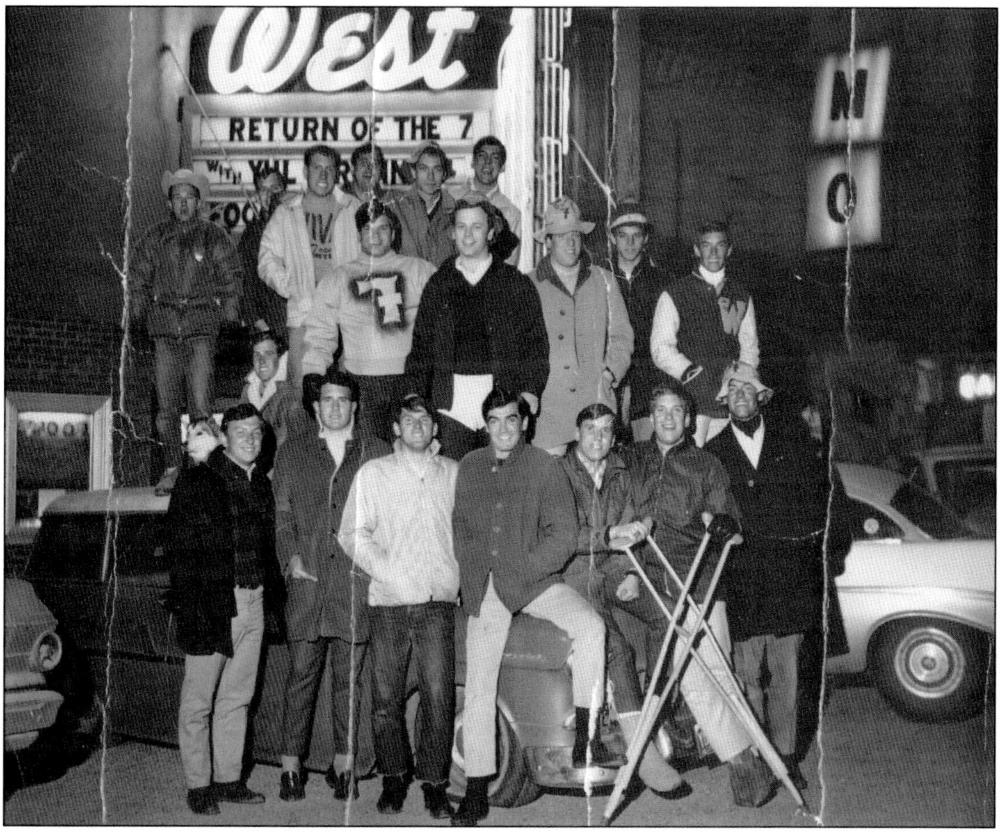

The "7." The Luftseben organization was based on the German word for seven. When the movie *Return of the* 7 came to Gunnison's West Theatre in 1966, it afforded a perfect opportunity for the Luftseben to take a memorable photograph next to the marquee. The student with a "7" on front of his sweater is John Knickerbocker.

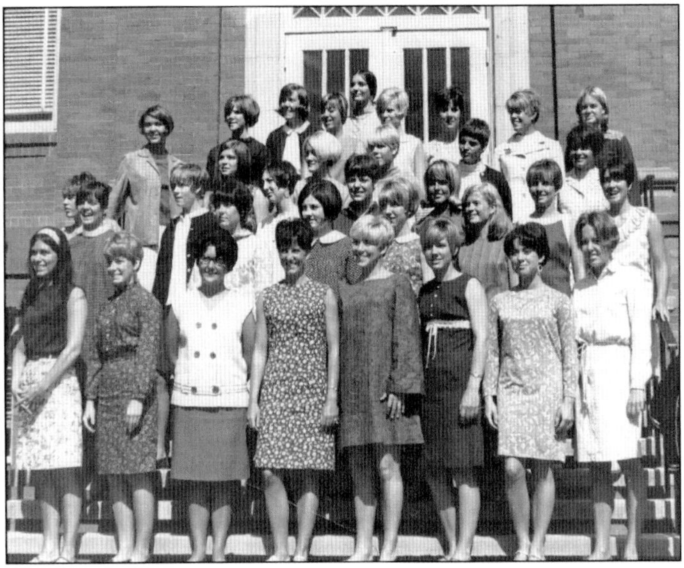

TKD's. The TKD's, affectionately known as "Tap a Keg a Day," was the Western State women's organization that rivaled the men's Luftseben. The women were usually at all Luftseben parties. Here, they pose for a formal picture in front of Taylor Hall in 1966. Identified in the first row are, from left to right, Susan Lyall, unidentified, Harriet Burch, Patty Baker, Lynn Van Horn, unidentified, Sandy "Jeep" Sterner, and Patty Ziegler.

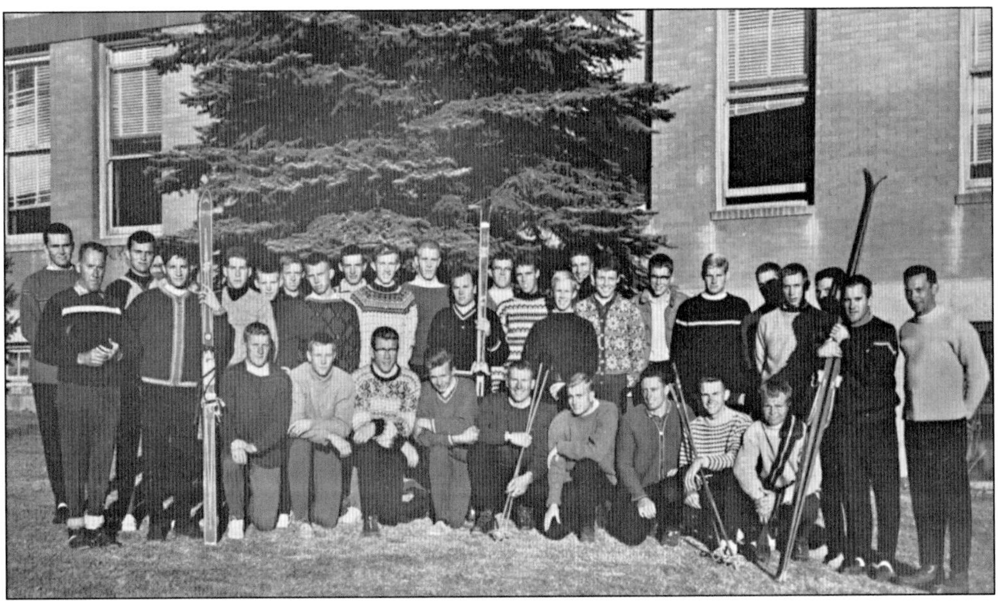

Greatness. One of the great ski teams in Western State history was the 1961 team. The team had great competitors in both alpine and Nordic events. Two-time US Olympic coach Sven Wiik recruited and led the team. Notables included Olympian Dave Gorsuch (kneeling in the first row with ski poles), Jennings Cress, NCAA skimiester (third from the right in the first row), Loris Werner (with skis front, second row, second from right), and Ken Phelps (third from the left of those standing).

Johnson Returns. Dr. John C. Johnson, member of the first faculty at Colorado State Normal in 1911 and founder of the Rocky Mountain Biological Laboratory at Gothic, returned to the college in 1966. The event was "Mountain Dewins," a series of skits at homecoming, and Dr. Johnson received a rousing ovation.

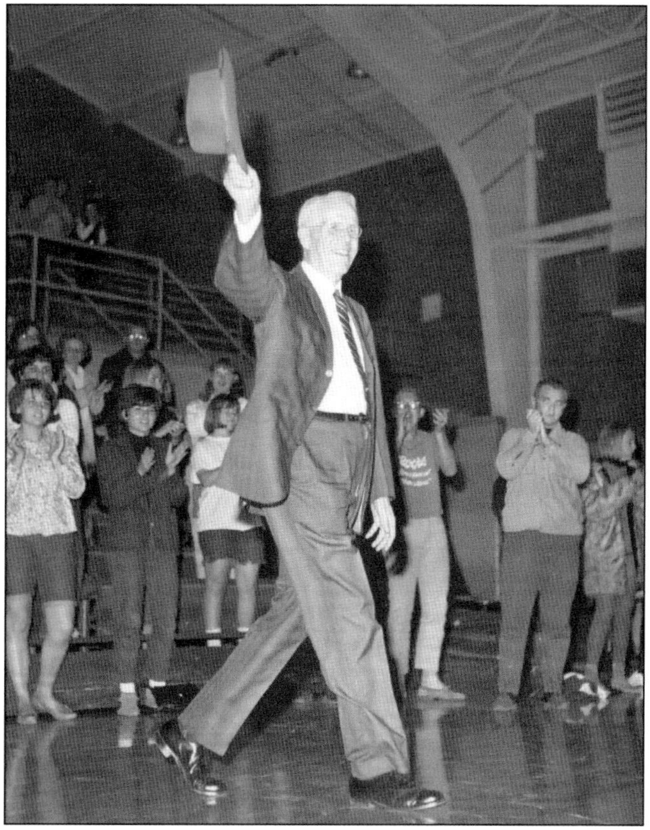

First Women's Ski Team. One of the first women's ski teams in Western State history poses for a photograph in 1964. Not yet an official sport, skiing became a club with the women competing and dominating throughout Colorado. Barbara Strawn and Patti Hippas are middle and right in front, and Sara Squires Davis is holding the skis on the left.

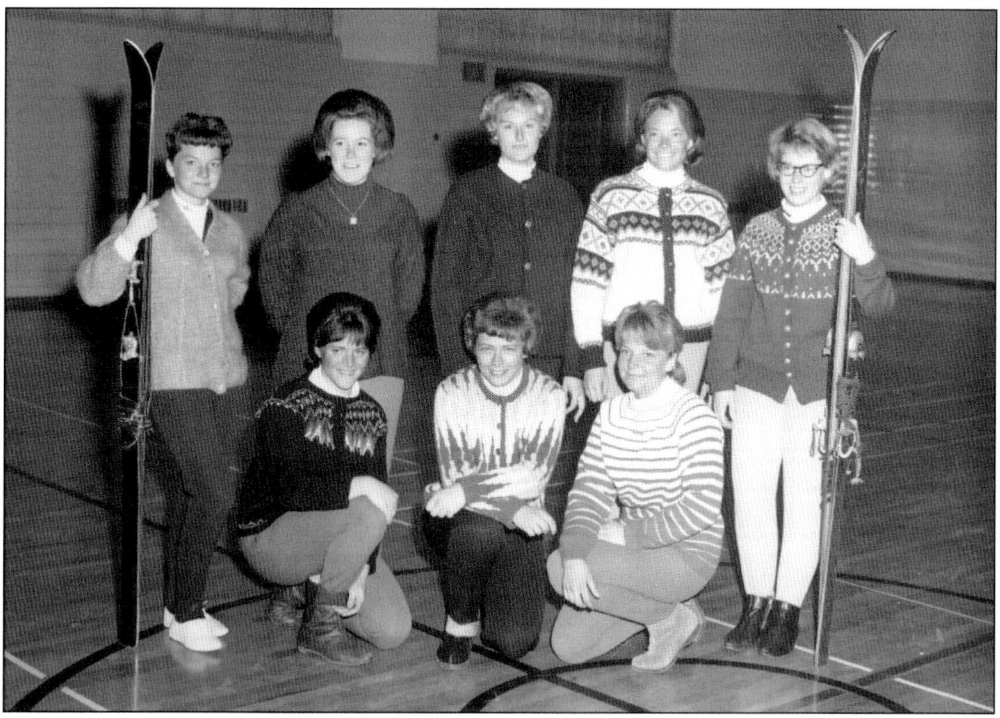

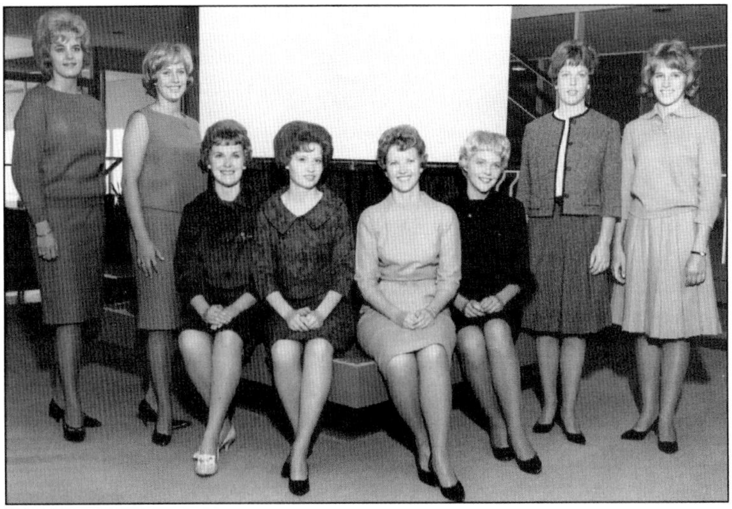

Queen Candidates, 1963. Eight attractive Western State women pose in Escalante Terrace before the selection of homecoming queen was made in 1963. Royalty, fraternities, and sororities were very important then, unlike today. (WSCU.)

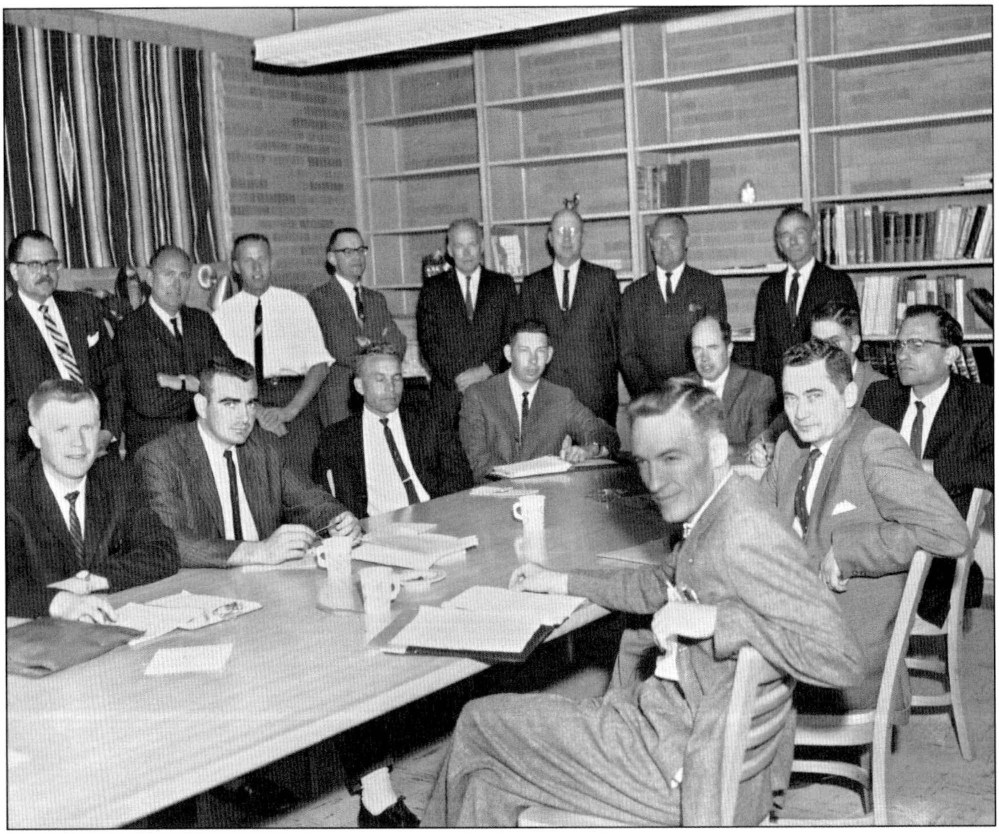

Social Science Department. Social science faculty, along with members of the Western administration, gather for a meeting in Kelley Hall during the fall of 1962. Some of the faculty and administrators include history professor Bill Edmondson (standing second from the left), Pres. Harlan Bryant and political science professor "Mac" McCulloch, (standing fifth and sixth from the left, respectively), and D.H. Cummins, dean of faculty (standing at the far right). (WSCU.)

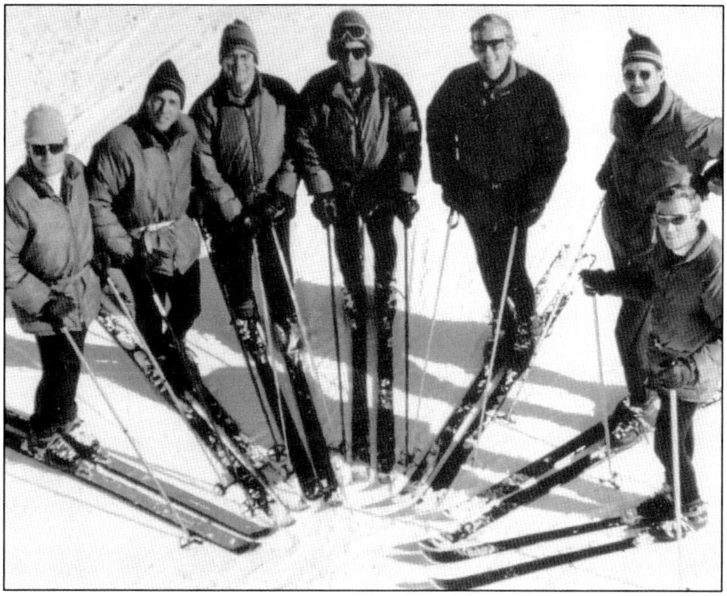

Early Ski Patrol. The Crested Butte Ski Area opened in 1961, and soon, most members of the ski patrol were Western State College students. The patrol of 1965–1966 included Western students, from left to right, Jeff Jacobson, John Burns, Mike Zahradka, Walt Frike, George Sibley, Don Bachman, and Bill Sweitzer. Sibley became a Western State professor.

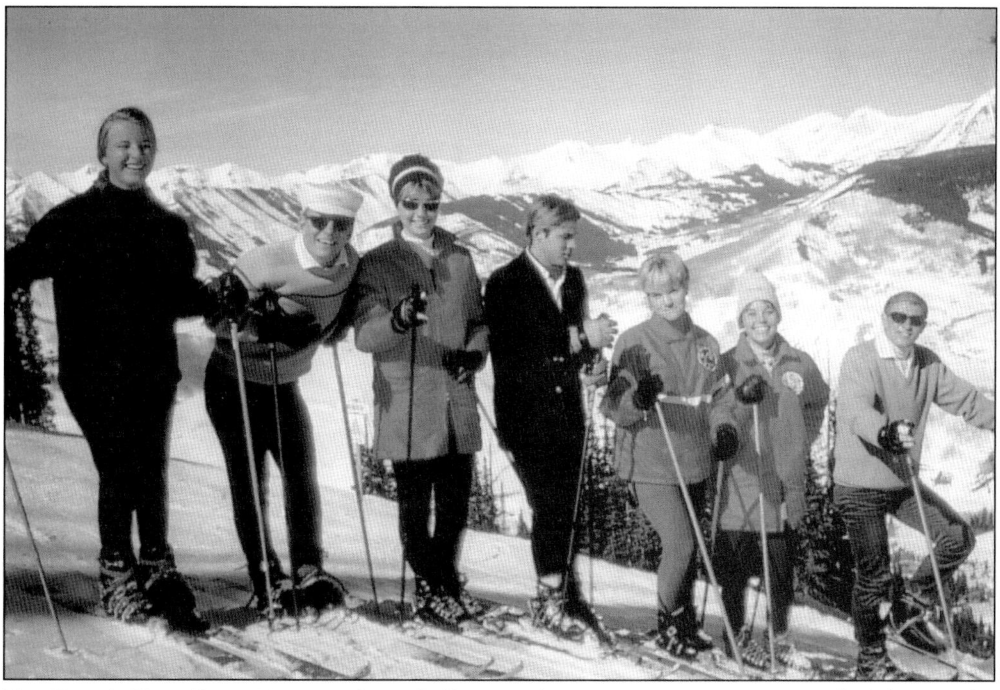

The Hawk's Nest. Seven Western State College students pose on a steep run called the Hawk's Nest at the Crested Butte Ski Area in 1968. From left to right are Joyce Saya, Ken LaCasse, unidentified, Don Trachte, two unidentified, and Jim Iverson. A 20-minute hike on skis got one to a sensational and steep powder run.

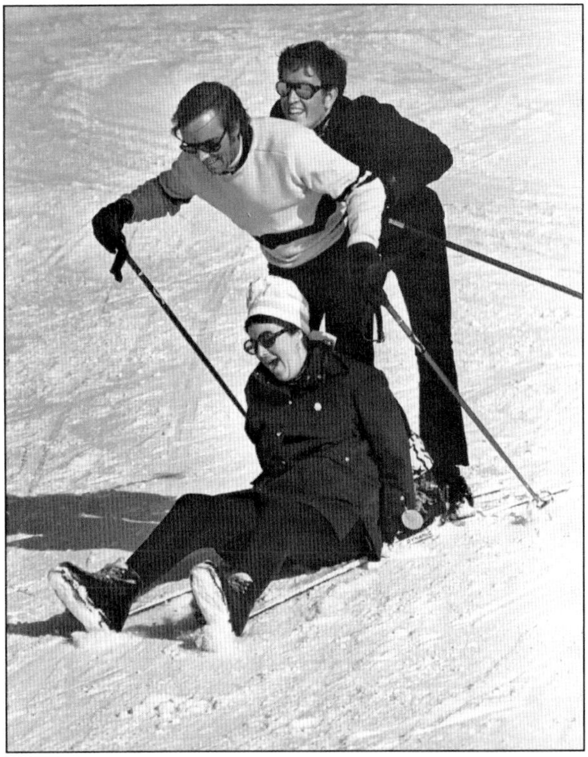

Hijinks. A spring skiing party is underway at the Crested Butte Ski Area in the 1960s. Bill Sweitzer is skiing near the bottom of the mountain with Ann Vitt riding in front and T.J. Sardy hanging on in back.

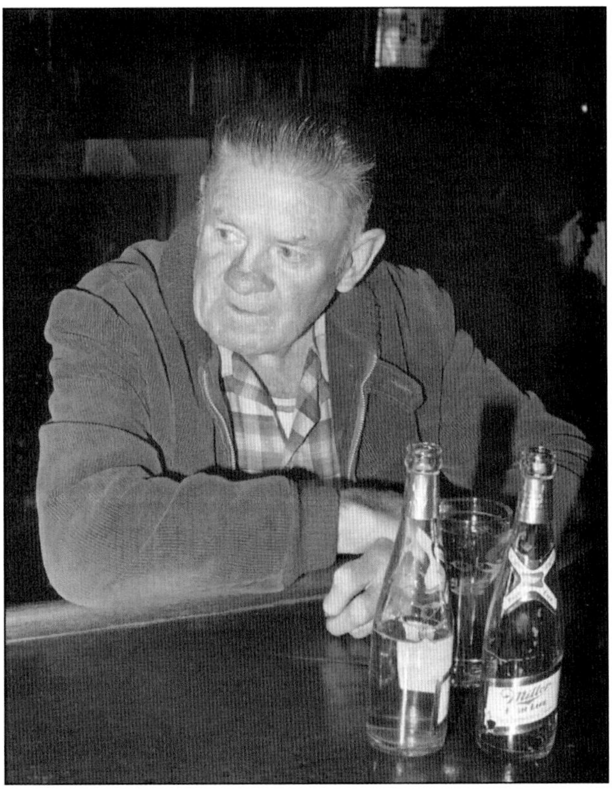

Pittser. One of the great old-timers of Crested Butte was Martin "Pittser" Sporcich. His family had migrated to the United States from troubled southeastern Europe, and Sporcich soon went to work in Crested Butte's coal mines. He became very popular with the young people, including many Western students, and loved baseball. Today, the softball field in Crested Butte is named for him.

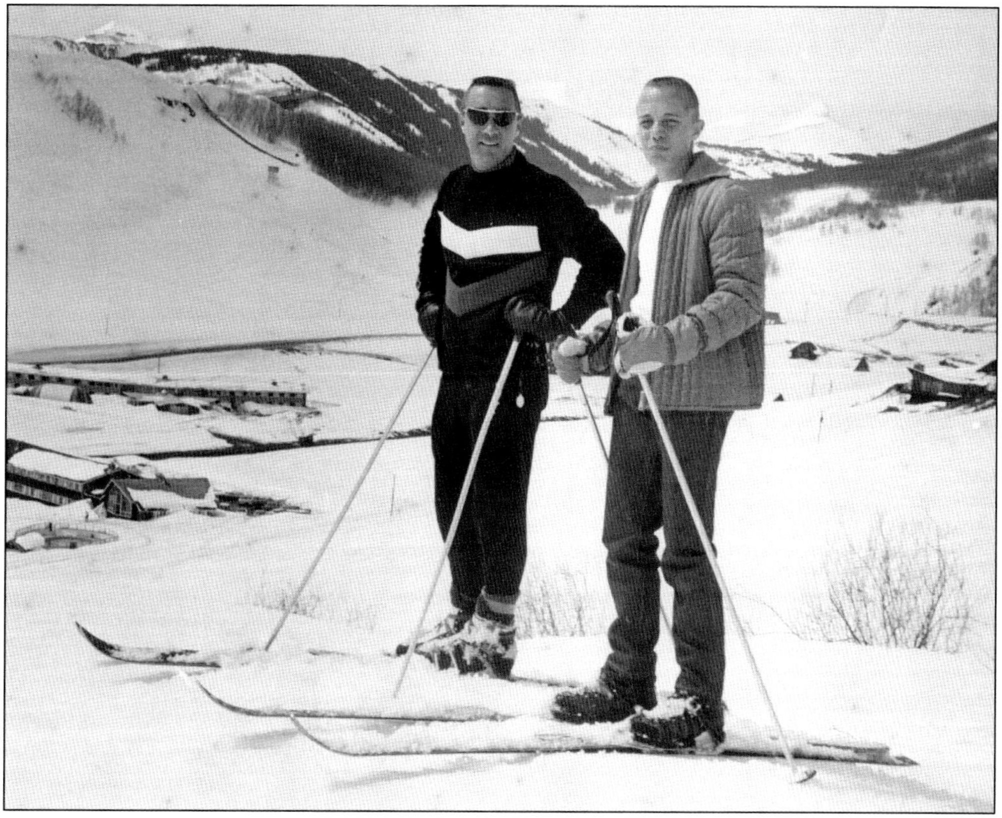

The Astronaut. One of the original seven astronauts, Gus Grissom, owned a house that looked like a space module at the Crested Butte Ski Area in the 1960s. Grissom (left) became a proficient skier and often talked to Western State science classes. He died in an accident while training for a mission at Cape Canaveral in 1967. (CBMHM.)

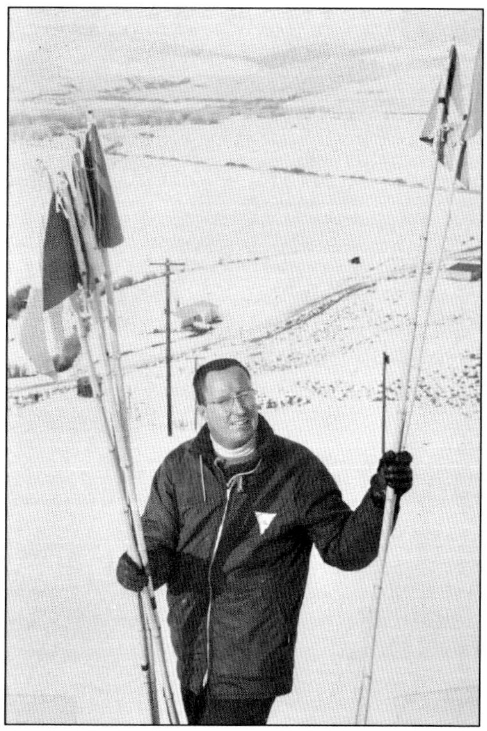

Ken MacLennan. Taking over for Sven Wiik as Western State's ski coach was Ken MacLennan, seen here setting poles at the Cranor Hill Ski Area. MacLennan was a great high school athlete at Ouray and continued as a member of Sven Wiik's great teams. MacLennan's teams also distinguished themselves, and he was elected to the WSC Hall of Fame for his accomplishments.

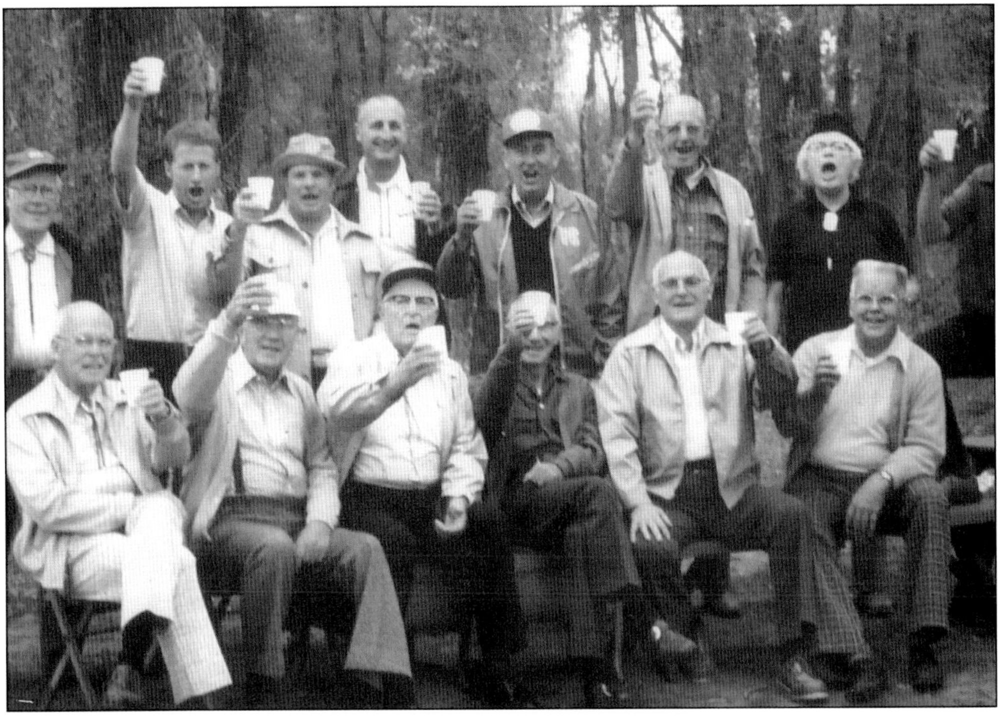

The Old Timers. In 1975, Mickey Zahradka and Duane Vandenbusche from Western State started "the Old Timers," 15 faculty members who gathered at Zahradka's cabin on the Gunnison River. It has met for 38 consecutive years and now includes 75 men from the Gunnison Country. From left to right are (first row) Harlan Bryant, Olaf Kjosness, Paul Wright, D.H. Cummins, Herb Dorricott, and Harold Binford; (second row) Chuck Wright, Duane Vandenbusche, Tracy Borah, Paul Coleman, Bill Edmondson, Bob Corneer, Bill Dorgan, and Bob Arnold (hidden). Mickey Zahradka (the 15th member) took the photograph.

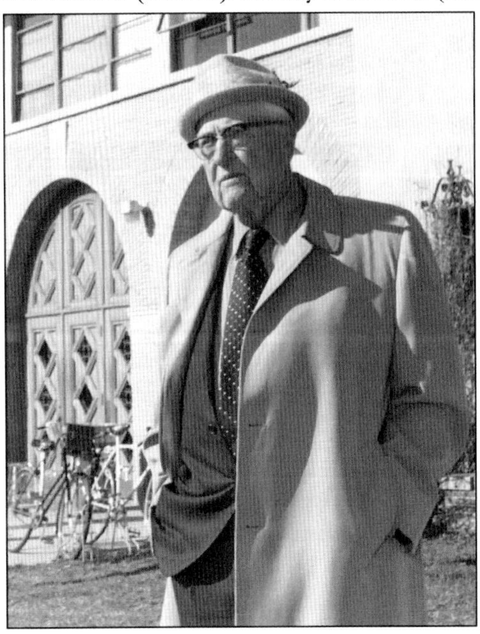

The Grand Old Man. Paul W. Wright was perhaps the most famous and influential faculty member in Western State history. An outstanding football player at the college, Wright coached many sports and is considered "the father of intercollegiate skiing" for getting that sport adopted by the NCAA. He also served as head of the physical education department and as athletic director. Wright Gym is named for him today.

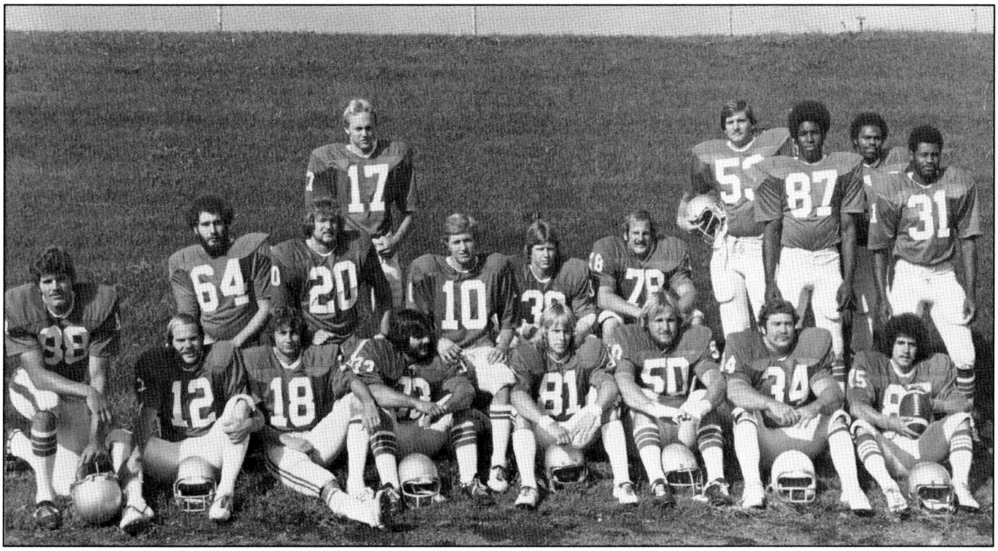

Western State Seniors. One of the greatest football teams in Western's history was the team of the 1970s. Included were All-American quarterback Charlie Thompson (10), All-American offensive tackle Mike O'Rourke (78), and tight end Tyron James (87). (WSCU.)

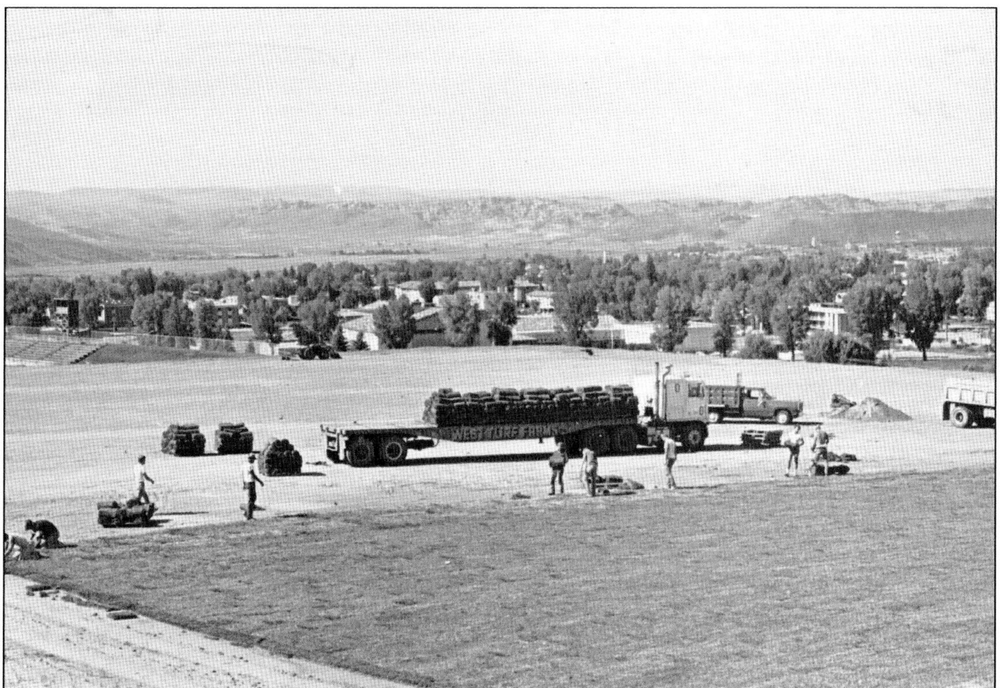

Crismon Field. Named for Lt. Scott Crismon, a navy pilot killed in the Vietnam War, Crismon Field was created above Mountaineer Bowl in the 1970s. The Army Corps of Engineers bulldozed part of a nearby hill to create a level field that was then sodded. Larry Means, head of WSC's foundation and an ex–Air Force colonel, was responsible for the Army Corps of Engineers' involvement. (WSCU.)

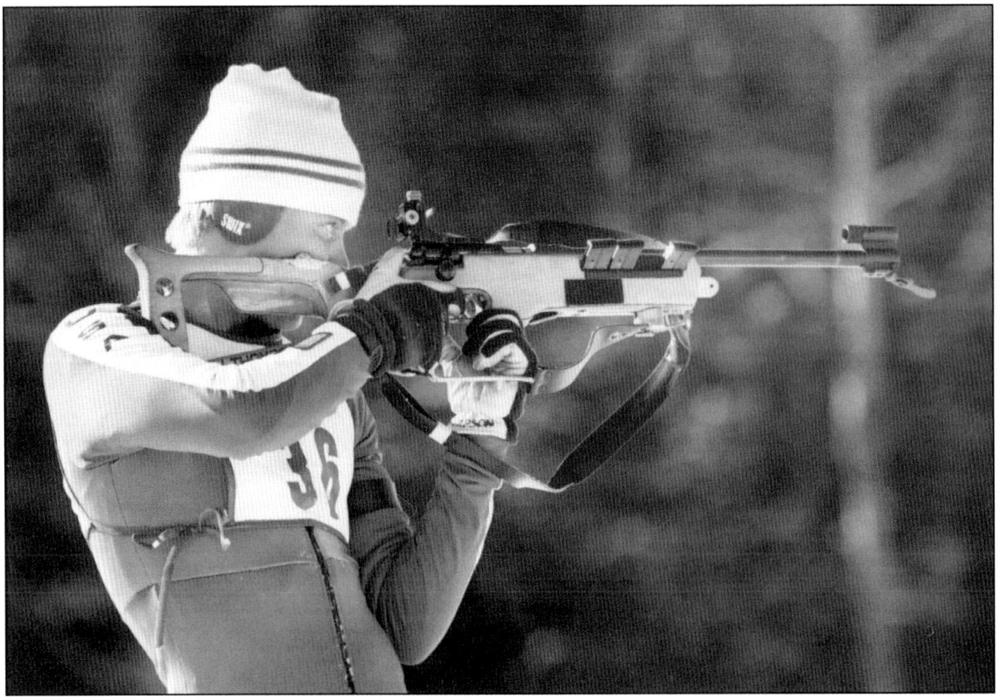

JOSH THOMPSON. One of Western State's greatest athletes, Josh Thompson, is seen here competing in the biathlon at the 1986 World Team Trials at Lake Placid, New York. Also an All-American cross-country runner, Thompson was a biathlete for the United States in the 1988 Olympic Games.

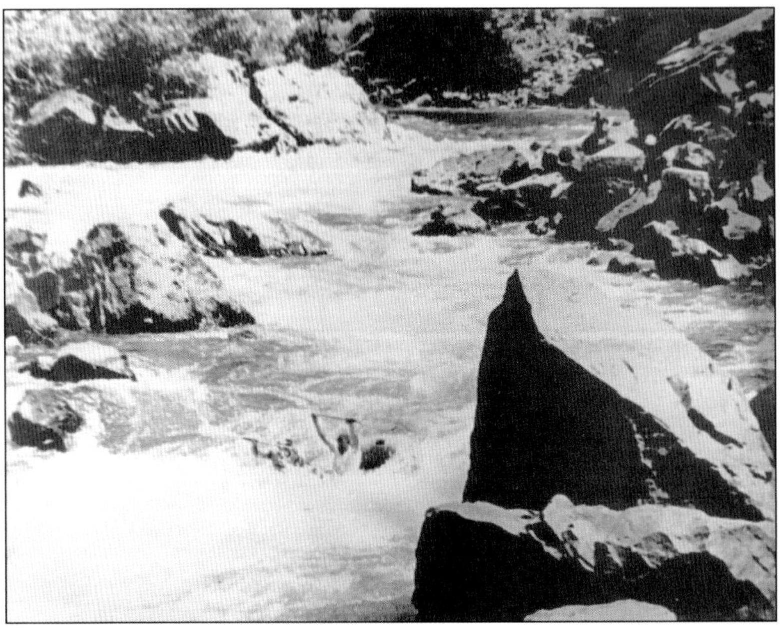

DOWN THE BLACK CANYON. Ed Nelson of Montrose and Fred Glass of Gunnison navigate a nasty section of the Gunnison River in the Black Canyon in 1962. Many Western State students ran rapids in the canyon with most using kayaks rather than rubber rafts.

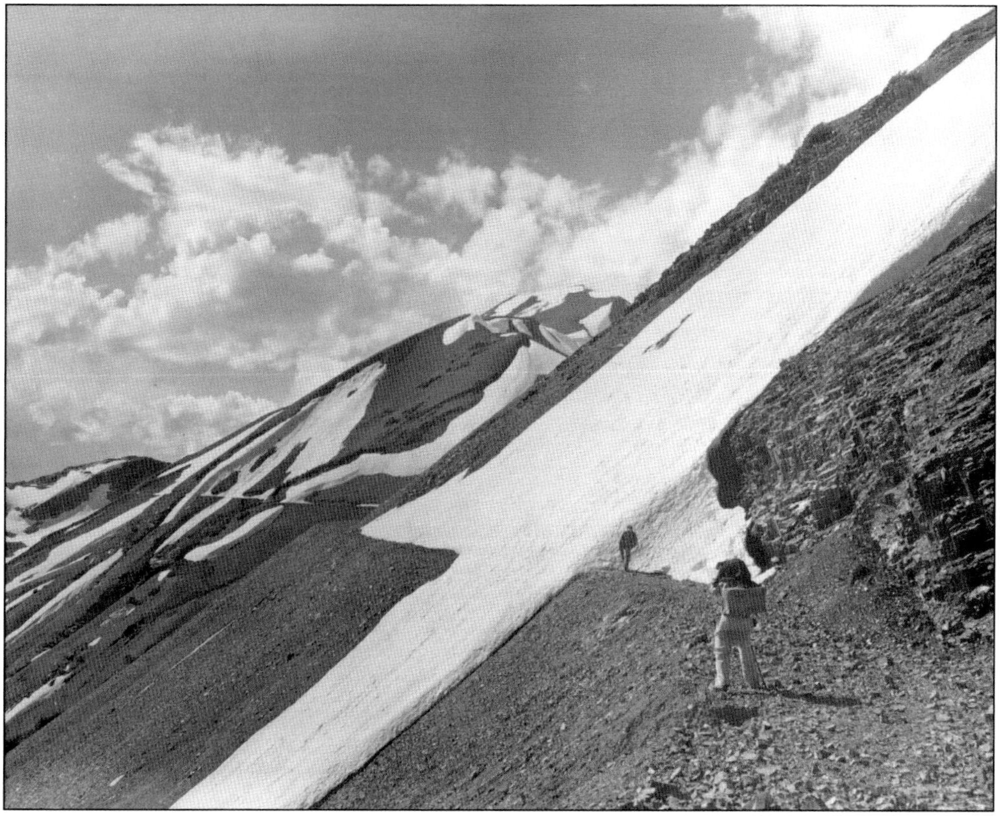

Yule Pass. Located between Crested Butte and the town of Marble, Yule Pass was used by early freighters. The pass is over 11,000 feet and in steep terrain, which led to many avalanches. The pass and road were very dangerous. In 1948, a party of Western State students, led by Dave Gaskill, spent four days skiing from Crested Butte to Marble under very dangerous conditions.

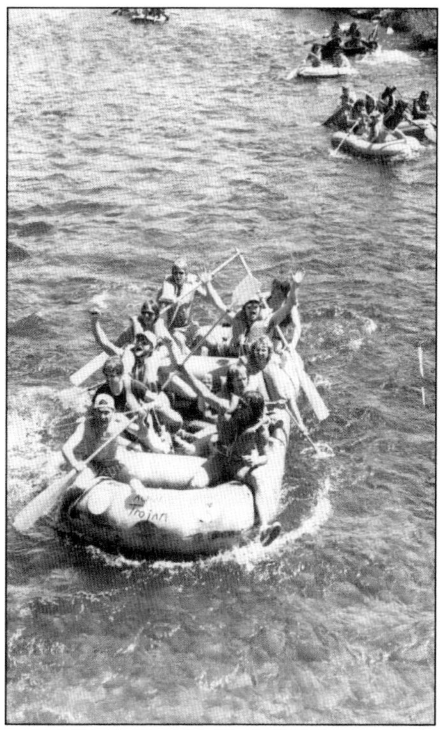

Springfest. For joyous fun, few celebrations at Western State could top Springfest. Every May, parties, dances, outdoor events, and a boat race down the swollen and roaring Gunnison River highlighted the celebration. (WSCU.)

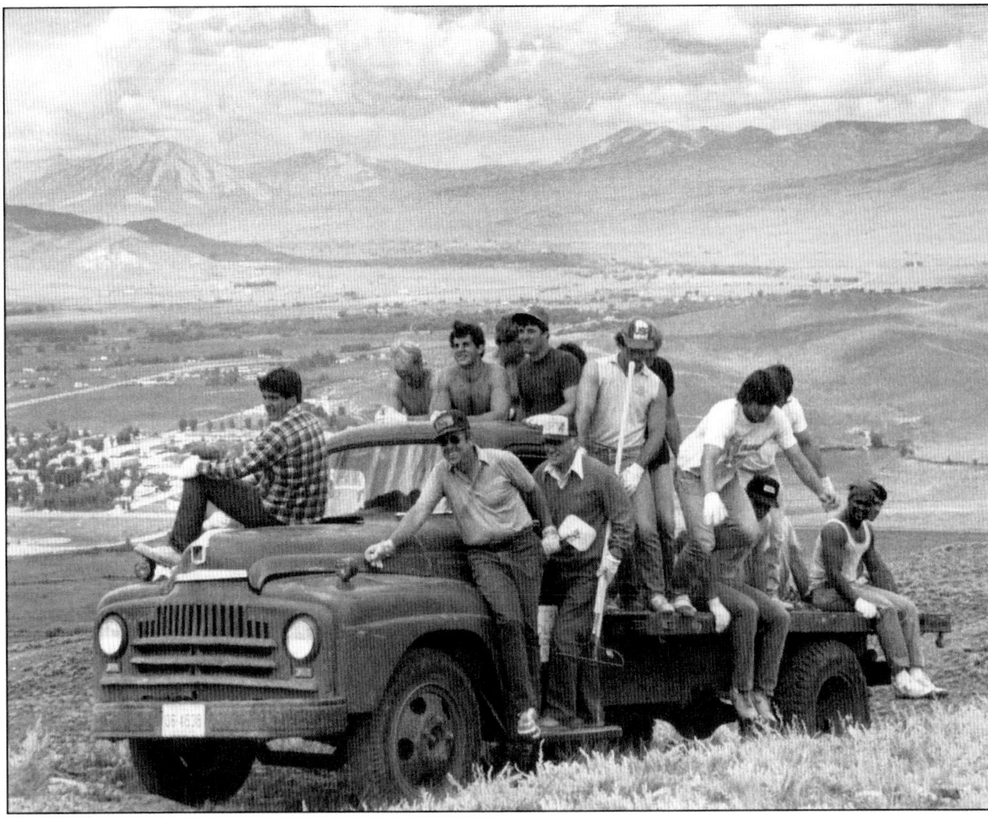

Preparing the "W." Before whitewashing the "W," Western State students and some faculty cut weeds, added rocks, and cleared debris. Riding on the truck running board near the top of W Mountain, registrar Wes Lazenby (left) and golf coach Ollie Woods (right) directed the work. Gunnison is in the background. (WSCU.)

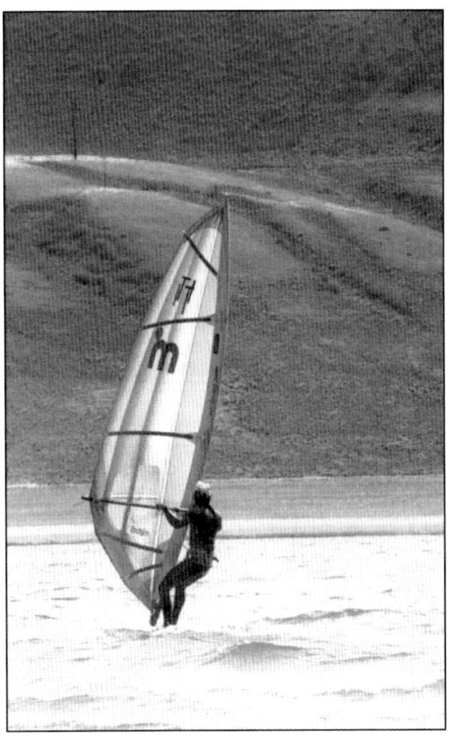

Windsurfing. A Western State College student rides the wind on his surfboard at the Blue Mesa Reservoir west of Gunnison in the 1970s. Windsurfing became a big sport for WSC students with the Bay of Chickens as the choice spot on the reservoir.

The "W." The largest college letter in the nation, 420 feet long and 16 feet wide and containing 20,560 feet of rock, was constructed in 1923 on the side of Tenderfoot Mountain overlooking Gunnison. The "W" was the brainchild of Dr. John C. Johnson of the Western State faculty. On May 2, students and faculty carried hundreds of rocks from the side of the mountain and placed them inside the borders of the lines of string that outlined the "W."

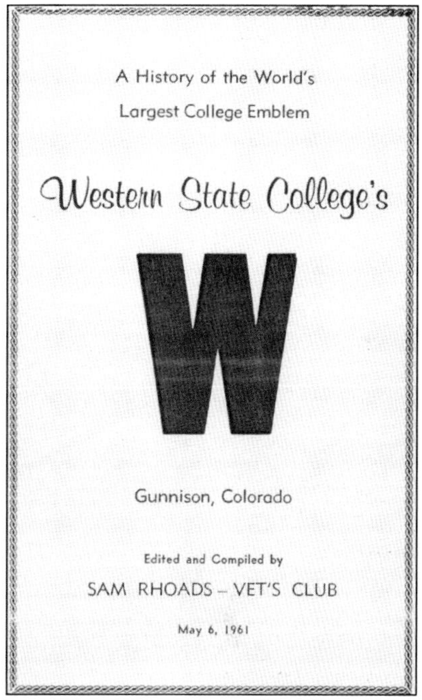

A History of the World's
Largest College Emblem

Western State College's

W

Gunnison, Colorado

Edited and Compiled by
SAM RHOADS – VET'S CLUB

May 6, 1961

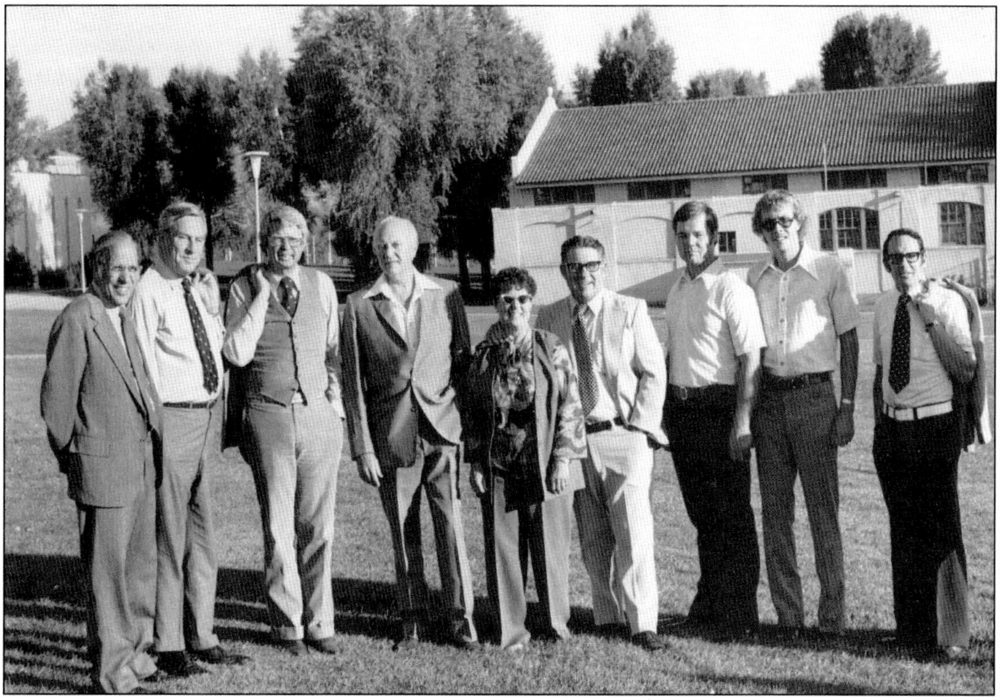

Water Workshop. Begun by lawyer Dick Bratton and history professor Duane Vandenbusche in 1975, the WSC water workshop has focused on the problems and importance of water in the West. In the 1970s, the workshop brought Gov. Richard Lamm and three ex-governors to Western to share their views on water. Pictured from left to right are historian David Lavender, ex-governor John Love, Lamm, ex-governor Steve McNichols, Helen Jensen, ex-governor John Vanderhoff, Gary Sherman, unidentified, and Dick Bratton.

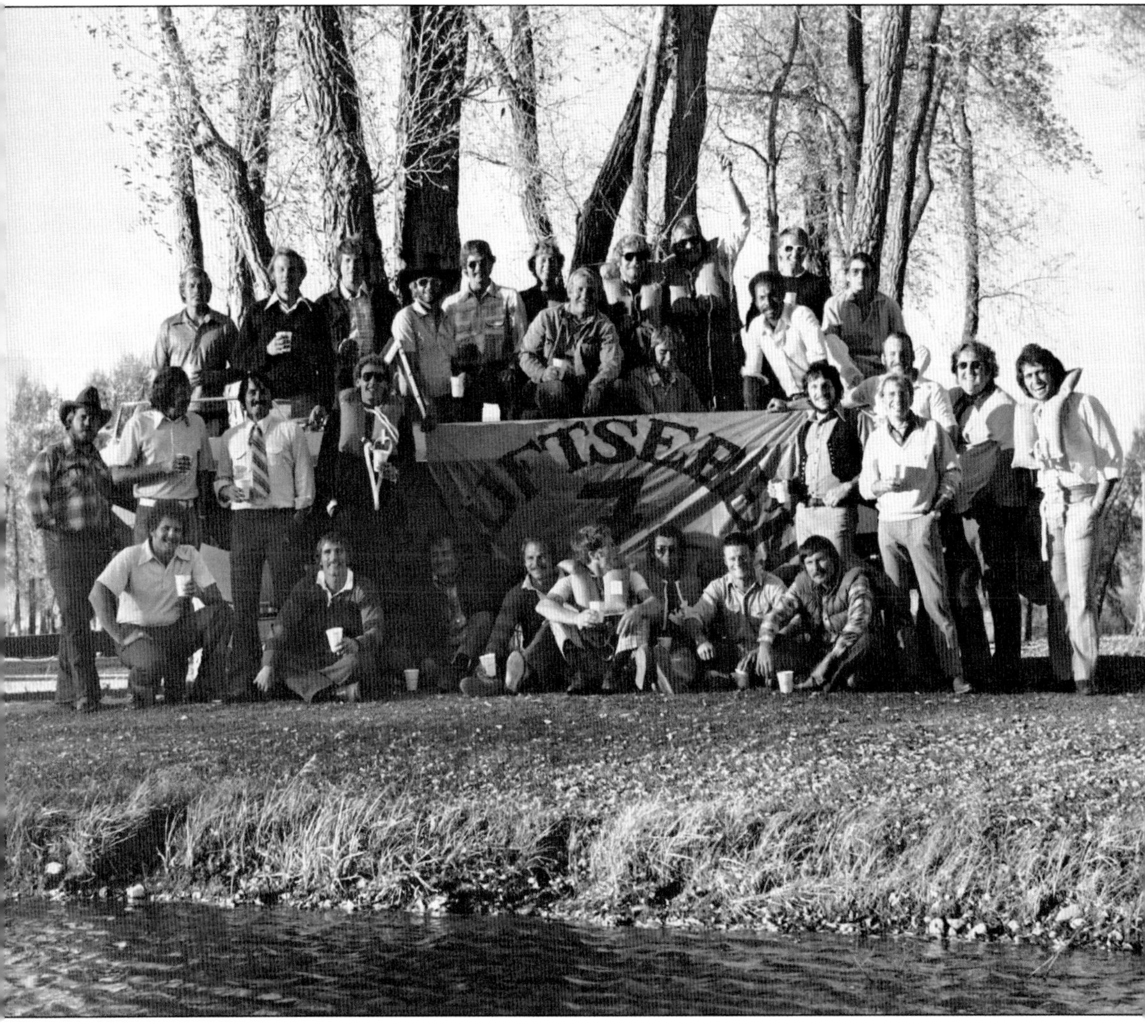

LUFTSEBEN. One of the great social organizations of Western State College was the Luftseben. Started by seven students in the early 1960s, the club threw great parties and engaged in all kinds of activities, including hijinks at the ski area. The fearless leader of the Luftseben was and is Ed Holthaus, now a successful realtor in St. Louis. Here, some of the younger members gather at the Dos Rios Golf Course during homecoming in 1975.

Eight

Stars of the High Country

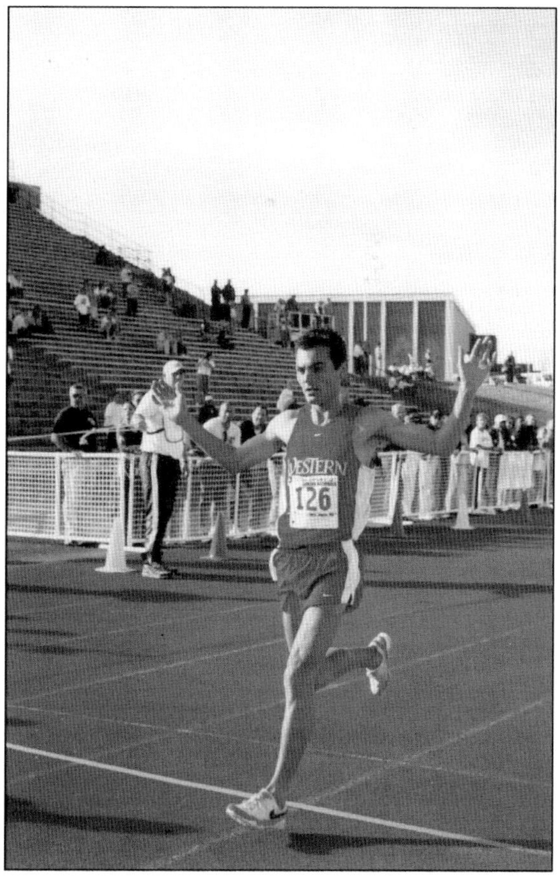

Michael Aish. Twelve-time NCAA National Champion in track and cross-country, Michael Aish crosses the finish line to win the NCAA cross-country championship at Joplin, Missouri, in 1999. Aish was the greatest runner in WSC history and represented New Zealand in the 2000 and 2004 Olympic Games.

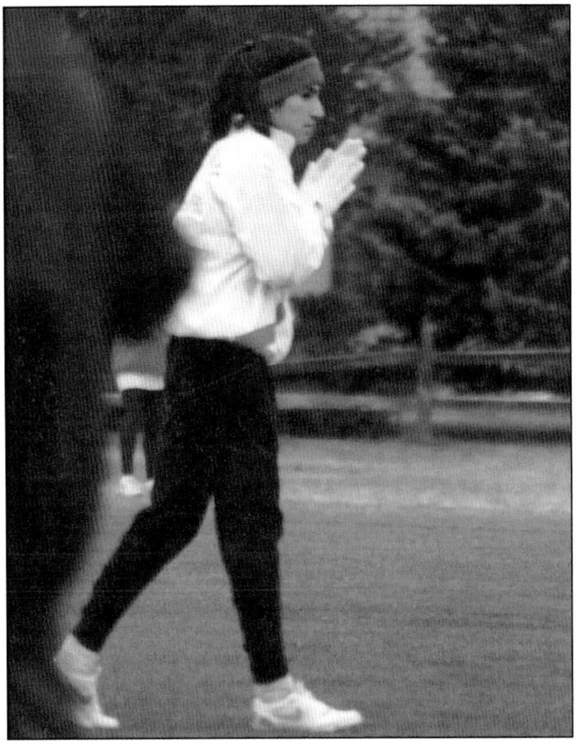

A Pensive Moment. One of the great athletes in Western State history, Elva Martinez Dryer is a measure of concentration at Kearney, Nebraska, in the fall of 1995. About an hour later, Martinez Dryer would win the NCAA regional cross-country meet, and two weeks later, she would win the NCAA national meet. She was a seven-time national champion in track and cross-country.

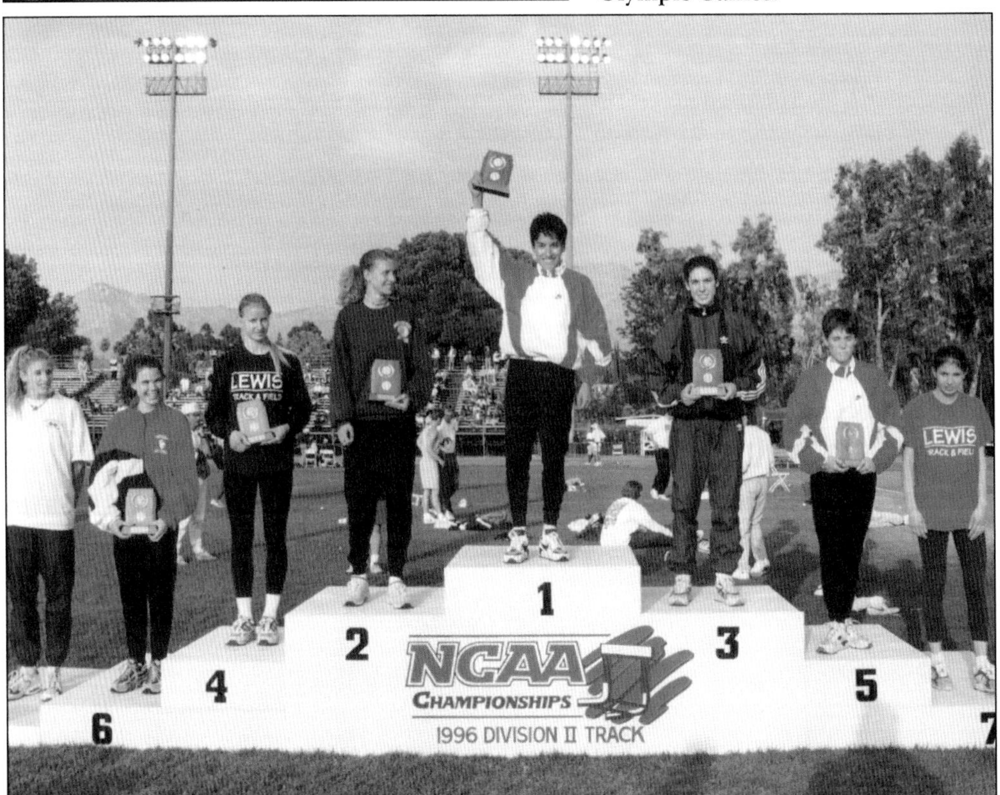

Elva Martinez Dryer. Western State's greatest woman distance runner, Elva Martinez Dryer, celebrates her 3,000-meter win in the NCAA meet in 1996. Martinez Dryer would go on to represent the United States in the 2004 and 2008 Olympic Games.

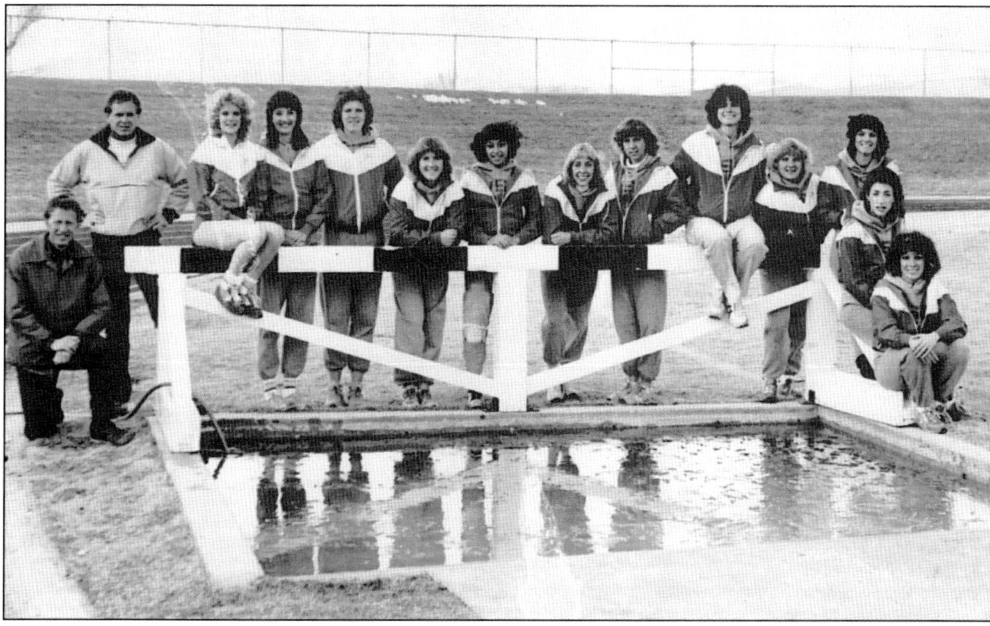

First Women's Track and Field Team. Women's track and field benefited from Title IX, equalizing opportunities for women. The 1983 women's track and field team was WSC's first. From left to right are head coach Duane Vandenbusche, assistant coach Mark Veneklassen, Mickie Kirkendall, Ginger Dowell, unidentified, Holly Binning, Kelly Smoote, Donette Schmiedbauer, Kris Marshall, Renee Foote, Shere Elliot, unidentified, Lori Kruse, and Wendy Damuth.

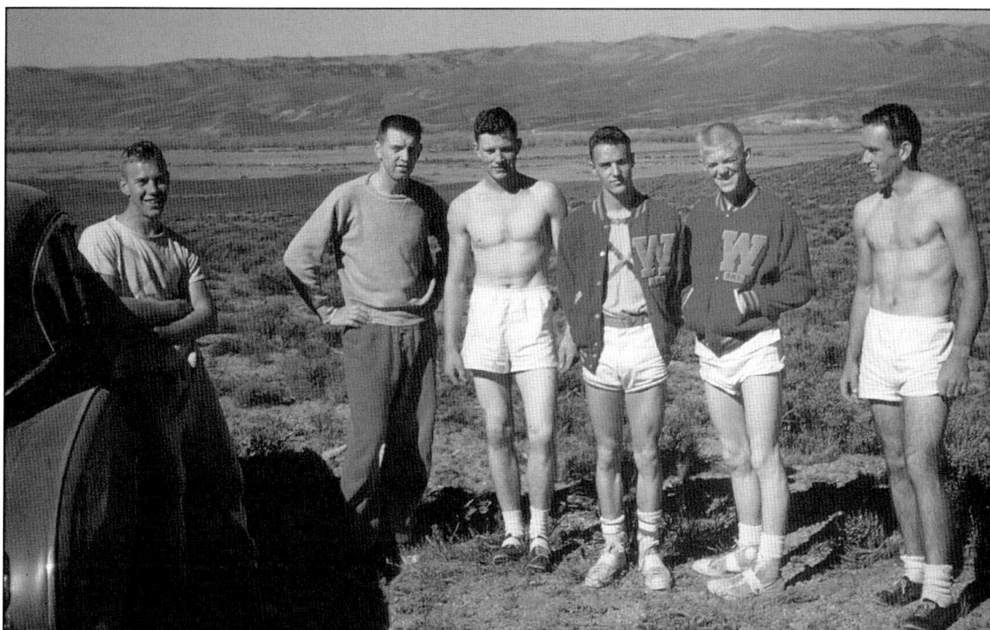

The Winner. Dick Mize (fourth from the left) has just won the W Mountain Race in the 1950s. Runner-up Walt Jackson is to the right of him. The 2.8-mile race followed a road to the top of the mountain, gaining almost 900 feet of elevation.

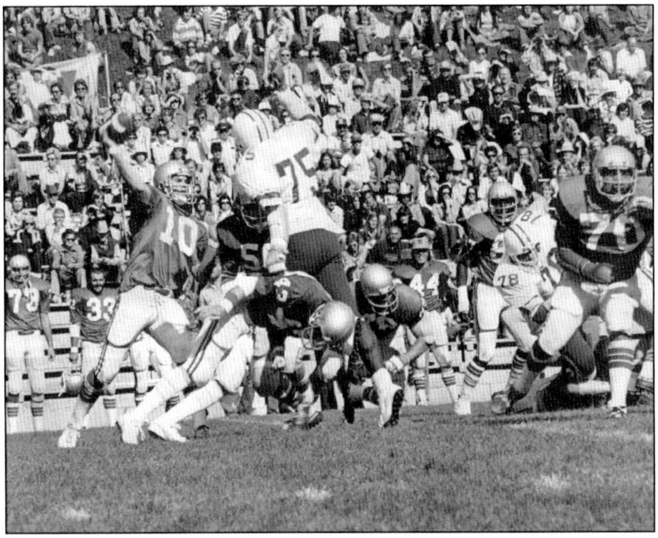

Mike Makings. One of the finest quarterbacks in Western's history, Mike Makings quarterbacked the Mountaineers in 1975 and 1976 and led two of the college's greatest teams. His father, Dick Makings, quarterbacked the Mountaineers in 1956 and 1957. Both were All-Conference quarterbacks.

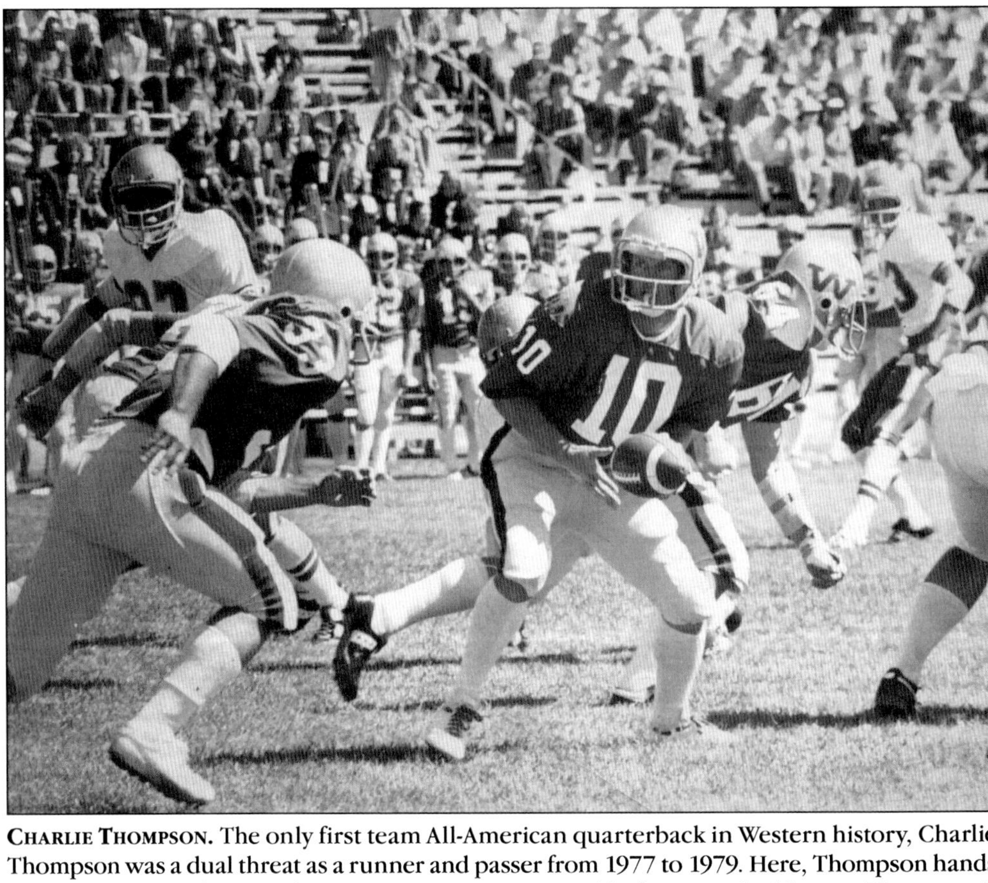

Charlie Thompson. The only first team All-American quarterback in Western history, Charlie Thompson was a dual threat as a runner and passer from 1977 to 1979. Here, Thompson hands off to running back Steve Plepson in Mountaineer Bowl before a packed house. Thompson's Mountaineers won several conference titles for coach Bill Noxon.

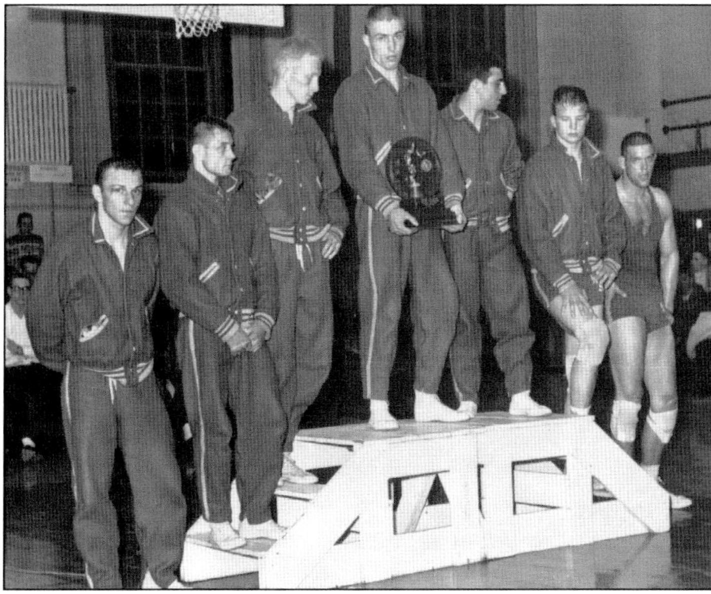

Wrestling Champions. Tracy Borah's wrestling team won its first NCAA title in 1963 and repeated in 1964. The national champions are on the podium with their trophy. From left to right are Joe Oldfield, Van Doughty, Bob Hollingshead, Truman Sandelin, Al Rende, Al Rozman, and Joe Kuhn. (WSCU.)

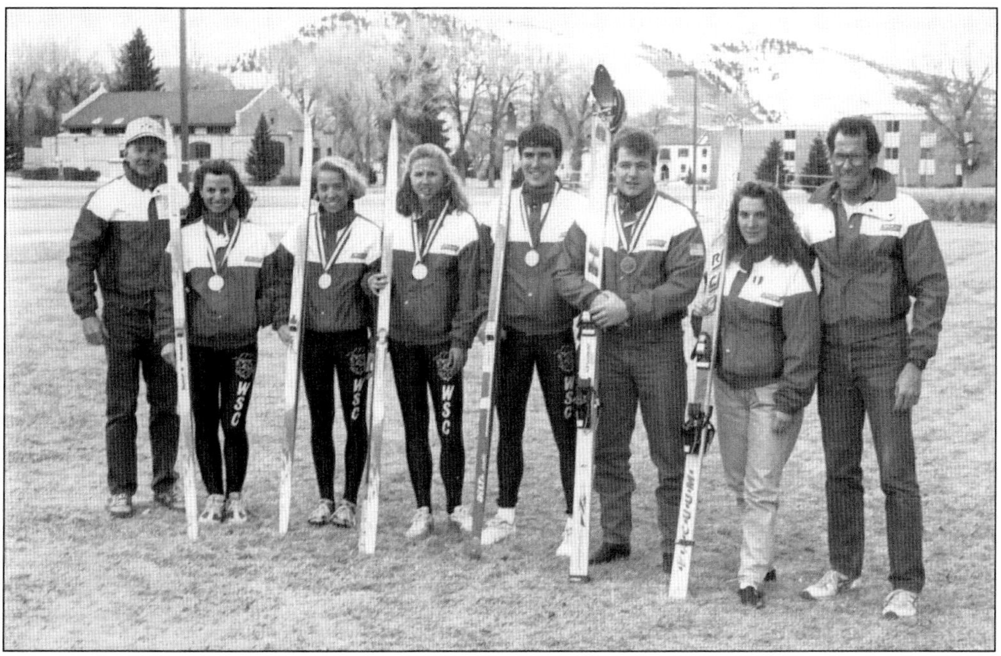

All-Americans. Six Western State skiers earned All-American honors at the National Collegiate Ski Association Championships in 1992. Pictured from left to right are coach Miles Minson, Susanna de Funes, Lynn Frank, Michelle Chupurdia, Mike Werner, Mark Norton, Kristina Bergstrand, and alpine coach Will Goldsmith.

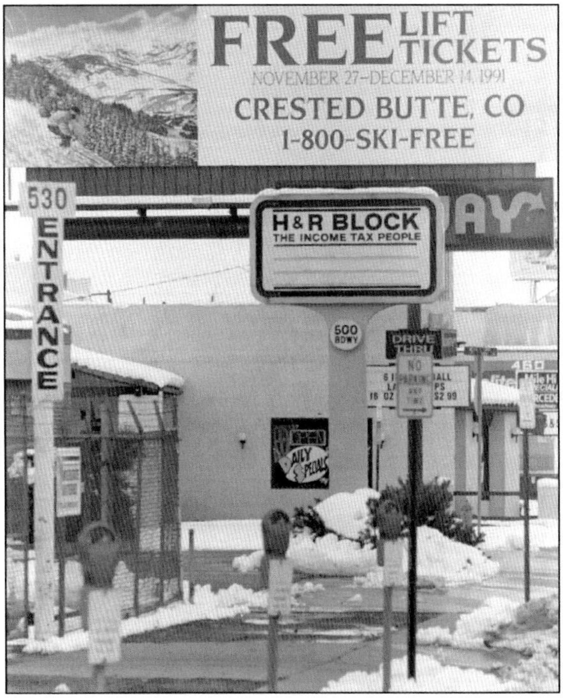

Free Skiing. One of the most successful promotions in ski-area history was the Crested Butte ski free program, which ran for more than two weeks in 1991. The brainchild of Crested Butte official John Norton, the promotion drew thousands of skiers and became a great recruitment tool for Western State College. The ski free program lasted for a number of years. (CBMHM.)

Running the Hurdles. Western State 220-yard low hurdler Gary Peyton clears one of the last hurdles in a 1950s race in Mountaineer Bowl. The WSC team was small throughout the decade but always had a few outstanding individuals, like Peyton. (WSCU.)

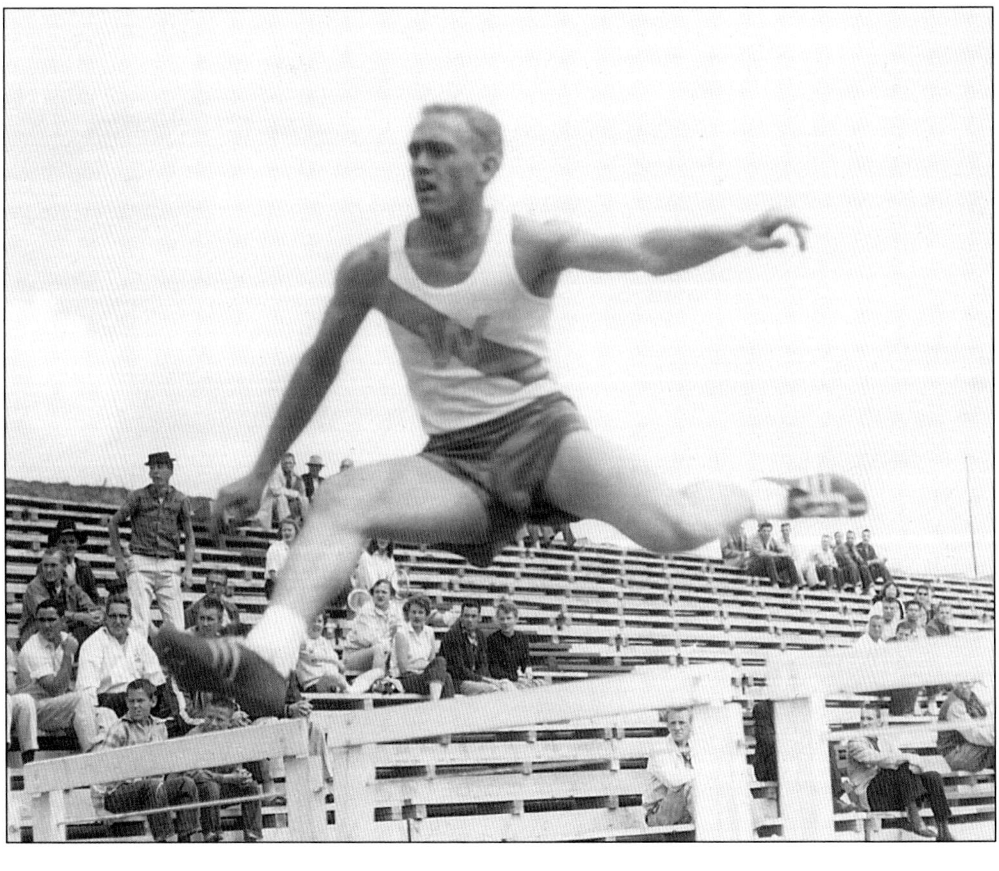

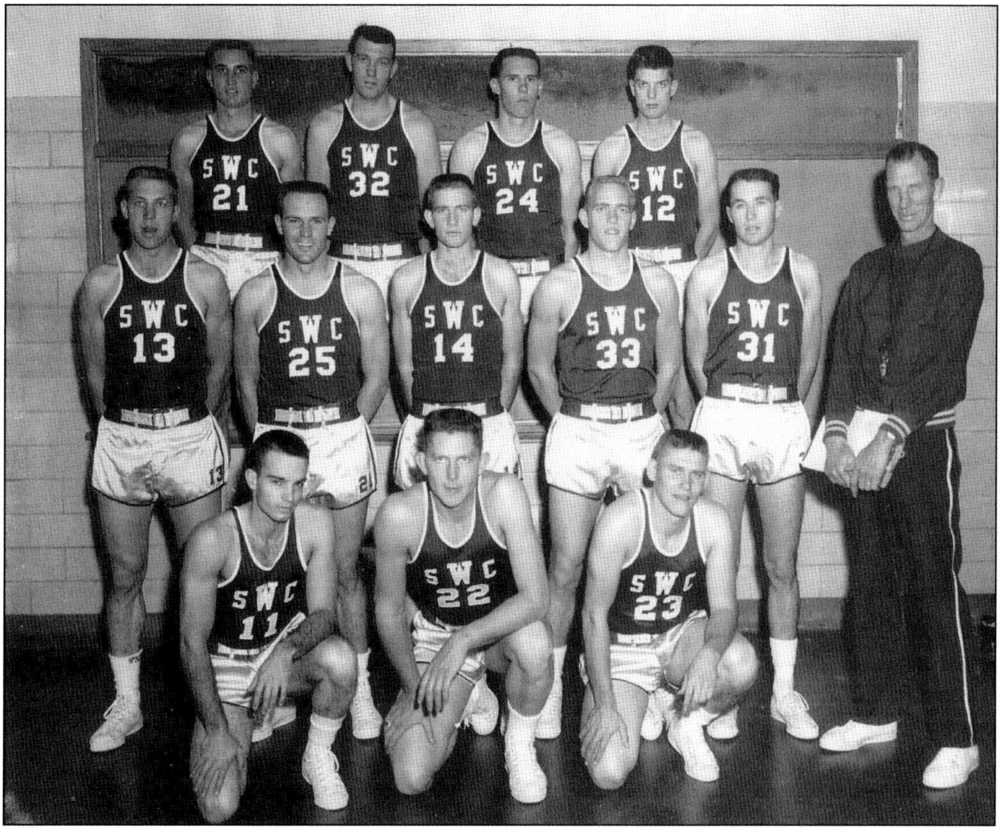

BASKETBALL TEAM, 1960. Pete Pederson coached both basketball and football until he left Western in 1961. His 1960 team included, from left to right, (first row) Dick Hime, Jon Hertzke, and Wally Reinhardt; (second row) Howard Roth, Glenn Richeson, Gale Filmore, Gary Payton, Lee Cox, and Pederson; (third row) Ed Hoffner, Wick Skipper, Rich Buck, and Rod Smith. (WSCU.)

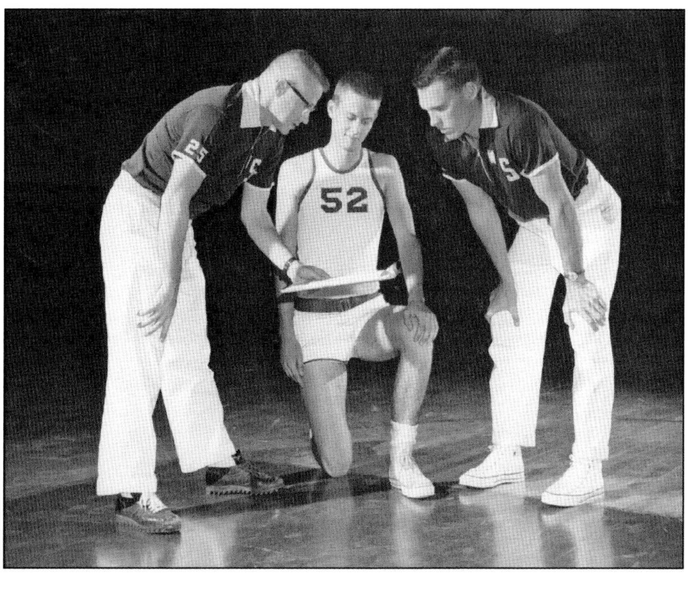

MOUNTAINEER BASKETBALL, 1963. Gene Anderson (left) came to Western State to replace Pete Pederson and had some outstanding basketball teams during his tenure. Here, he goes over strategy with center Dick Wilson and assistant coach Rich Buck. (WSCU.)

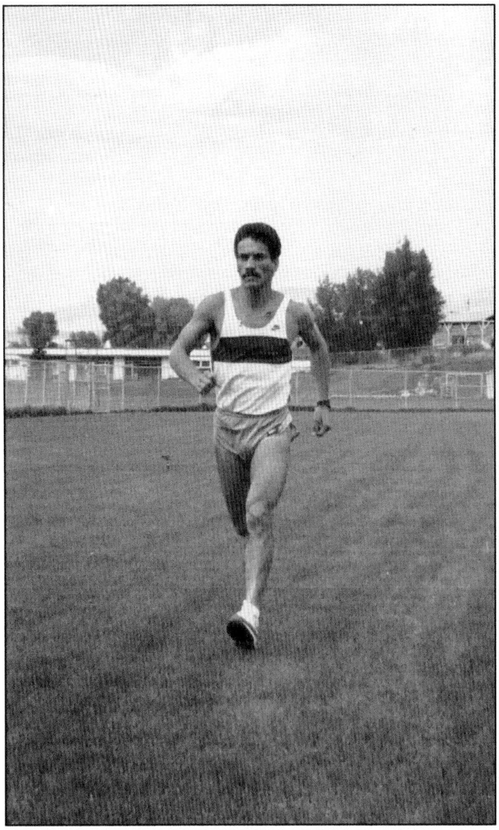

"The Tiger." From Venezuela, Eduardo Navas was a five-time national champion for Western State in distances from 1,500 to 10,000 meters. He was known as "the Tiger" because of his tremendous kick at the end of races. Navas later became the Venezuelan National Track coach.

National Champions. The first of many national championships for the Western State men's cross-country team was won in 1986 in Kenosha, Wisconsin. Pictured from left to righ are head coach Duane Vandenbusche, Eduardo Navas, Steve Roch, Doug Meade, Frank Oropeza, Steve Cathcart, Juan Diaz, Jose Rojas, and assistant coach Dennis Leck.

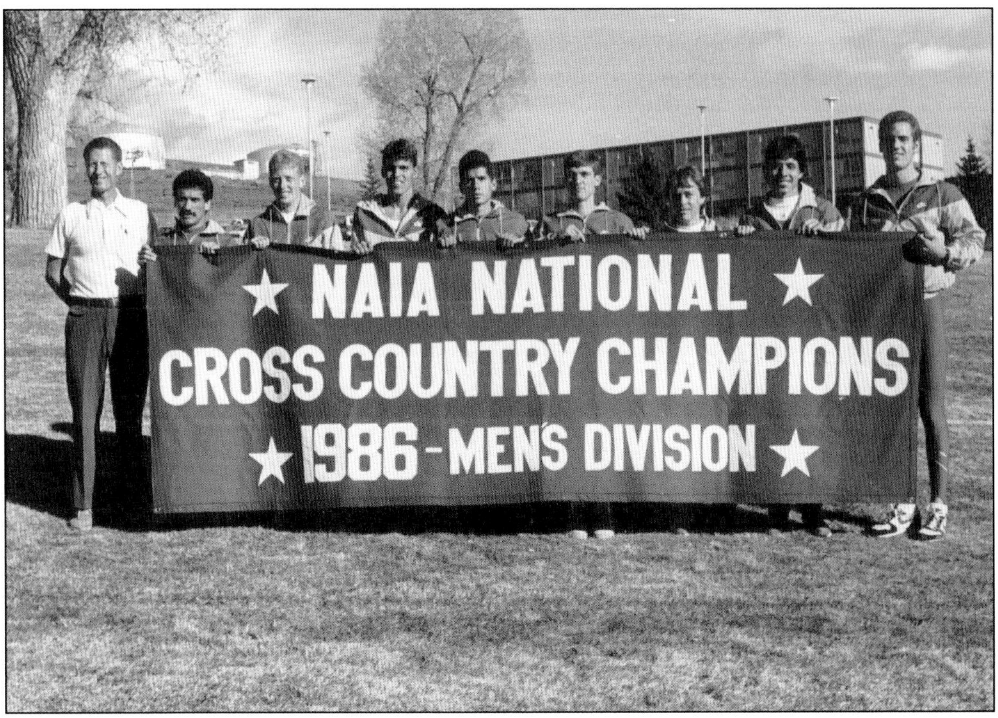

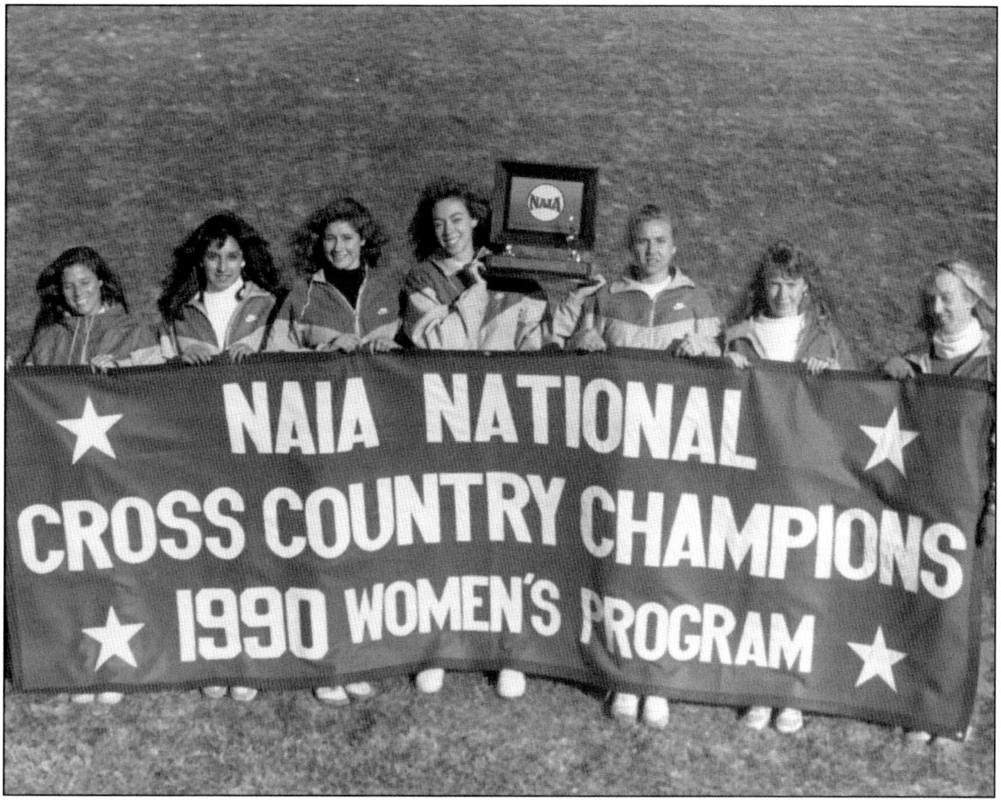

First Title. The Western State women's cross-country team won the school's first title for women in any sport by winning the NAIA championships in 1990. From left to right are Cassie Henkiel, Elva Dryer, Juli Cyrus, captain Jolynn Hutchinson, Michelle Chupurdia, Nicole Small, and Amy Cope.

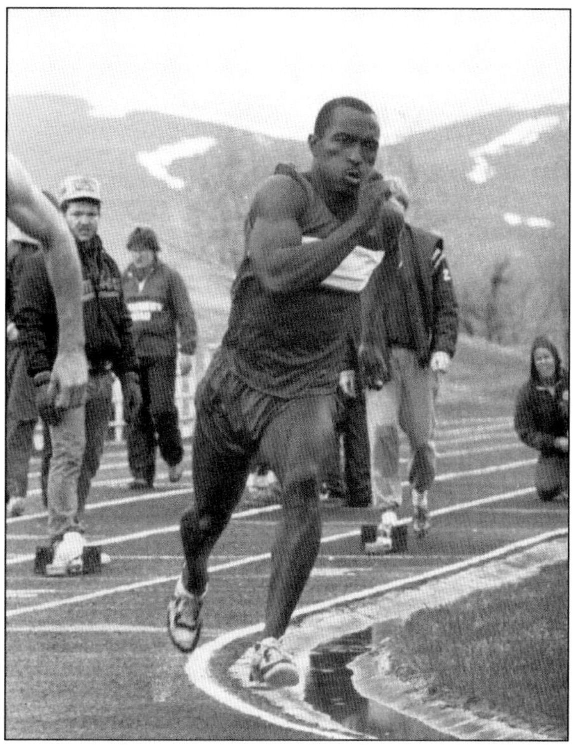

Sam Seale, Track Man. The greatest track and field sprinter in Western State history, Sam Seale set field house and outdoor track records in the 100 and 200 meters across Colorado during his career from 1984 to 1988 and was a many-time All-American in those events.

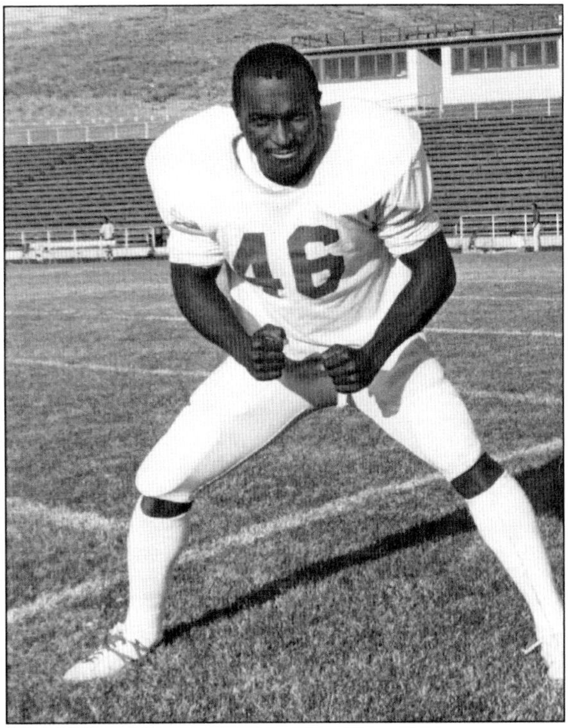

Sam Seale, Football Player. In addition to his track and field greatness, Seale was also an outstanding football player. A running back for Western, he played nine years of professional football as a defensive back for the Oakland Raiders and the San Diego Chargers.

Western State's Best. Some of the greatest women distance runners in Western's history are at the starting line at the home meet in Gunnison in 1995. From left to right in the white uniforms are (first row) Tuma Urio, cross-country and track national champion; Sarah Horan, New Zealand National runner; and Elva Dryer, seven-time NCAA champion and two-time US Olympian; (second row) Nicole Jefferson, five-time NCAA Champion; and All-American Renee Retherford.

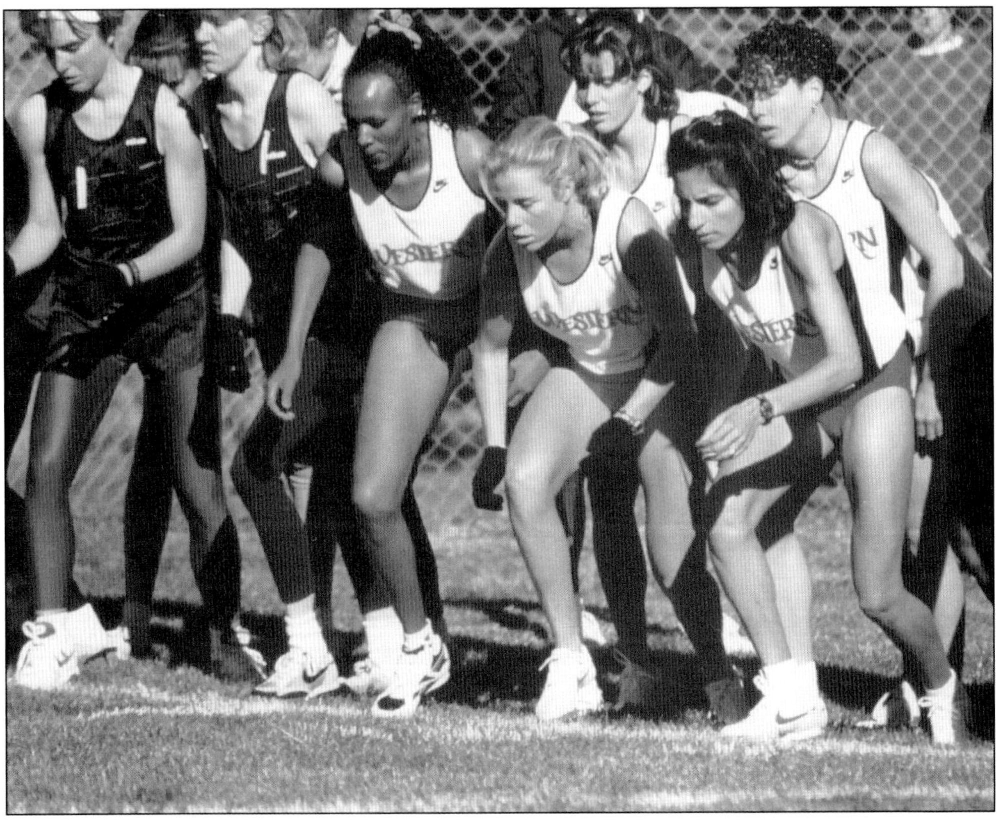

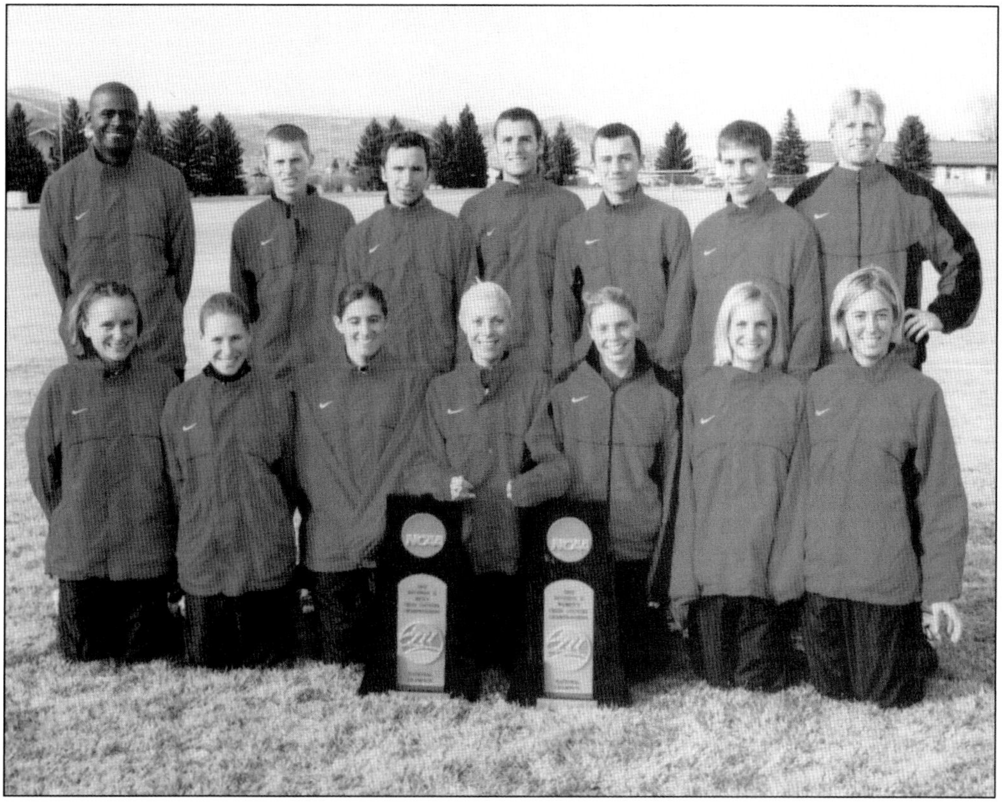

NATIONAL CHAMPIONS, 2002. Both WSC men and women won NCAA cross-country titles in 2002. The men's team, pictured standing from left to right, are Will Banks, Chris Siemers, Rubin McRae, Josh Eberly, Phil McPherson, Tim Parr, and Kelly Christensen. The women, kneeling from left to right, are Hannah Lawrence, Kristen Toney, Lori Hubbart, Rebecca Mackie, Lisa Bloome, Alisha Williams, and Maren Shepherd.

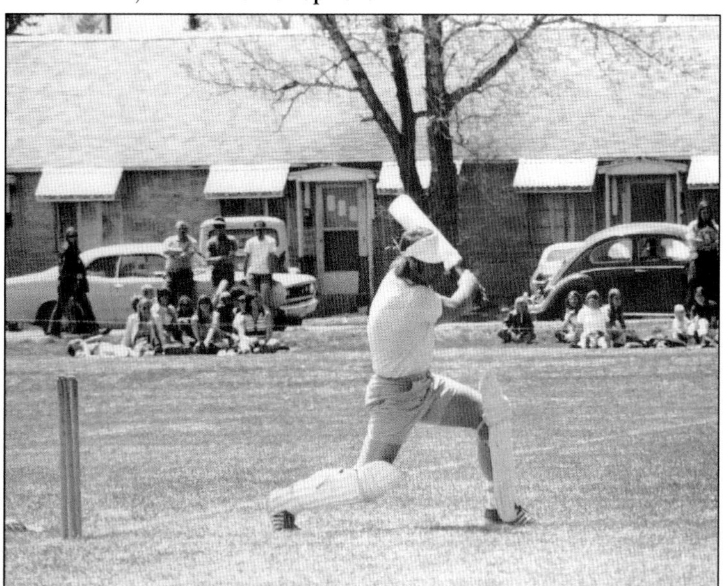

CRICKET. Started by Western State professor Bill Edmondson in 1970, Western State had one of the few college cricket clubs in the nation. The faculty took on students annually, and clubs journeyed as far as UCLA to play matches. (WSCU.)

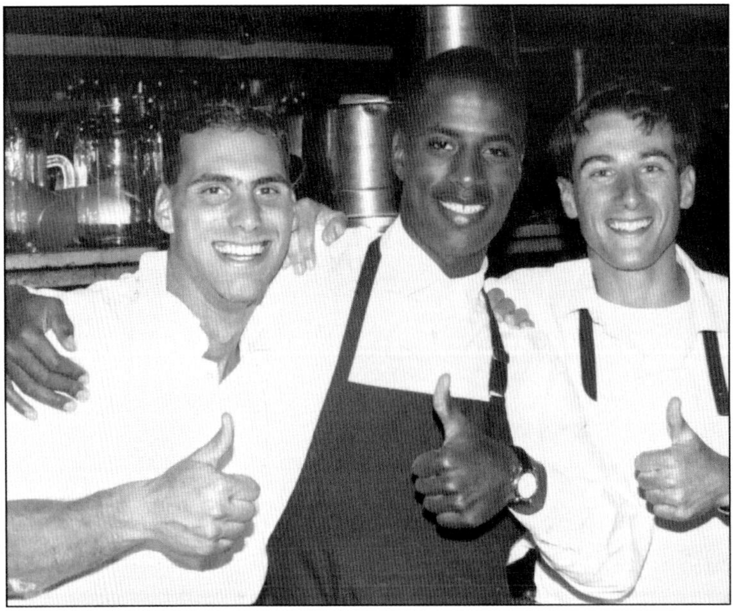

The Happy Trio. From left to right, Neal Sherbyn, Tyrone Johnson, and Philip Spratley work as servers at a Western State Hall of Fame Dinner in the 1990s. Sherbyn was a top sprinter and football player, Johnson was a conference champion in the 400 meters and a top receiver in football, and Spratley, a New Zealand native, was an All-American in cross-country and track.

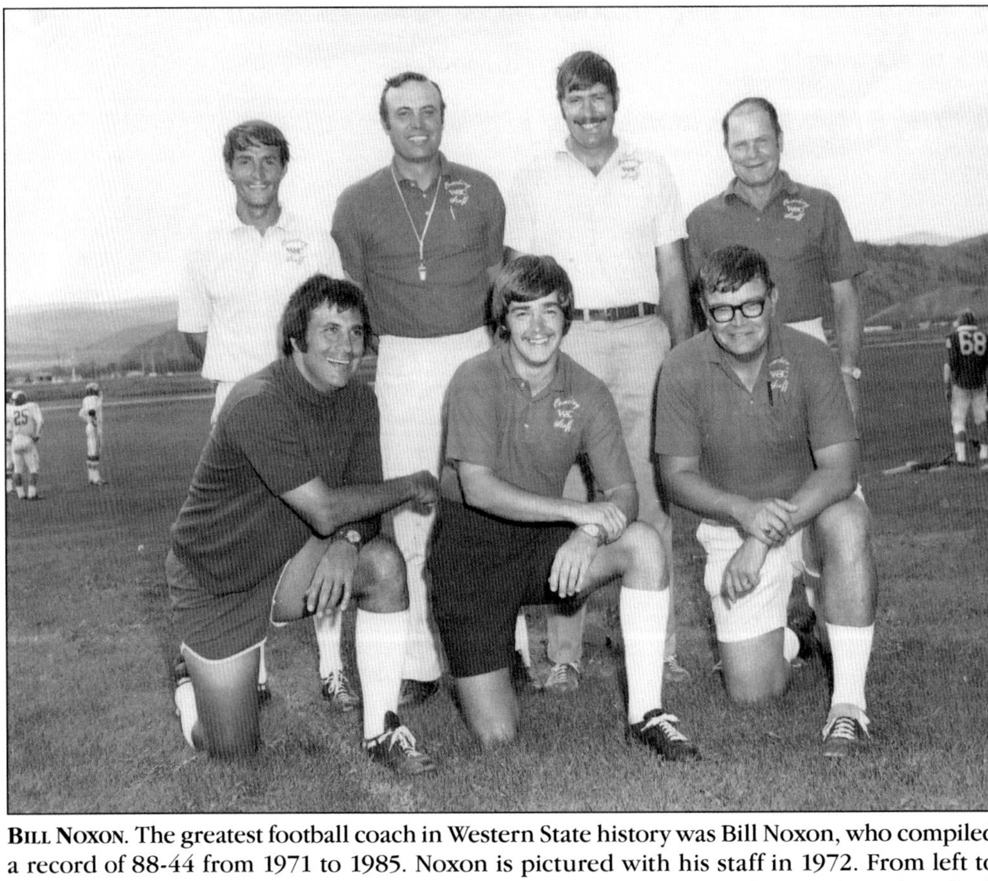

Bill Noxon. The greatest football coach in Western State history was Bill Noxon, who compiled a record of 88-44 from 1971 to 1985. Noxon is pictured with his staff in 1972. From left to right are (first row) graduate assistants John Henderson, unidentified, and unidentified; (second row) Dick Newman, Noxon, Marv Allen, and Tracy Borah. (WSCU.)

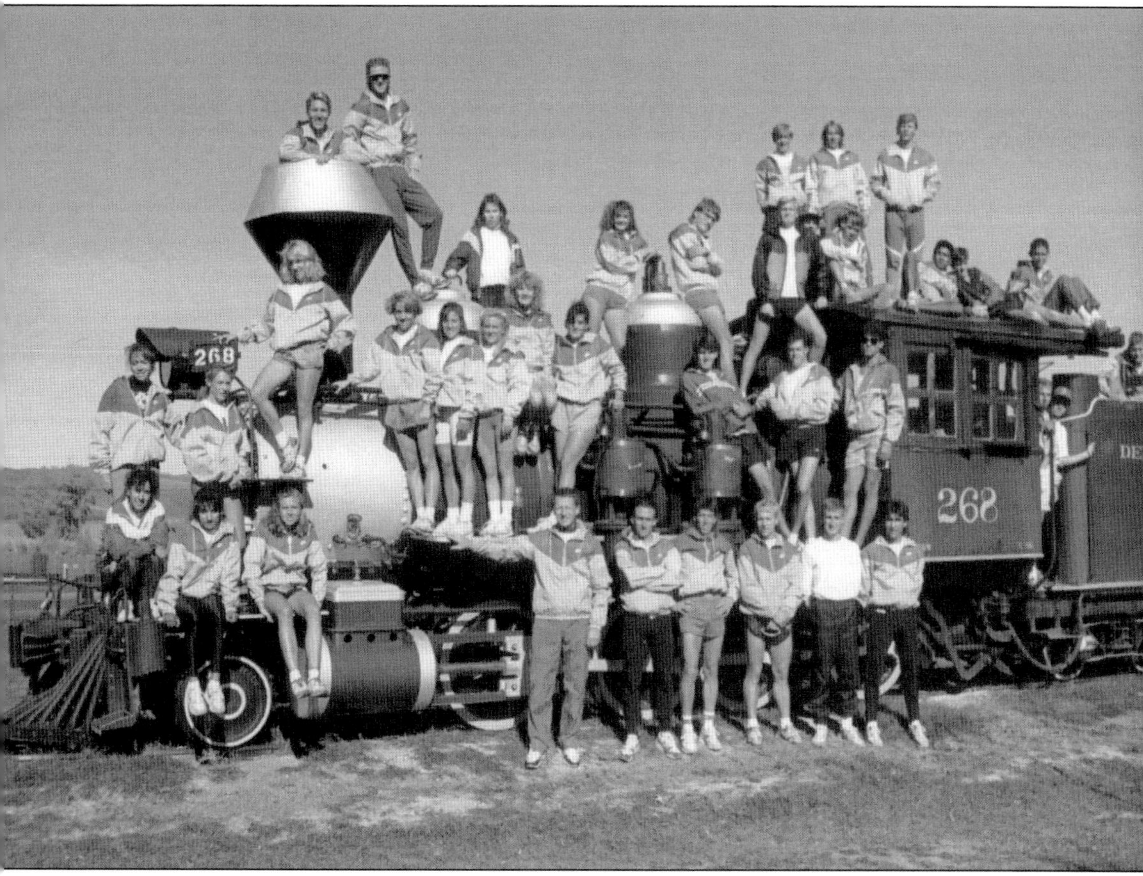

Denver & Rio Grande Runners. Western State men's and women's cross-country teams inhabit narrow-gauge engine no. 268 in 1992. The engine is on the track at the Gunnison Pioneer Museum; it had a long history in the Gunnison Country.

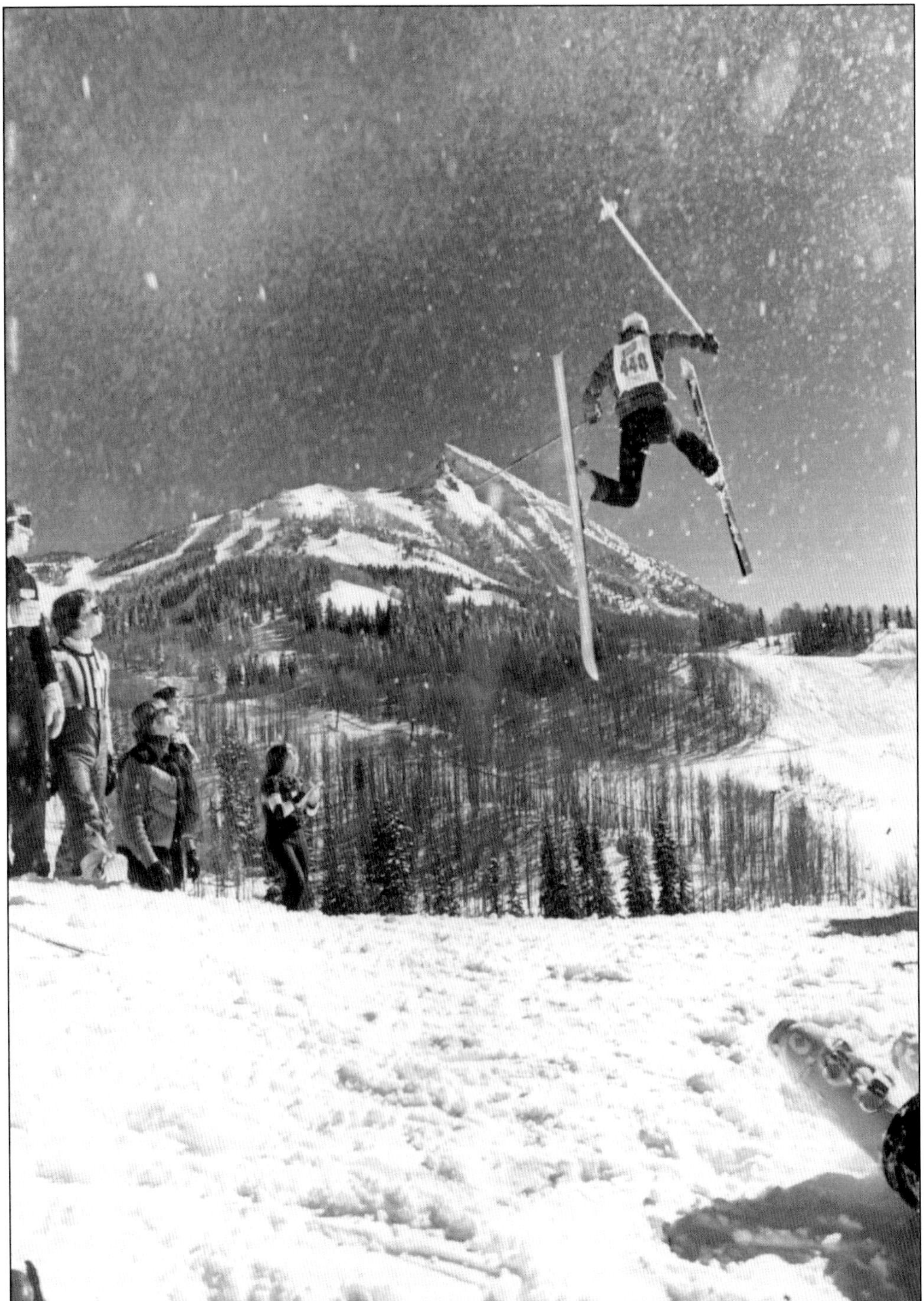

BIG AIR. A Western State College student sails high off a jump and does a "daffy" during competition at the Crested Butte Ski Area in the early 1970s. Mike Graizer, Scott Magrino, Paul Hitchcock, and Ron Boar—all Western students—were among the top Gelande jumpers in the nation. (CBMHM.)

Nine

WINTER WONDERLAND

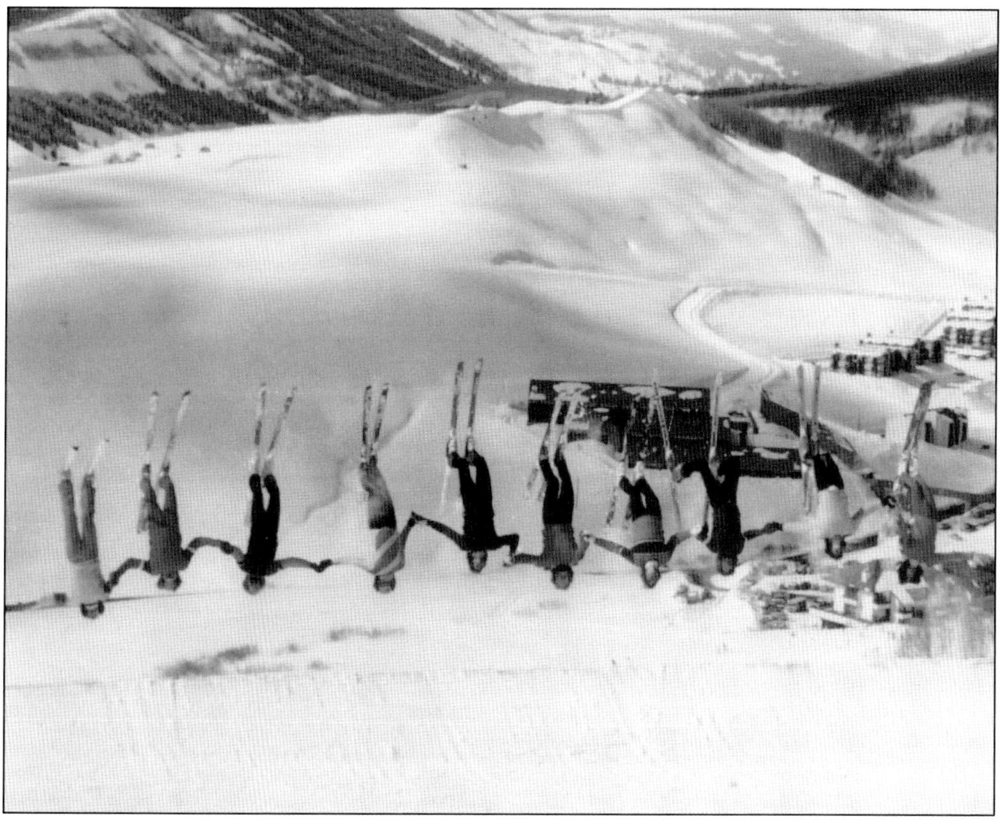

THE FLYING BAMBINI BROTHERS. In January 1974, seven Western State College students, calling themselves the Flying Bambini Brothers, did a back flip on skis on a run off of the T-bar lift. In an incredible feat, they landed successfully, still holding hands. The picture was taken by G.J. Santelli who, with Chris Osmundson, now owns Flatiron Sports at Mount Crested Butte. From left to right are Brian Faisano, Peter Brewster, Roger "Ram Jet" Evans, Michael Graizer, John Bush, Rick Wood, Tony Nepa, and three Steamboat Springs skiers. (GS.)

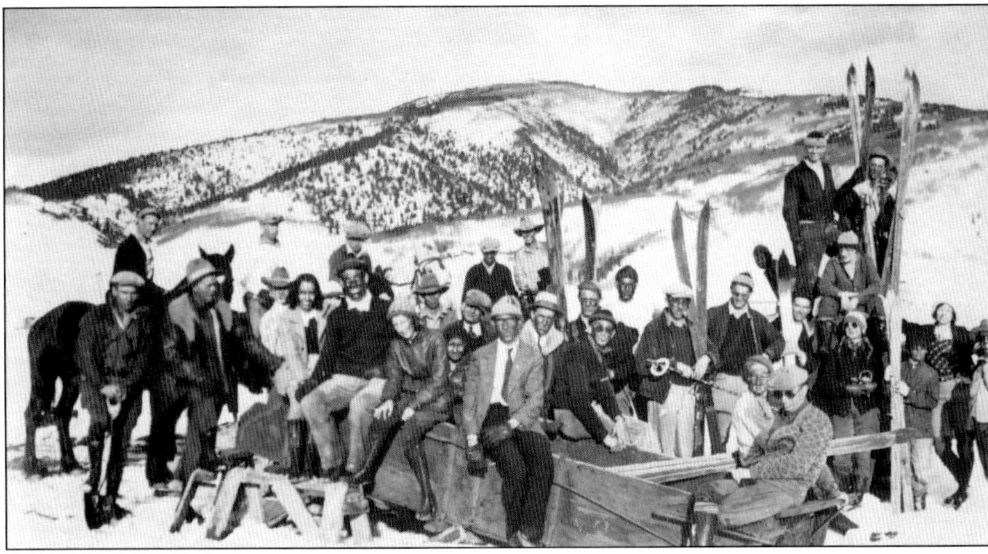

Winter Gathering. The Western State Hiking and Outing Club poses for a picture at Quick's Hill before a ski outing in 1932. The wooden skis seen here were 9 to 10 feet long and very difficult to turn. One simply went downhill and attempted to slow down by traversing the hill.

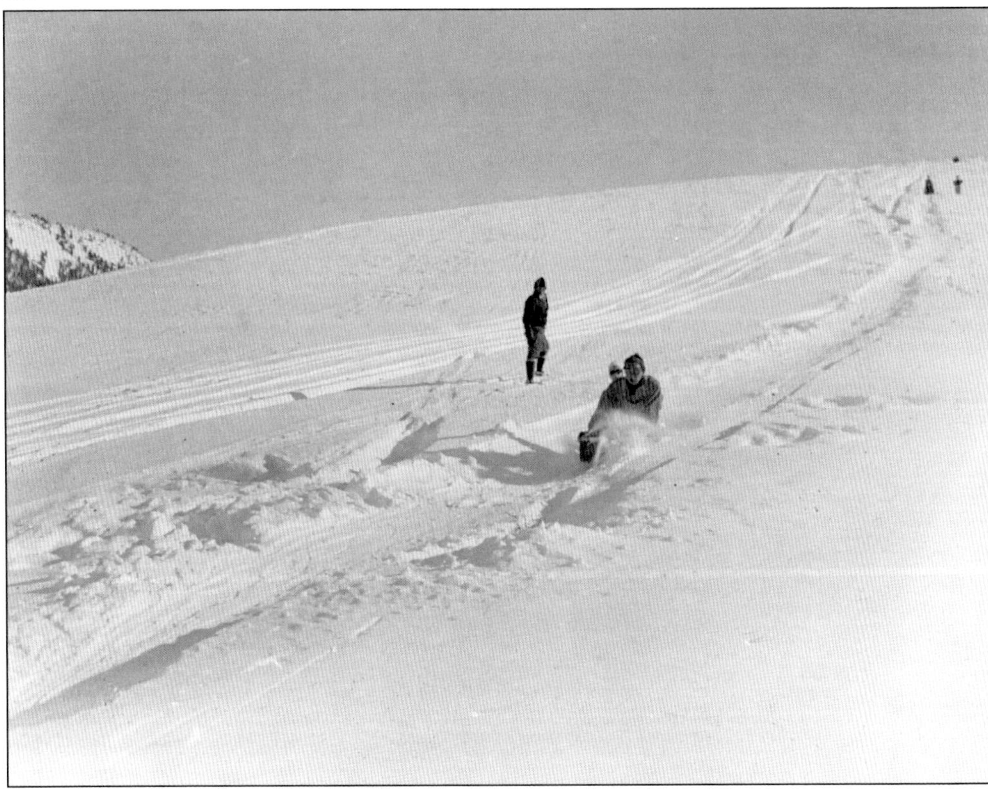

Toboggan Run. Two Western State College Hiking and Outing Club members roar down the toboggan run on Quick's Hill in the 1930s. The run ran for over a quarter-mile complete with turns and jumps leading to spectacular spills.

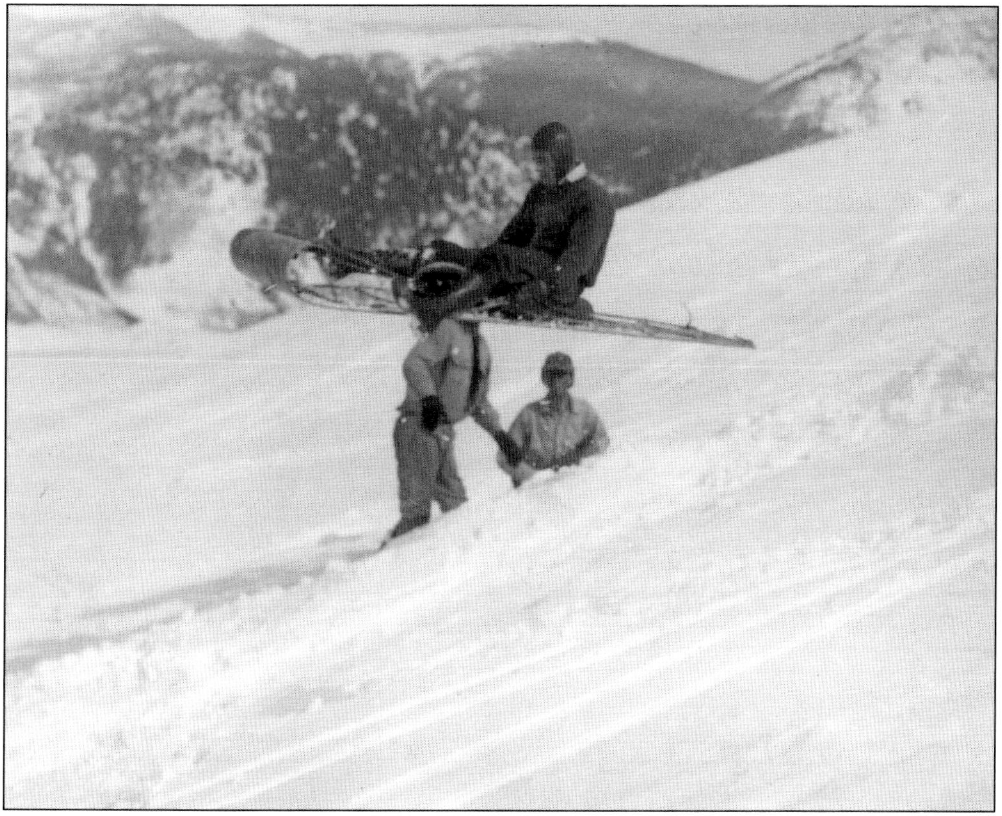

Aloft at Quick's Hill. Fred Brand, a 21-year-old Western State student, soars off a toboggan jump on Quick's Hill in 1932. The hill was steep, and Brand recalled, "We were all a little scared going off that jump at a speed we calculated at 35 miles an hour."

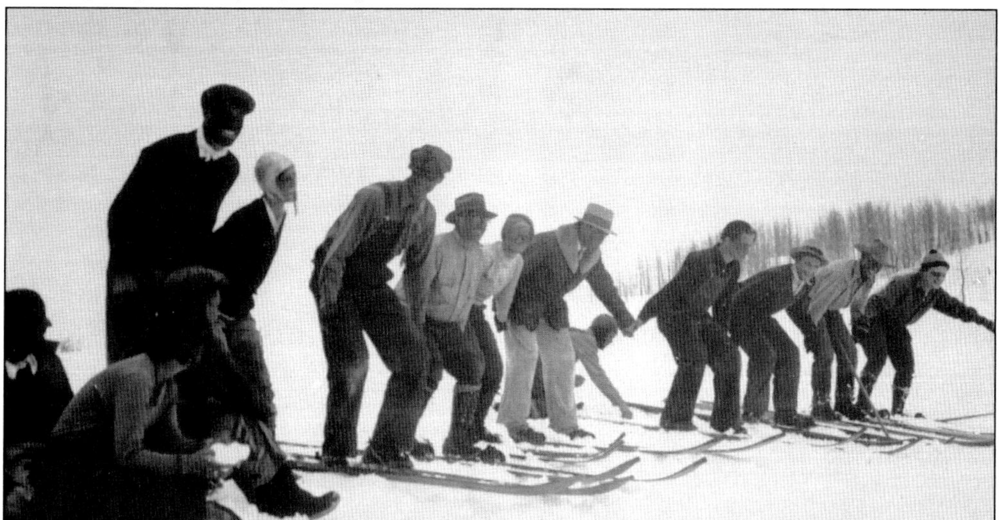

Ski Race. With no poles, hiking and outing club members get ready to race on Quick's Hill in February 1932. There were no turns; the first one down to the bottom standing won. Many times, club members would play crack the whip on the hill with disastrous results.

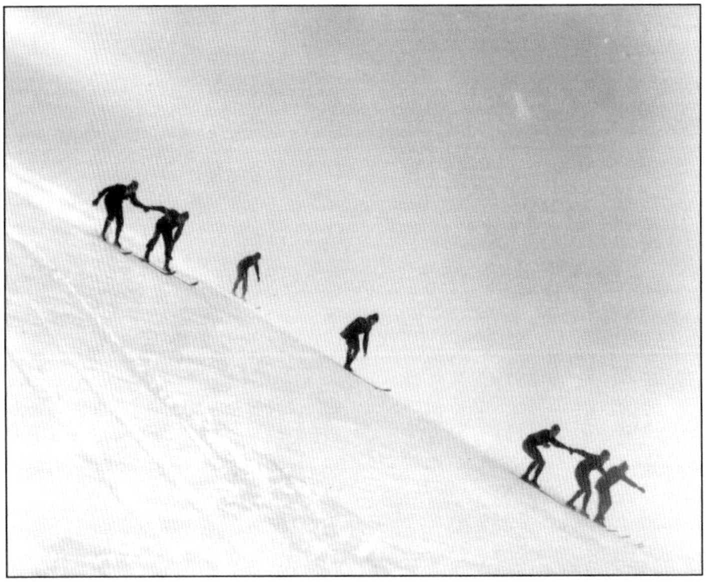

Crack the Whip. Western State students hold hands and play crack the whip on Quick's Hill, located eight miles south of Crested Butte, in 1932. The steep hill was the major ski hill used by Western State students prior to a ski lift built at the nearby Pioneer ski area in 1939.

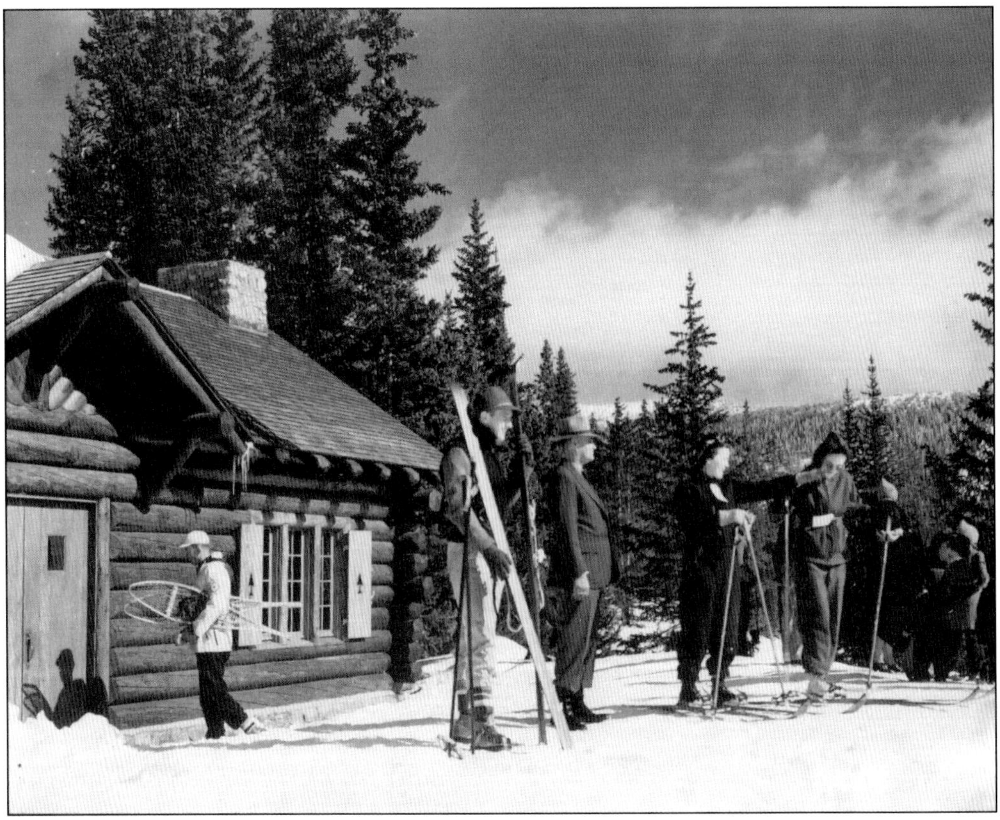

Monarch Warming House. The Monarch Ski Area, situated 44 miles from Gunnison, opened in 1939. The warming house was called the Inn Ferno after Salida mayor Claude Ferno, who was key in getting funding for the ski area. Monarch averages over 350 inches of snow a year and has some of the finest powder skiing in the Rockies. Many Western State College students were and are today regular visitors to the ski area.

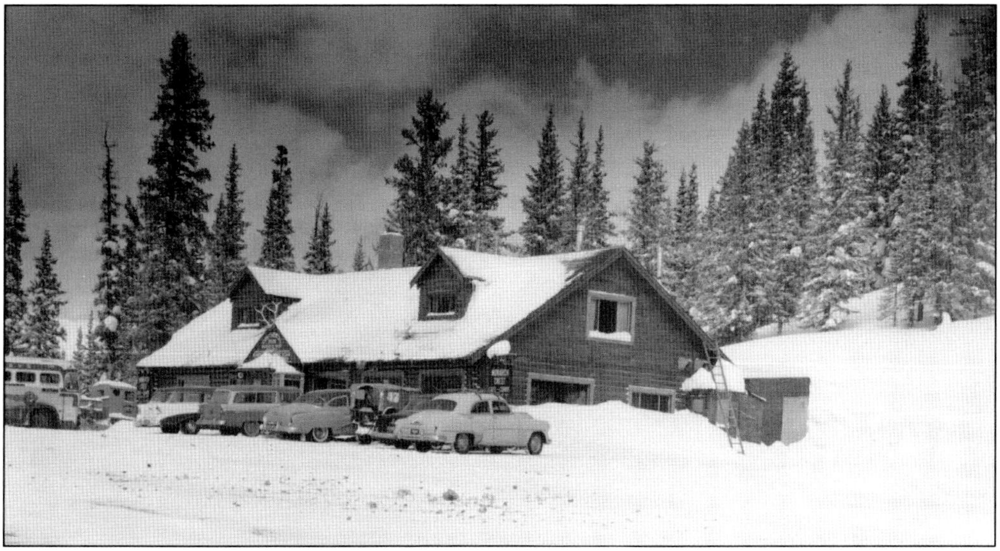

Monarch Crest. Built by entrepreneur Elmo Bevington, the Monarch Crest building sat on top of the Continental Divide at 11,312 feet. After the initial building was destroyed by fire, a new structure was built, and today, thousands of tourists stop to rest and take spectacular photographs of the surrounding Rocky Mountains.

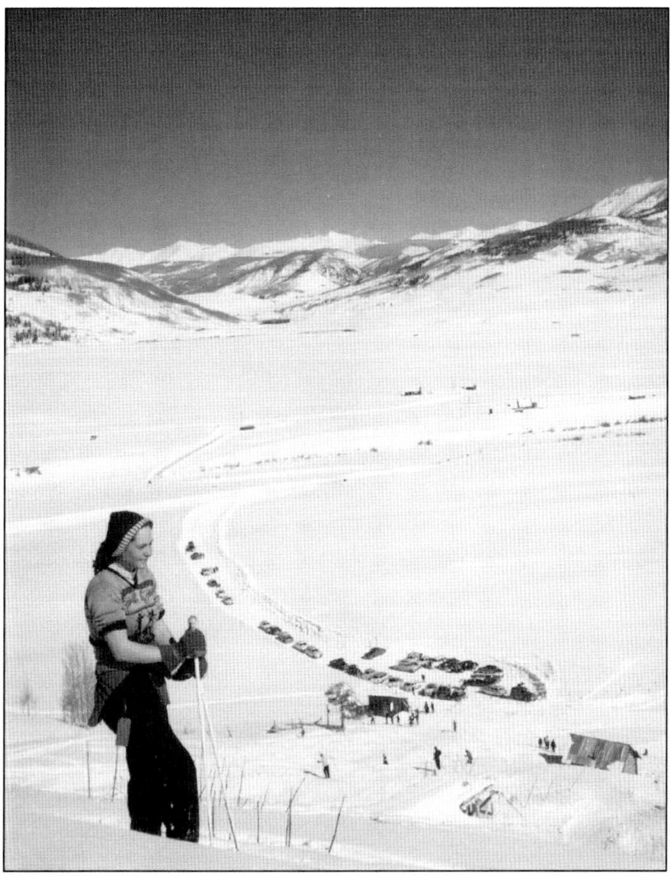

Rozman Beauty. Rozman Hill, located on John Rozman's ranch, replaced the Pioneer Ski Area in the Gunnison Country, opening during the winter of 1949–1950. The new ski area had a jumping hill and rope tow and was located just off Highway 135 from Gunnison. Rozman was in the middle of incredible beauty at the edge of the Elk Mountains.

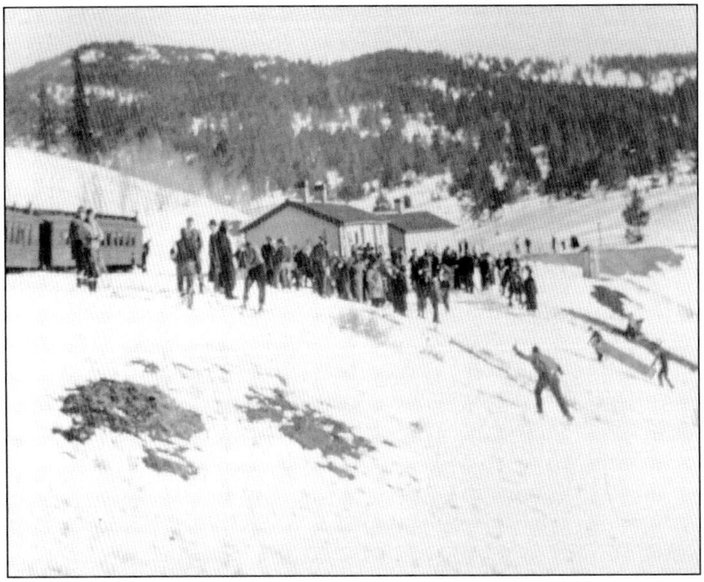

MARSHALL PASS SKI TRAIN. In the late winter of 1938, the Salida and Gunnison Sports Clubs charted a Denver & Rio Grande train to take skiers to Marshall Pass on the Continental Divide. Over 500 skiers, including many Western State students, skied from one to three runs down the pass; some received ski lessons, and some brought their toboggans.

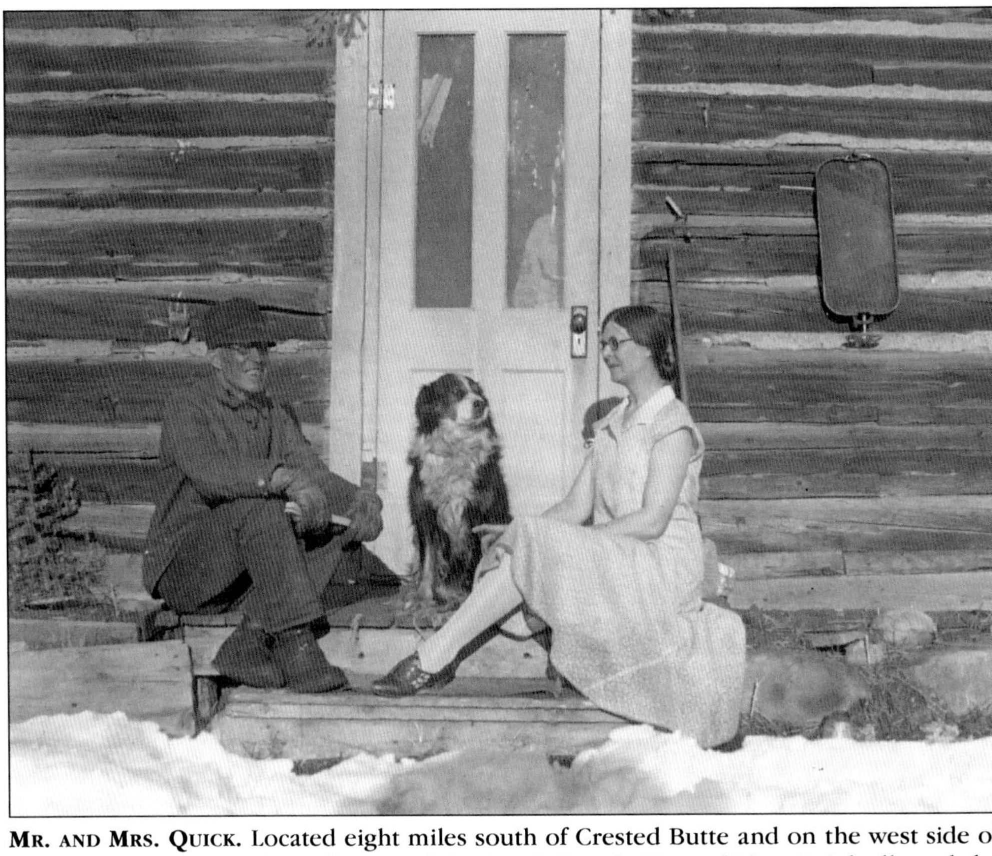

MR. AND MRS. QUICK. Located eight miles south of Crested Butte and on the west side of Highway 135 was Quick's Hill, part of the Quick Ranch. Mr. and Mrs. Quick allowed the Western State Hiking and Outing Club and locals to use their hill for skiing and tobogganing during the 1920s and 1930s. There was no lift; foot power got one to the top of the 400-foot-high hill.

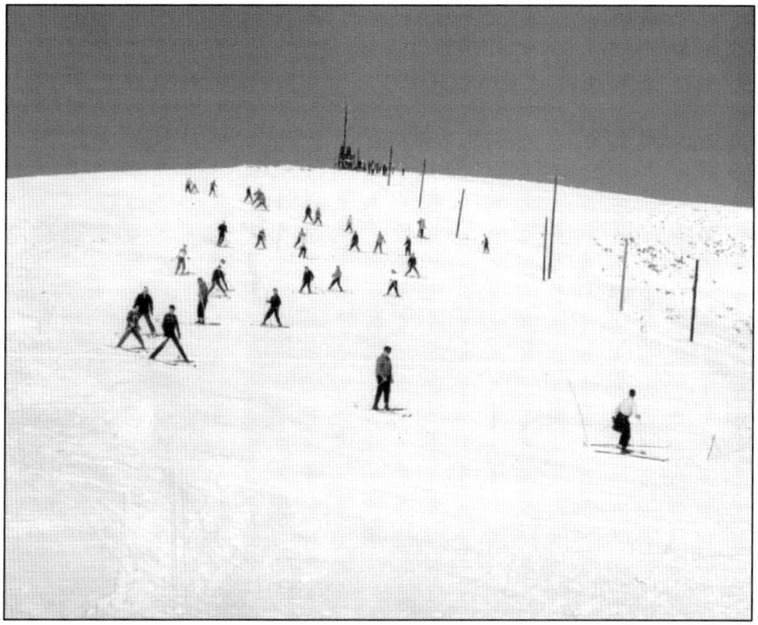

Zip and Walk a Mile. The Cupola Ski Area on top of Cupola Hill, just north of Taylor Hall, opened on January 10, 1941. The course ran 400 yards down the hill, gradually widening from 20 yards at the top to 100 yards at the foot of the hill. Before the lift was put in, locals skied Cupola and referred to the run down as "zip" and the hike back up as "a mile." (WSCU.)

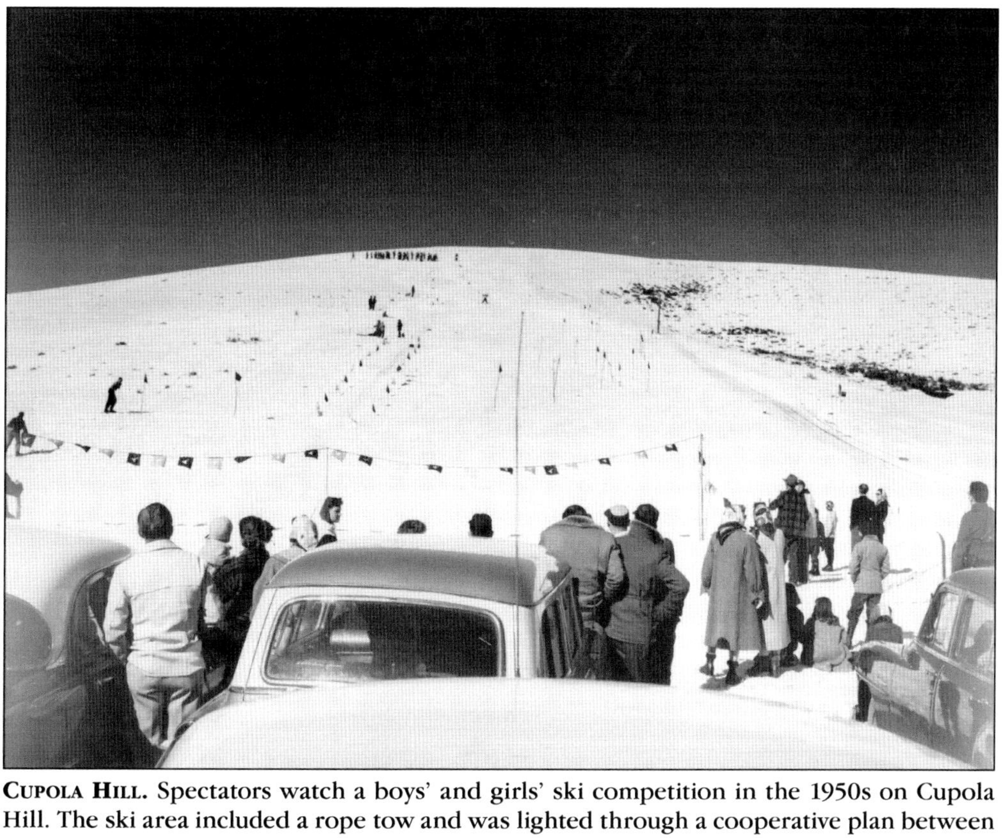

Cupola Hill. Spectators watch a boys' and girls' ski competition in the 1950s on Cupola Hill. The ski area included a rope tow and was lighted through a cooperative plan between Western State and the City of Gunnison that furnished power for the 2,000 feet of wiring used in lighting the area. Cupola's last year of operation was 1956; it was replaced by Rozman Hill. (WSCU.)

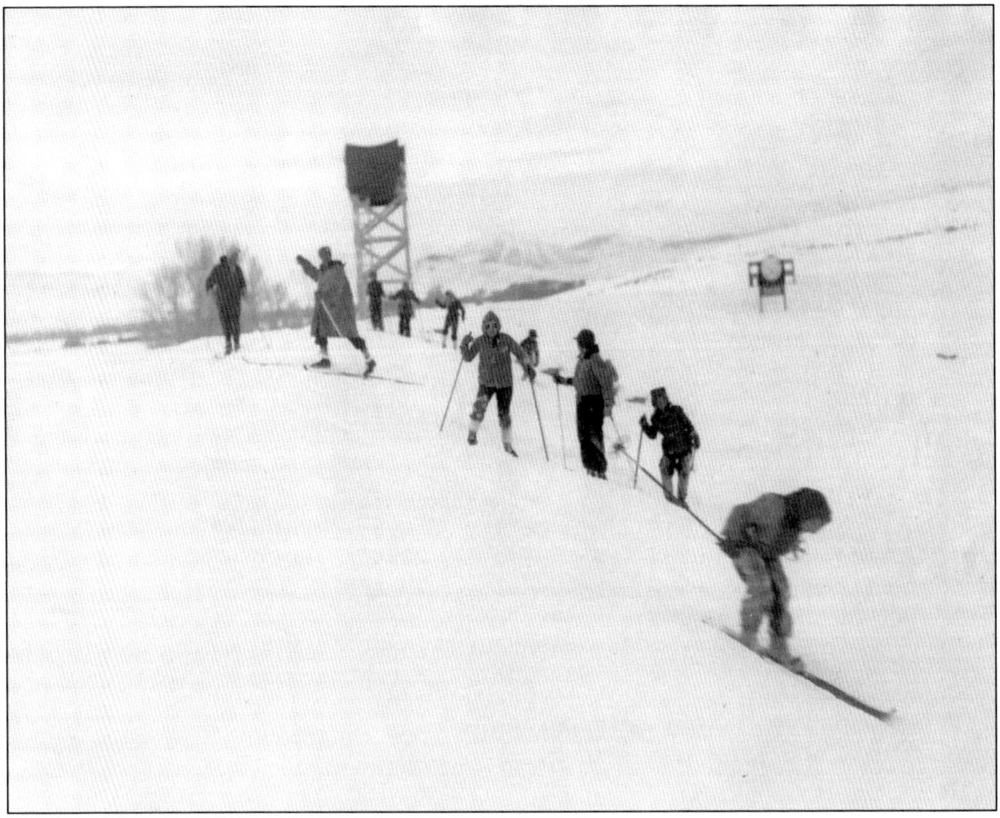

Young Skiers. Sven Wiik, Western State's ski coach, had a great program that introduced hundred of skiers to the sport for the first time. The youngsters are practicing here inside Mountaineer Bowl in the 1950s with long skis and Beartrap bindings; learning the new sport was tough.

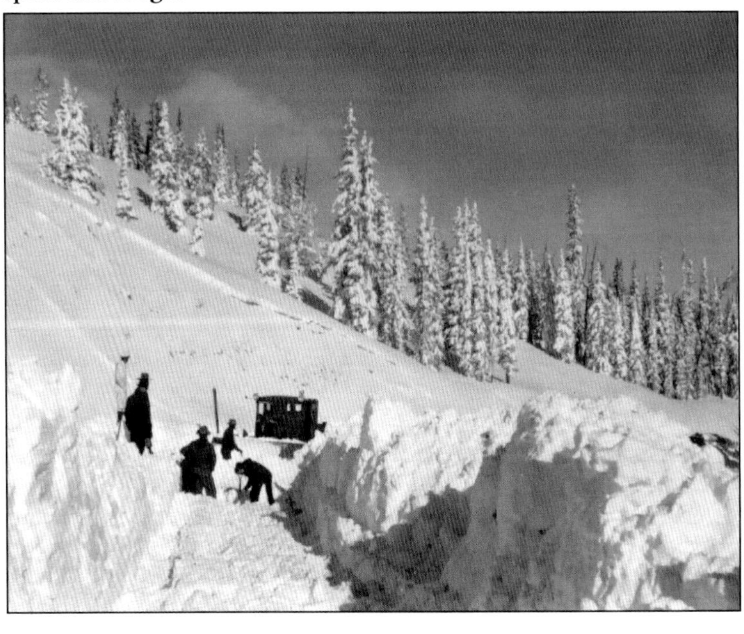

Monarch Avalanche. The Monarch Ski Area opened in 1939 on the east side of the Continental Divide with the base area at over 10,000 feet. It received over 350 inches of snow a year, and avalanches were often a problem, closing Highway 50 to the ski area. A massive avalanche in the 1940s has closed the pass; it took days to reopen.

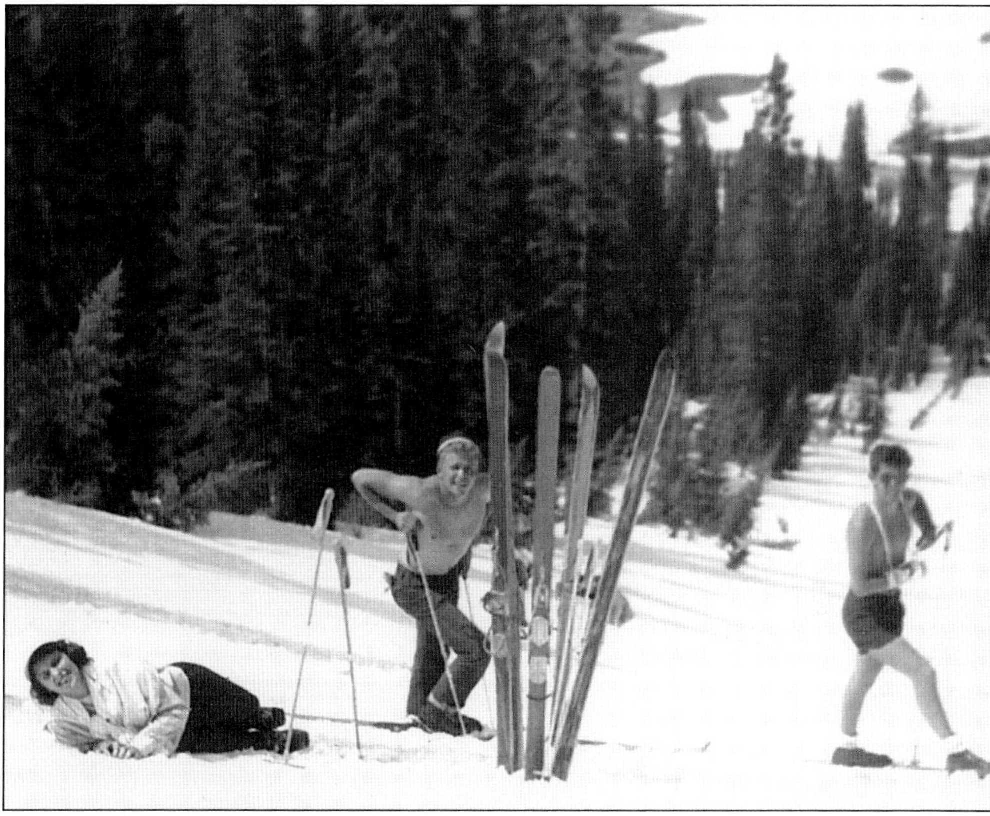

Spring Skiing. When ski areas closed by mid-April, spring skiing began in the Gunnison Country. Western State skier Dolph Kuss (right), Wayne Johnson, and an unidentified female student enjoy skiing in May 1950 near the top of 10,000-foot-high Kebler Pass. (WSCU.)

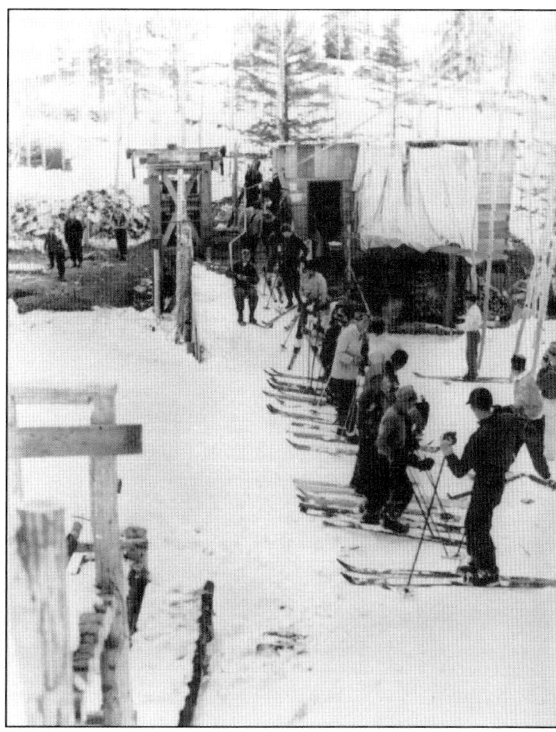

Loading the Chairs at Pioneer. The Pioneer Ski Area towers and cables were taken from the Blistered Horn Mine near Cumberland Pass and the old mining camp of Tin Cup. The single chairs were made by Gunnison locals. Pioneer was the first ski area in Colorado to have a chairlift.

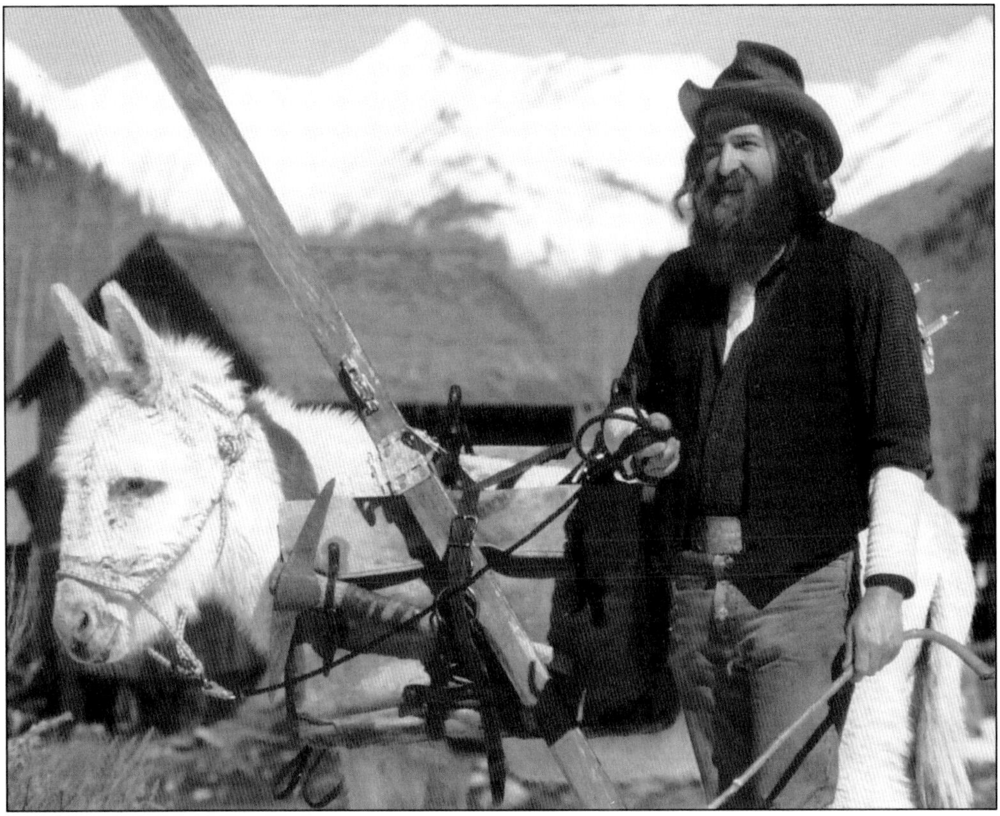

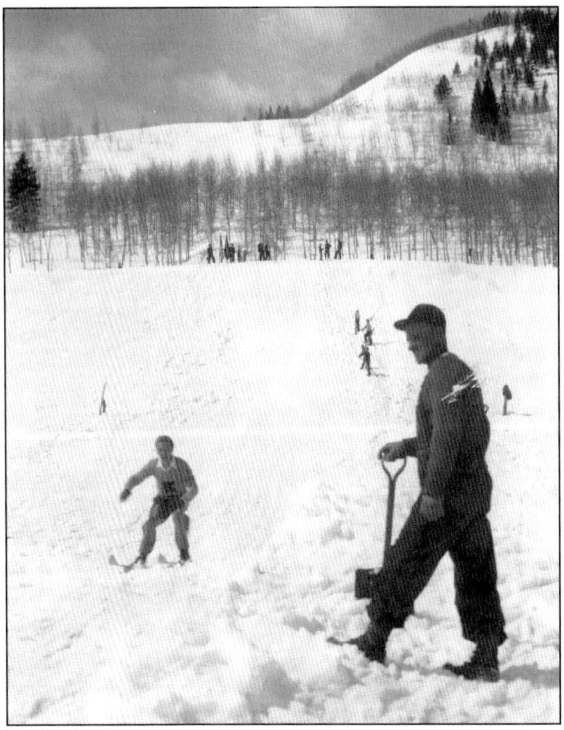

Crested Butte Publicity. When the Crested Butte Ski Area opened during the winter of 1961–1962, it wished to present an image of the Old West. This publicity photograph depicts an old miner with his burro and skis heading to a mining camp in the nearby Elk Mountains.

Pershing Mine Hill. Just north and west of Crested Butte, the Pershing Hill Ski Area opened and ran in the early 1950s. The hill was located near the Old Pershing Mine and had a jump and rope tow. Here, children from Crested Butte, along with Western State students, learn to ski.

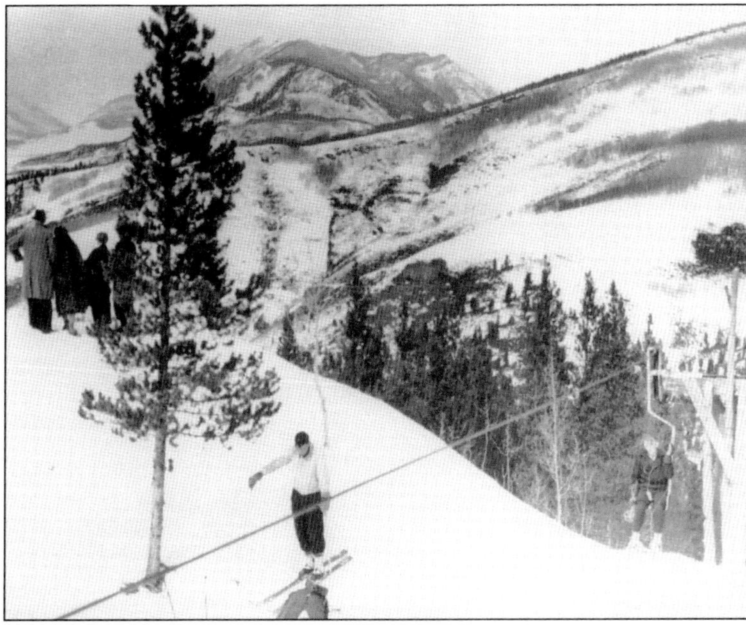

Pioneer, 1946. The Pioneer Ski Area opened in the Gunnison Country during the winter of 1939–1940. The area closed because of World War II but reopened in 1946. Pioneer was located three miles up Cement Creek and eight miles south of Crested Butte Mountain, seen in the distance.

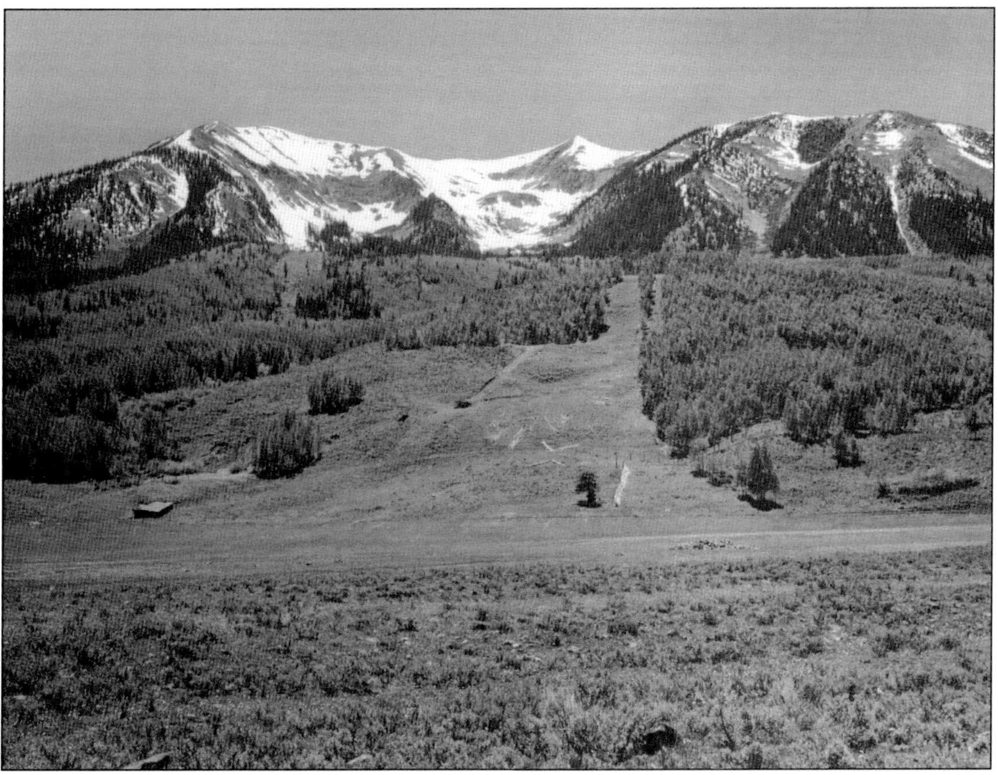

Building Rozman Hill. When the Pioneer Ski Area neared the end of its existence, the Western State ski team needed a new ski hill. They found one on the flank of Mount Whetstone on the John Rozman Ranch, five miles south of Crested Butte. Rancher John Rozman allowed the team to use the hill without compensation. Rozman Hill is shown here during construction in 1950.

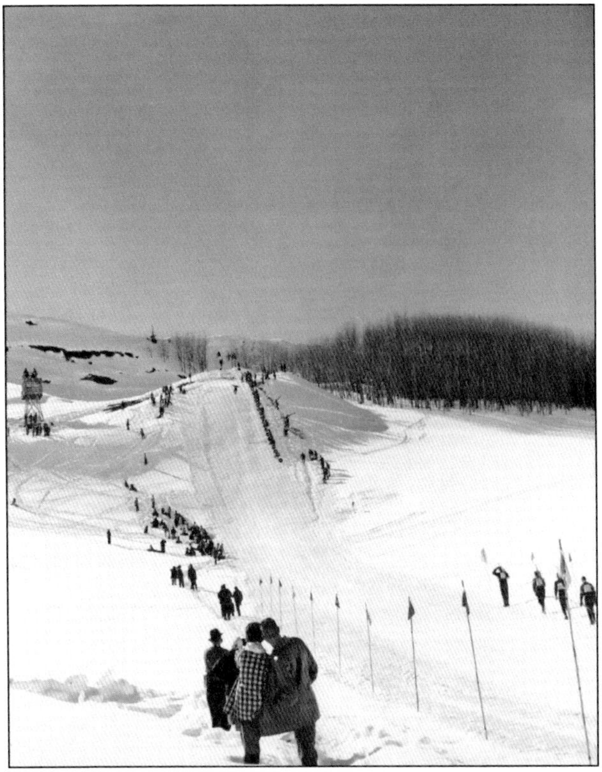

Rozman Jump. A jumper is in full flight off the 150-foot jump during an intercollegiate meet at Rozman Hill in 1953. The judges' stand can be seen on the left. Rozman was one of the very few jumping hills in Colorado.

First Year. The Crested Butte Ski Area opened during the winter of 1961–1962. The Warming House had just been built, and the T-bar was the major lift. A gondola, which carried skiers to over 11,000 feet on the mountain, did not open until January 1963.

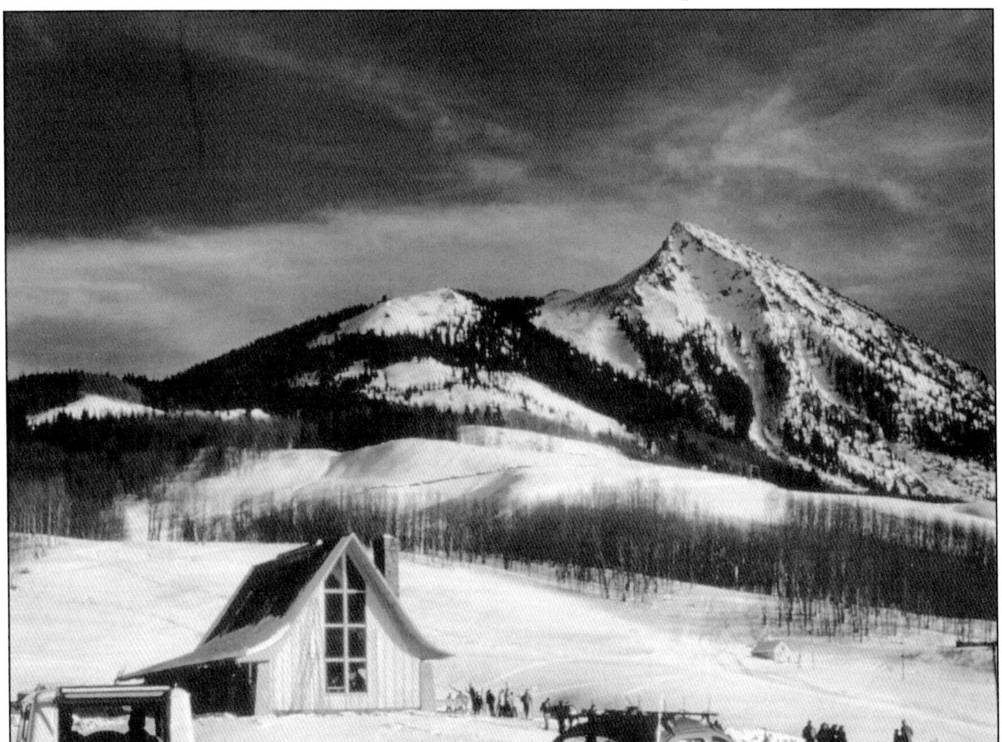

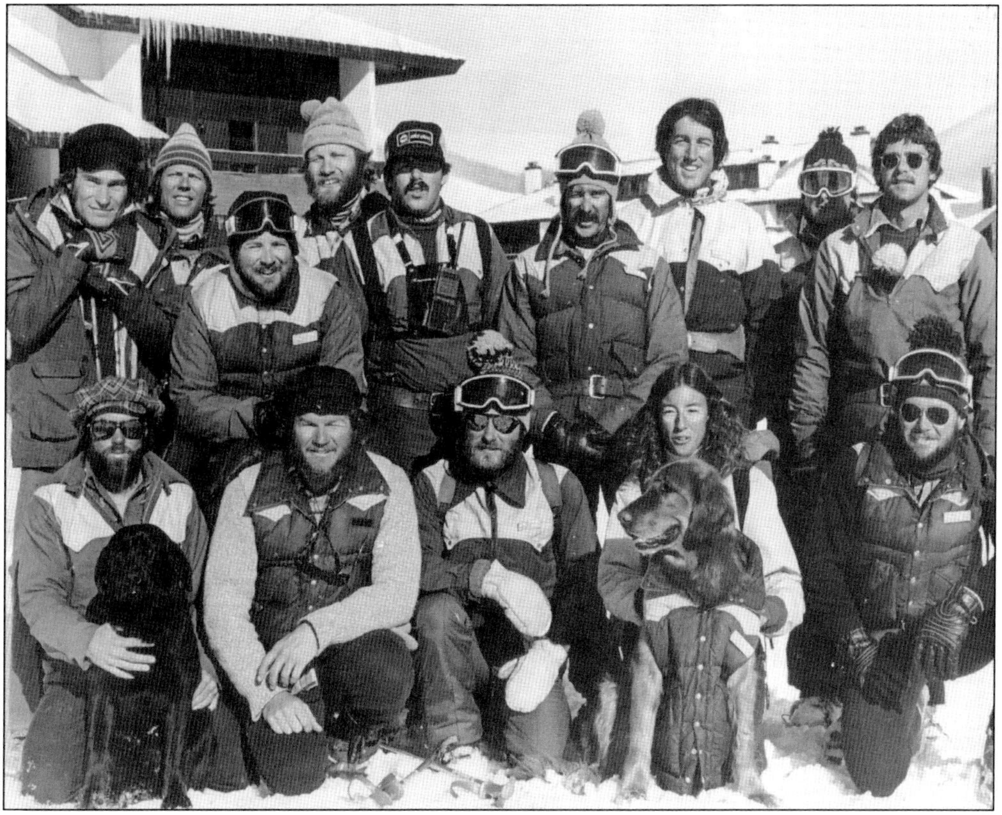

CRESTED BUTTE SKI PATROL. One of the finest ski patrols in the Rockies poses at the Crested Butte Ski Area in the early 1970s. It was comprised almost entirely of Western State students; all were superb skiers who could ski the spectacular extreme terrain at the ski area.

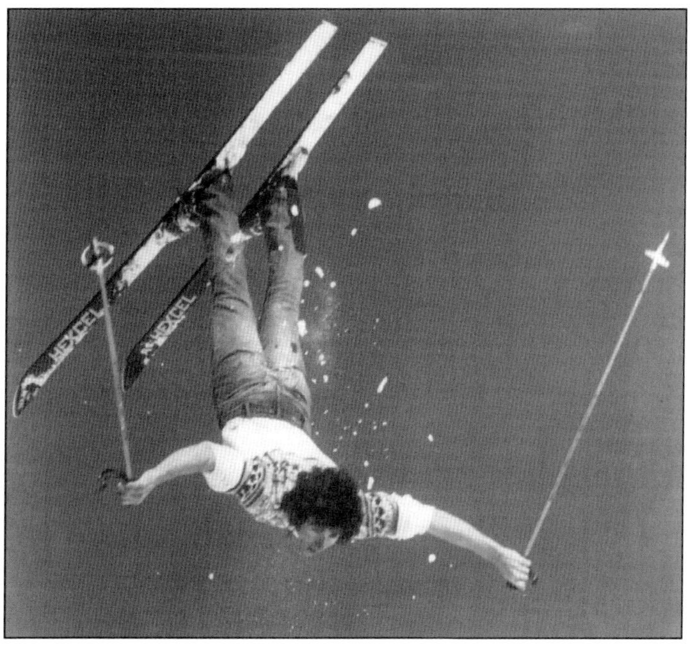

ACROBATIC JUMPING. Western State College students were among the best in the nation in Gelande jumping in the 1970s. The jumps were exciting and dangerous and drew huge crowds. Here, a WSC student sails high in the air doing a back flip near Tower 7 at the Crested Butte Ski Area.

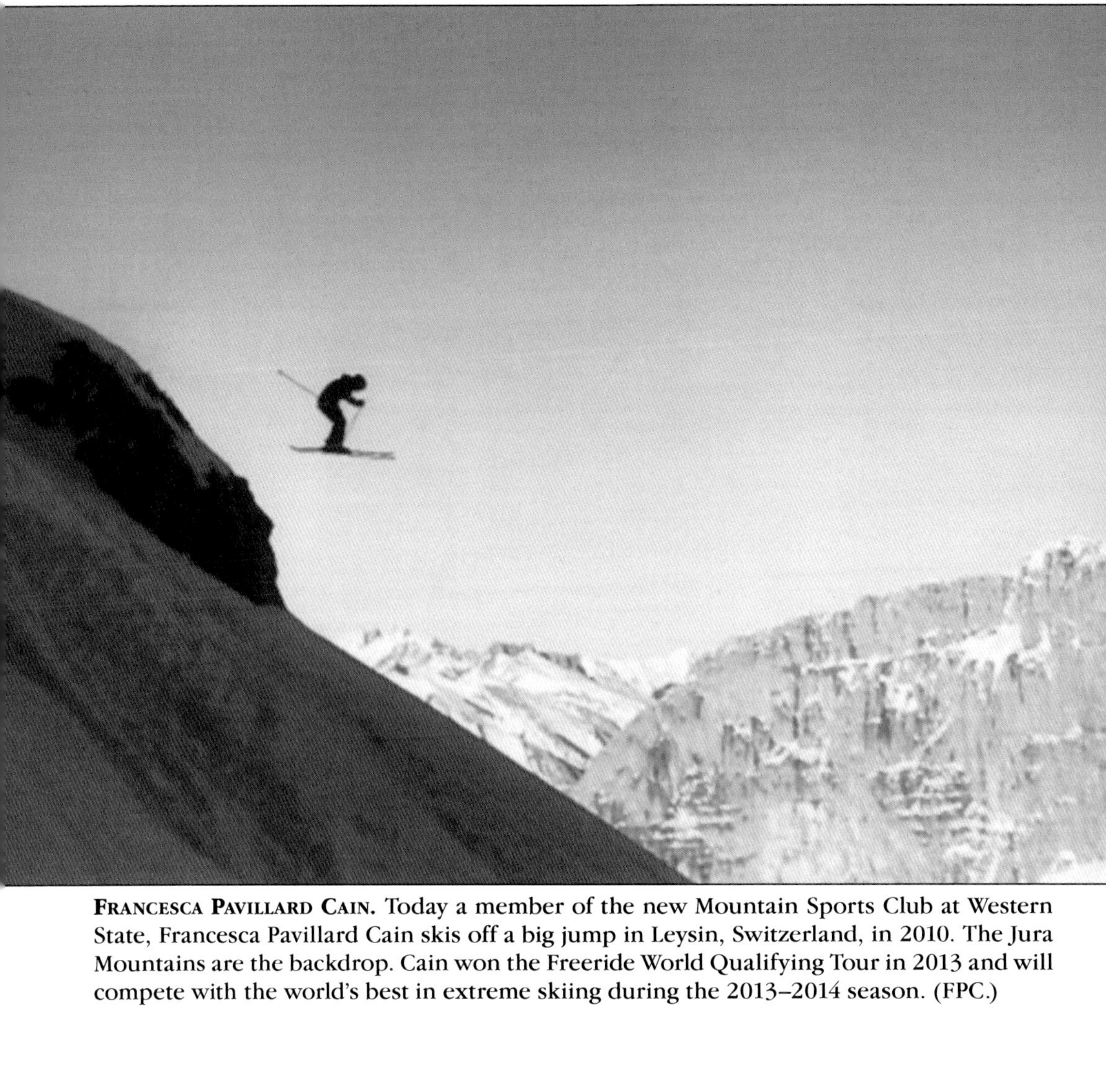

Francesca Pavillard Cain. Today a member of the new Mountain Sports Club at Western State, Francesca Pavillard Cain skis off a big jump in Leysin, Switzerland, in 2010. The Jura Mountains are the backdrop. Cain won the Freeride World Qualifying Tour in 2013 and will compete with the world's best in extreme skiing during the 2013–2014 season. (FPC.)

Ten

POTPOURRI

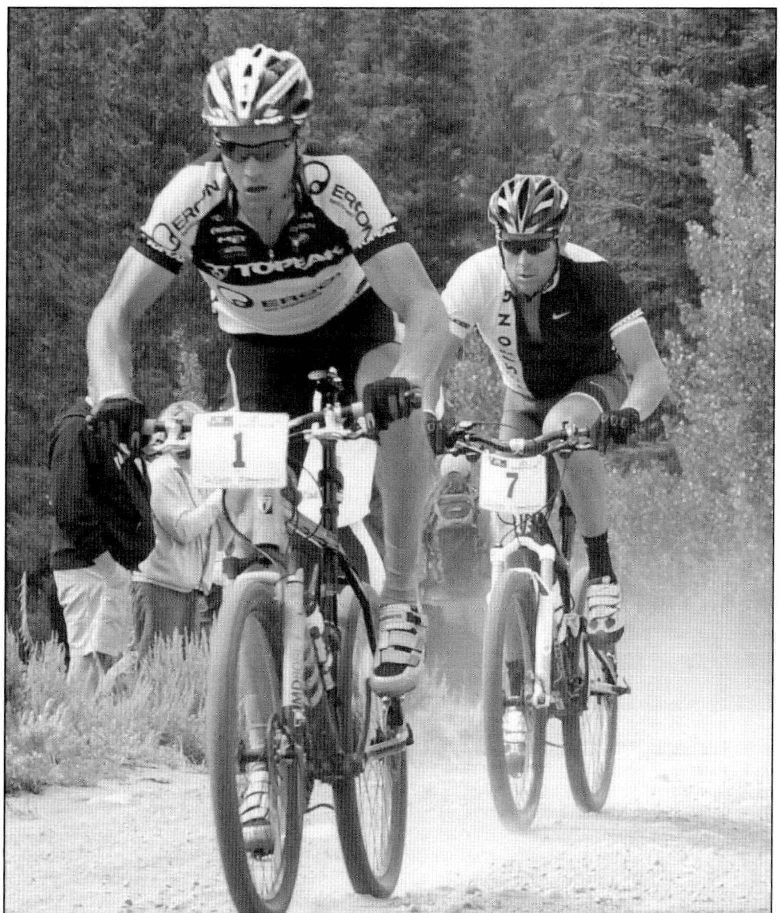

DAVE WIENS. A 1990 Western State College grad, Dave Wiens is recognized as one of the greatest mountain bikers of all time. He has won the Leadville 100-mile race six times, defeating Tour de France winners Floyd Landis in 2007 and Lance Armstrong in 2008. Here, Wiens leads Armstrong at the 75-mile mark in the 2008 race. Wiens is currently the head of Western's highly successful Mountain Sports Club. (DC.)

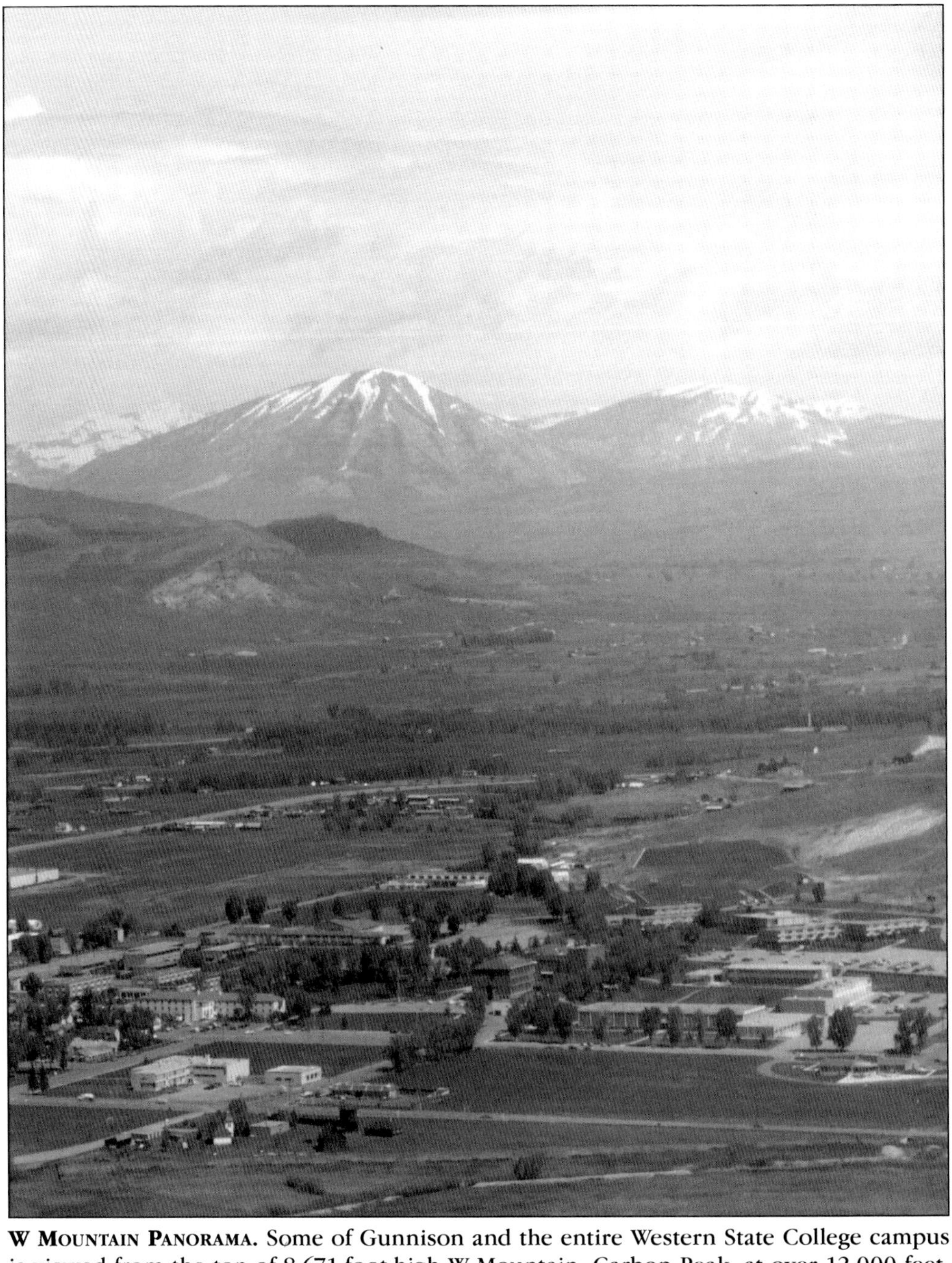

W MOUNTAIN PANORAMA. Some of Gunnison and the entire Western State College campus is viewed from the top of 8,671-foot-high W Mountain. Carbon Peak, at over 12,000 feet, towers in the background.

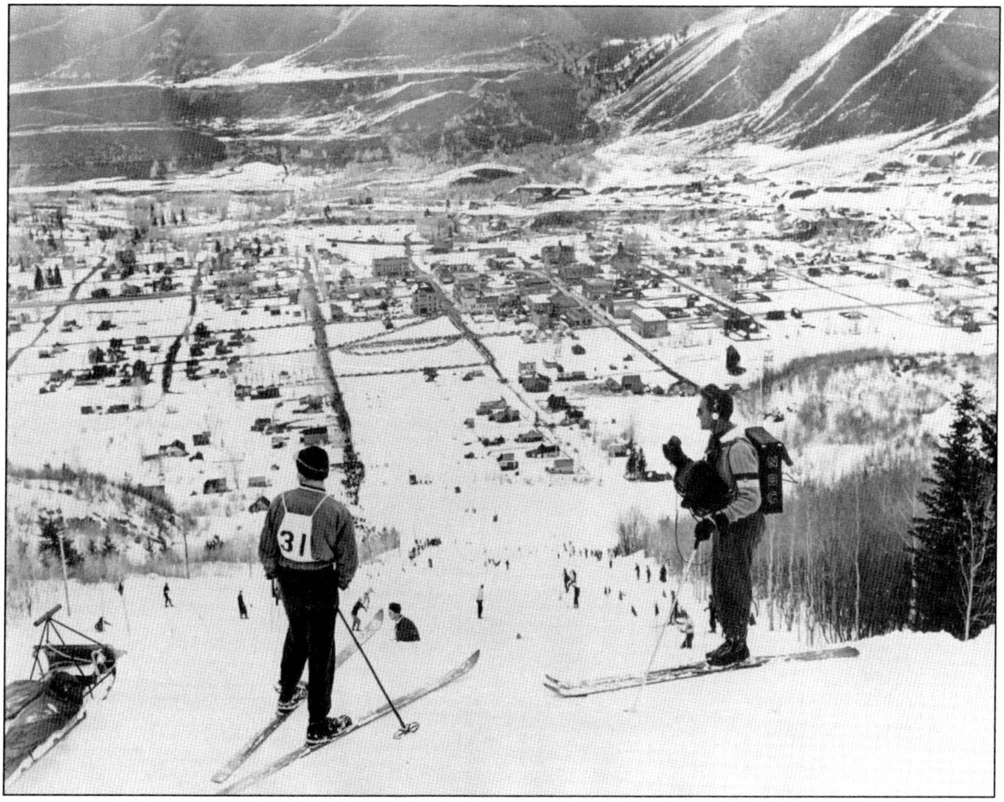

Aspen, 1947. A Western State College skier looks over the race course on Little Nell on Aspen Mountain in 1947. Unlike the bustling town it is today, Aspen then was simply a mining camp that had hit on hard times. The Aspen Ski Area had just begun.

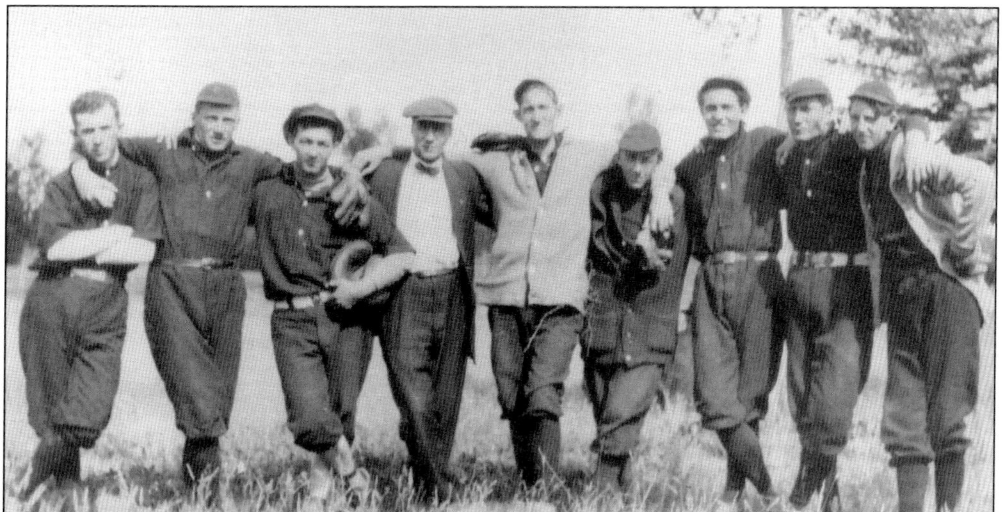

The Gunnison Nine. In the days of legendary Major League Baseball players like Ty Cobb, Honus Wagner, and Cy Young, baseball was truly the national pastime and was played in Gunnison and nearby mining camps. The Gunnison team of 1910 played against teams from nearby mining camps like Baldwin, Crested Butte, Pitkin, and Lake City. (GPM.)

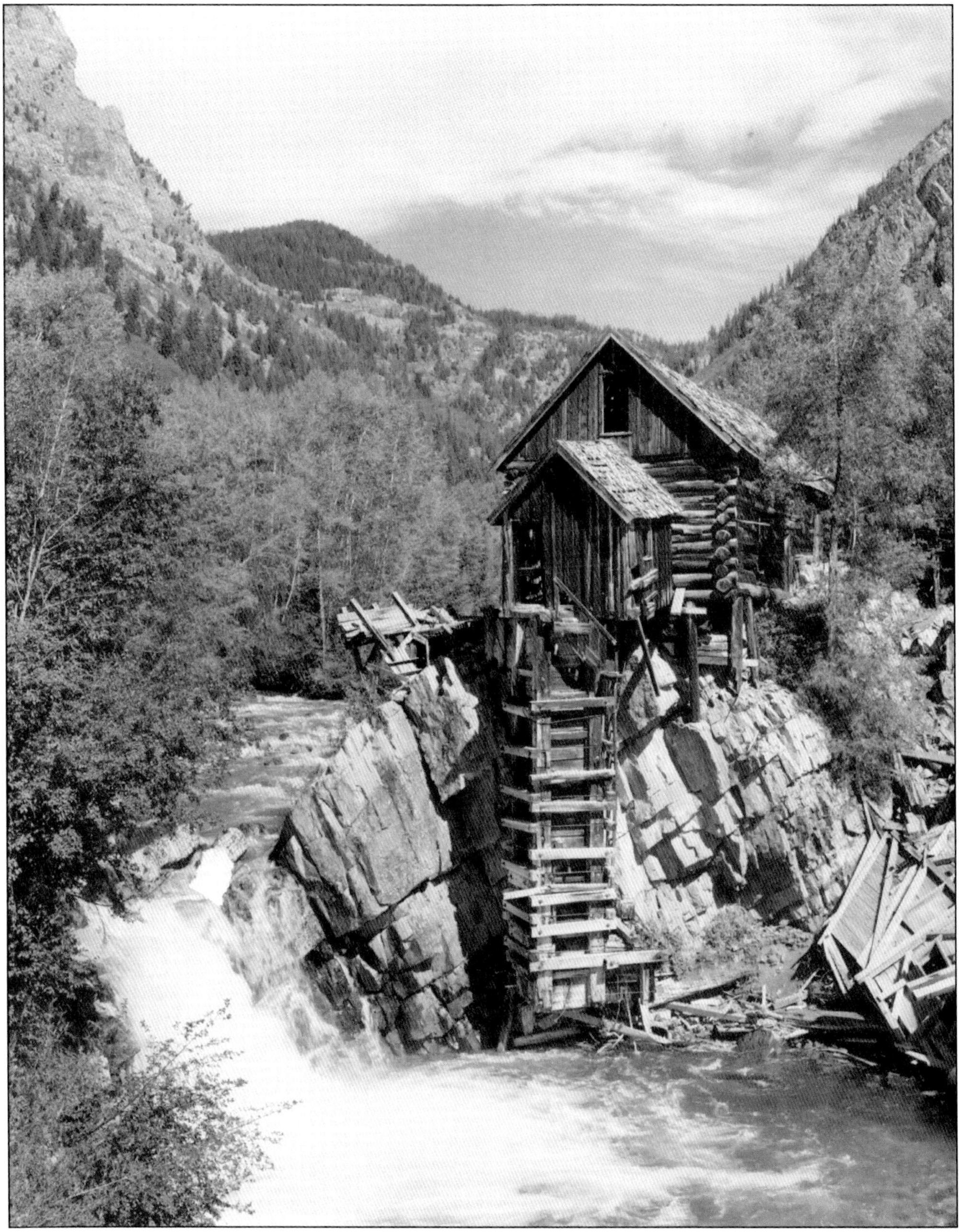

Crystal Mill. One of the most photographed sites in Colorado, the Crystal Mill is located on the beautiful Crystal River, 20 miles north of Crested Butte. The mill used a generator belted to a waterwheel to power three silver mines on the other side of the mining camp.

Alisha Williams. One of the most decorated athletes in Western State history, Alisha Williams won six NCAA championships in track and field and was a many-time All-American in cross-country from 2001 to 2005. Today, she is one of the top women 10,000-meter runners in the nation and just missed making the 2012 Olympic team.

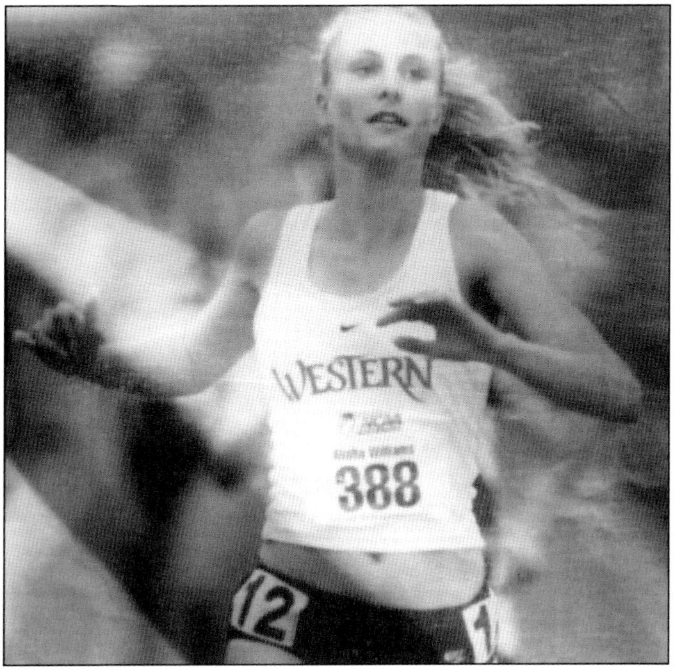

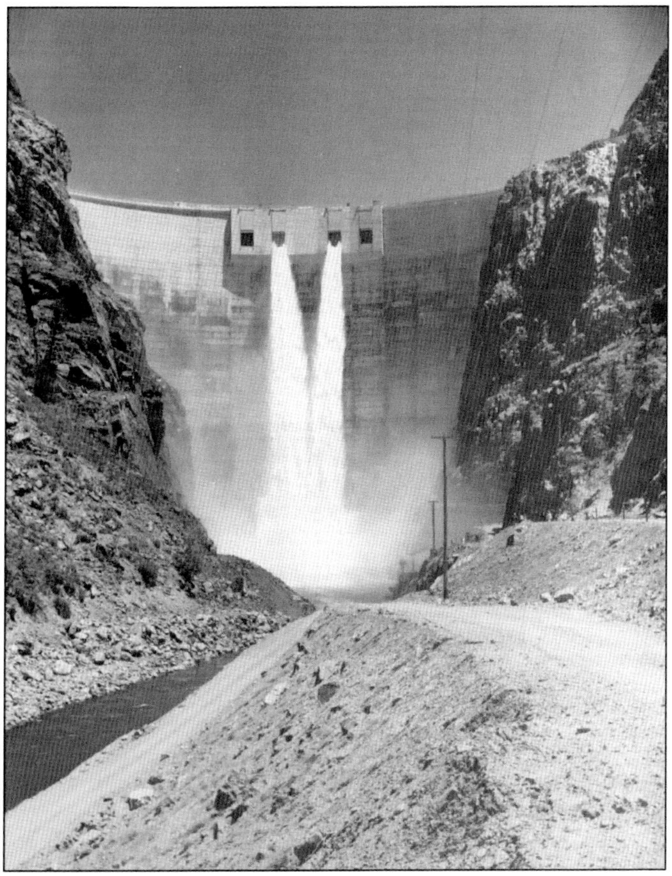

Morrow Point. The US Bureau of Reclamation built a thin-arched, double-curvature high dam called Morrow Point in the Black Canyon of the Gunnison in 1968. This type of dam was very rare at the time. The dam was 468 feet high and built for power generation. Here, two gates of the spillway overflow in the 1970s.

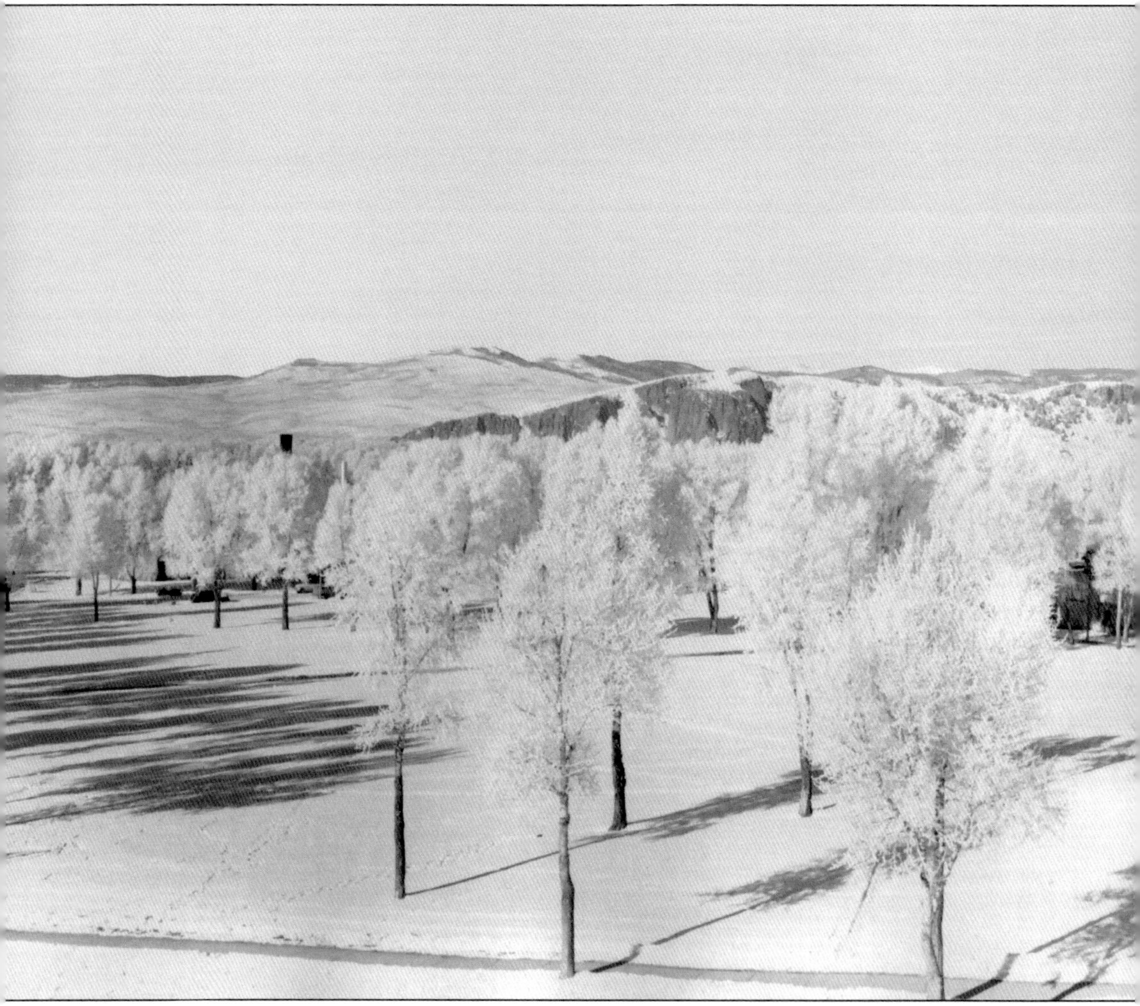

WINTER SPLENDOR. Hoarfrost covering trees on the Western State campus in front of Taylor Hall provides spectacular beauty. Four to five times every winter, conditions exist to give Western students a view they will not soon forget. (WSCU.)

CLIMBING CLASS. A group of Western State College students practices rappelling on a steep cliff near the junction of Spring Creek with the Taylor River, 17 miles from Gunnison. Through the years, several WSC graduates have become world-class climbers. (WSCU.)

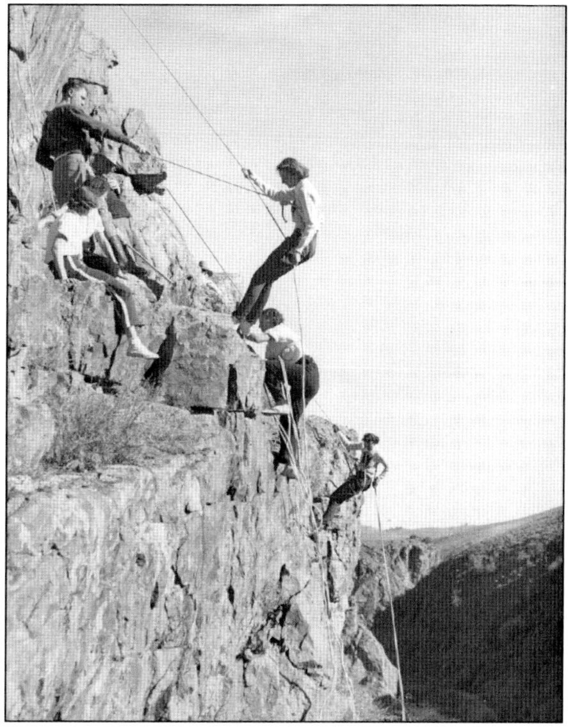

FLYING HIGH. Tobogganing and sledding have always been popular winter activities on the Western State campus. The hill on the west side of Mountaineer Bowl is steep and long, and great speeds can be obtained. Here, an unlucky tobogganer has hit a jump wrong and is high in the air and moving fast. (WSCU.)

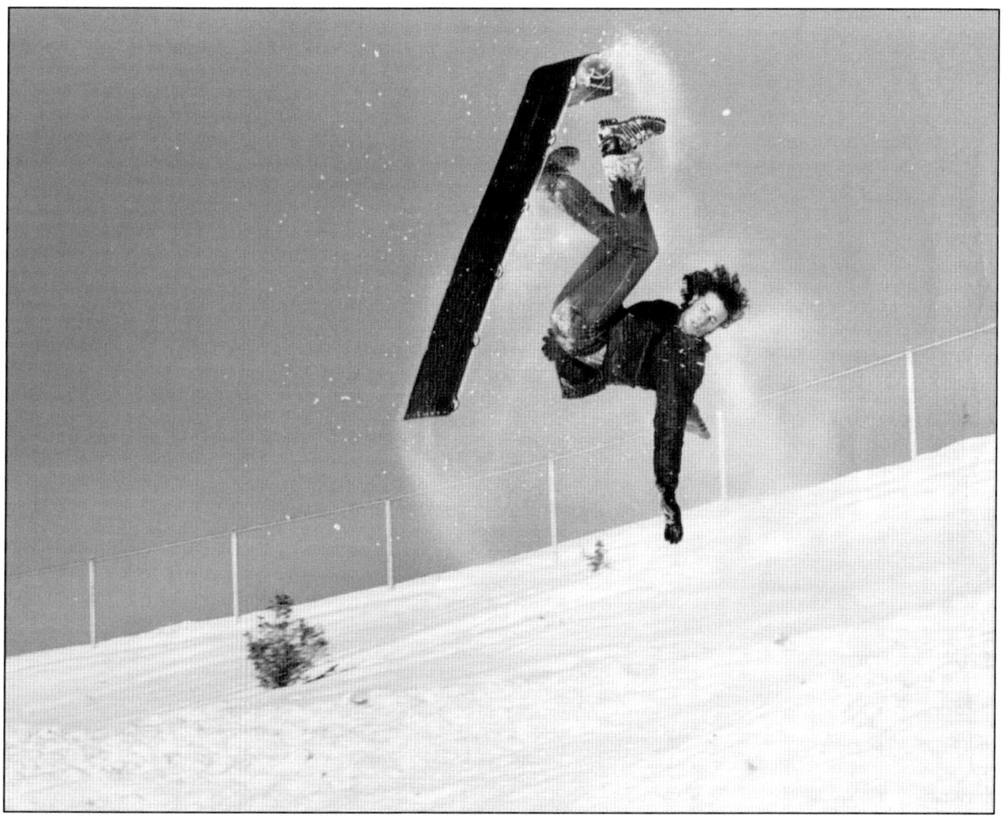

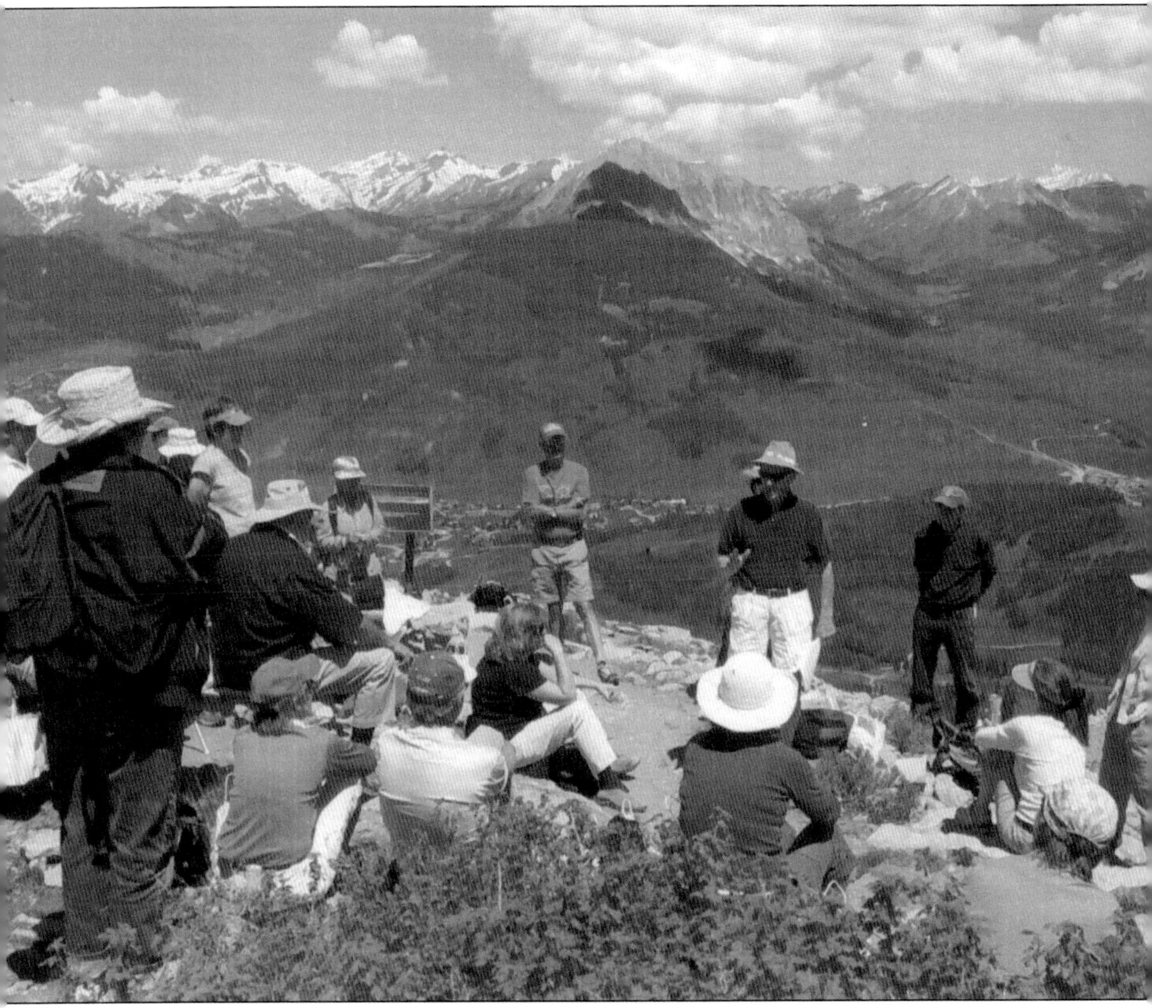

EXTENDED STUDIES CLASS. One of the most popular academic departments at Western State is extended studies. Here, a history class is in session near the top of the Crested Butte Mountain with Gothic Mountain, the Elk Mountains, and the East River Valley in the background.

Bibliography

Cope, John, Martin Hatcher, and Charles Miller, eds. *Looking Back at 100 Years of Western State College*. Gunnison, CO: Western State College, 2001.
Curecanti, Western State College yearbook, 1925–1989.
Fay, Abbott. *Mountain Academia*. Boulder: Pruett Press, 1968.
Vandenbusche, Duane. *The Gunnison Country*. Gunnison, CO: B&B Printers, 1980.
Wallace, Betty. *History with the Hide Off*. Denver: Sage Books, 1964.

Personal Interviews

Ed Ali. Los Alamos, NM: May 24, 2012.
Bob Arnold. Gunnison, CO: January 17, 1992.
Carol Baird Izett. Whitefish, MT: March 24, 2011.
Jim Balfanz. Stockbridge, MA: December 5, 2013.
Marvin Bohman. Loveland, CO: April 26, 2009.
Molly Gratton Fisher. Breckenridge, CO: June 13, 2012.
Thor Groswold. Montrose, CO: December 17, 2007.
Rial Lake. Gunnison, CO: August 5, 1975.
Bruce Palmer. Grand Junction, CO: December 17, 2007.
Crosby Perry-Smith. Ouray, CO: December 17, 2007.
Sven Wiik. Steamboat Springs, CO: December 15, 2007.

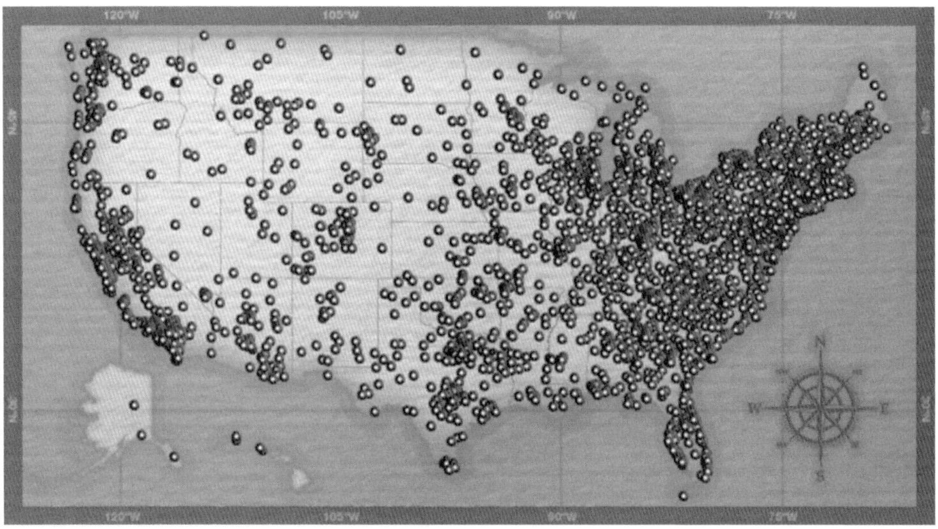